CAMP WITH COACH WOODEN

Camp

WITH COACH

WOODEN

GREG HAYES

Published by Greg Hayes
Santa Clarita, CA, U.S.A.

Printed in the U.S.A.

Attributions for all copyrighted material were sought.
If I have inadvertently missed anyone, please contact me.

Library of Congress Registration Number: TX 8-182-417
ISBN 978-0-9969315-0-2 (trade paper)

For additional information,
please visit our Facebook page Camp with Coach Woodpen.

Cover and interior design by InsideOut CreativeArts

DEDICATION

To Mom, Dad, Megan, and Kara.
This book is written that others might know
who and what we can never forget.

"Love is the medicine that can cure all the ills of the world."

JOHN WOODEN

Contents

INTRODUCTION

The Untold Story of Coach Wooden's Camps

John Wooden was a legendary coach and person. *Sporting News* magazine named him the greatest coach of all time, and the ESPN sports channel named him the greatest coach in any sport for the twentieth century. While the head coach at University of California Los Angeles (UCLA) from 1948–1975, Coach Wooden developed and led one of the greatest sports dynasties of all time. While at the helm at UCLA, his teams won an amazing ten national championships and set numerous impressive records. Yet his greatest achievements may not have been during March Madness—college basketball's annual spring tournament—but rather during the summers of his life after he retired from coaching at UCLA.

Coach Wooden was in many ways even more successful in the thirty-five years after he coached his last game in 1975 than he was during his coaching heyday. Those thirty-five years were characterized by love. Throughout his life he had been first and foremost a beloved son, a loving husband, a devoted father and grandfather, and a doting great-grandfather, but after retiring that love overflowed to more and more people from all walks of life, and he was greatly loved in return. In particular John Wooden deeply loved his wife, Nell, and it almost broke his heart when she passed in 1985. But his hurt and loss eventually grew in him a greater capacity for love that he poured into his family and into the lives of numerous people. His modest condominium in a middle-class neighborhood in Encino, California, became a destination for countless people who sought an audience with him and a chance to gain timeless wisdom.

In the final years of his life, Coach Wooden also became an internationally known motivational speaker, the author of numerous inspirational books, and the subject of books and documentary films. Streets, awards, events, and scholarships were named after him—even the post office in Encino bears his name. President George W. Bush honored him with the Presidential Medal of Freedom award, the highest award given to an American citizen. All this adds up to a tremendous legacy.

But one aspect of Coach Wooden's accomplishments that has gone under the radar is the tremendous impact that Coach had, and continues to have, through the John Wooden Basketball Fundamentals Camp that he ran from 1971 to approximately 1988.[1] At these weeklong summer camps for boys ages seven through seventeen, Coach molded, mentored, taught, and inspired young players from California, around the country, and even around the world as well as coaches of all ages and many others. Perhaps the greatest influence Coach had during those years, other than on his family, was on those he interacted with at his summer basketball camps. These people were, in a very real way, like family to him too. That is what this book is about.

His autobiography is titled *They Call Me Coach*, and those involved with John Wooden at camp referred to him (and still do today) as "Coach"—a term of respect and endearment. "Coach was relevant his entire life," said Chris Smith, a close friend of Coach and director of Sportsworld, Max Shapiro's San Diego sports-camp business that sponsored the Wooden basketball camps. "For thirty-five years after he retired, he grew as a person, and his influence grew and expanded."

This book contains the rich untold story, told from a coach's perspective, of the wonderful summers that Coach shared with so many young basketball players. It is written as a memoir of sorts in the hopes of recreating the typical camp week. All the quotes from

Coach are taken directly from camp videos, articles, or my personal camp notes or are paraphrases of conversations that my camp colleagues and I had with Coach. Every story in the book comes from my own experiences or those of more than seventy former campers and staff members who contributed their own remembrances to this book. It is my hope that everyone who reads this book, including the most dedicated Wooden reader, will gain new insights from Coach and discover new ways in which he expressed his timeless ideals.

The people in this book are all real individuals who were part of Coach Wooden's camps throughout nearly two decades. However, for the sake of simplicity and clarity, I have chosen to combine their stories into one camp experience, set in 1988, in the year that Coach Wooden expected to be his final camp (he later came back and did a couple more in the early 1990s). Coach Wooden and his camps left an indelible impact on each of these people. I have mentioned many people by name, but there are many more people and many more stories that could be told. If you were part of Wooden camps and not noted here, know that you too were important and some of your contributions were drawn from and are compiled into this story.

• • • •

I participated in my first Wooden camp as a twenty-two-year-old counselor straight from my UCLA graduation in 1977. I continued for twelve summers after that as a camp coach. But Coach Wooden was a unique person in my life long before that. Other than my parents and my two daughters, Coach Wooden has had more influence on me than anyone in my life.

I saw my first UCLA basketball games in 1964. I sat on my dad's lap watching on a nineteen-inch black-and-white television as the Bruins battled the University of San Francisco and then Seattle University in the NCAA West Regionals. Even at a young age I understood the excitement of the undersized UCLA team that full-court pressed and fast breaked its way to a perfect 30–0 season and to Coach Wooden's first National Collegiate Athletic Association (NCAA) title.

I was hooked. I followed the team closely from then on, often staying up late to watch the eleven o'clock television replay, even if I already knew who had won—which was almost always the Bruins.

Watching the way Coach Wooden led his teams to victory impacted me, but Coach affected me in more ways than through basketball. In junior high I started reading the Bible daily because I read in the newspaper that Coach said it was important to do. In high school, through reading his autobiography, *They Call Me Coach*, and learning his famous Pyramid of Success with its building blocks for true success in life, I learned many important personal and character lessons. I was better at football and baseball than at basketball and was offered opportunities to play at small colleges for those sports, but I wanted to go to UCLA because Coach Wooden was there. I was not quite good enough to make any Bruin teams, but I played a mean trumpet, and UCLA welcomed me with open arms.

Though no one knew it at the time, my first year on campus, 1973–74, was Coach's next-to-last year. The first time I saw Coach on campus, he smiled and said hello to me in a friendly and sincere manner. I was thrilled that he had taken notice of a kid he didn't know. The next school year, I traveled with the UCLA Band on my first plane trip ever to Portland, Oregon, for the 1975 NCAA Western Regionals. The band and the basketball team flew together, and Coach Wooden came to the back of the plane and visited with the band members and the cheerleaders. It was a memorable and exciting experience.

After graduating, in a most unlikely way, I went from being a trumpet player directly to being a UCLA graduate assistant basketball coach. Coach Wooden had retired by then, but his top assistant and former Bruins player, Gary Cunningham, a wonderful man and coach, was in charge by this time. Also on that staff were coaches Jim Harrick, Larry Farmer, and Craig Impelman. Harrick was a future UCLA head coach, and Farmer had been a Bruin and would also one day be head coach at UCLA. Impelman would one day marry Coach's granddaughter, Christy, and become the father of Coach's great-grandchild, John, who would himself become a future college coach. Coaching on that staff remains one of the greatest privileges of my life.

After coaching at UCLA I became a high-school teacher and basketball coach. My UCLA professors had prepared me well, but I learned more about classroom teaching from Coach—through his books, his Pyramid of Success, and personal interaction with him at camp—than I did from all my education classes combined. In later years I had incredible coaching opportunities that I had never imagined possible, all because of my association with Coach Wooden and UCLA basketball.

Eventually my own daughters came to appreciate and esteem Coach. My older daughter Megan's inspirational teacher, Dana White Lindvall, a former UCLA cheerleader, first introduced Megan to Coach Wooden's principles, and in 2014 Megan graduated Magna Cum Laude in nursing from UCLA. My younger daughter, Kara, in her own sixth-grade year, read a book by Coach called *My Personal Best* and came to deeply appreciate Coach's love for his wife, Nell. Megan and Kara first met Coach as preteens, years after the last camp. Coach was in his mid-nineties by them. He gave them his full attention, treated them as if they were particularly special, and signed our family's copy of his children's book *Inch and Miles* with "Love, John Wooden." Both Megan and Kara were impressed that Coach remembered me some fifteen years after I had last coached for him at his basketball camp.

• • • •

That was Coach—a humble hero who did not disappoint. He seemed to remember and care about everyone. At camp that meant that the campers were his players, the camp personnel his team, and the coaches his coaches. He worked the campers as if they were his own team, put on informal clinics for the coaches, met with visitors, and ate breakfast and lunch in the Cal Lu cafeteria with everyone daily. He explained his famed Pyramid of Success at every camp—his own definition of success that had more to do with becoming the best one could be than with winning the most games or becoming the most famous. He even taught us how to properly put on our shoes and socks and inspired us with a story about a little chap. We all felt honored, blessed, and forever grateful to have coached at his weeklong basketball camp.

As a camp brochure from 1975 said, "There is no secret as to why Coach Wooden is basketball's greatest coach. It is in large part because of his unequalled knowledge and ability to communicate with young men."[2] Tens of thousands of campers took that knowledge with them and used it for years to come. Coaches and counselors likewise were impacted and forever changed and went back to their schools and communities to collectively influence tens of thousands more students, athletes, educators, and others. Coach's words and example became clearer, more relevant, and truer to each of us the older we got.

This book is my recollection of those wonderful camps. It is my hope that this story represents, with love and balance, the experiences and memories of thousands who have been forever influenced by Coach John Wooden to be the best that they are capable of becoming. May former counselors, coaches, campers, campers' relatives, and camp personnel find this book to be a true representation of Coach Wooden's basketball fundamentals camps. And just as importantly, may a new generation of young people find timeless basketball and life wisdom from the greatest coach who ever lived and an even greater person—Coach John Wooden.

1

Meeting a Legend

It is a lazy, midsummer day in Southern California. The freeway traffic is light on this Sunday morning in 1988, with cars headed toward Dodger Stadium, Santa Monica beach, and Disneyland. As I drive north on the 101 freeway toward California Lutheran College in Thousand Oaks, my excitement about the week ahead of me builds.

It has been a great summer so far. The high-school basketball team that I coach has worked hard and improved; the Shot Doctor Camp that I ran in Payson, Arizona, was a huge success; and the ten-day tournament in the USSR, where I coached a high-school team, was a remarkable experience.

But the best week of the summer begins today—the John Wooden Basketball Fundamentals Camp put on by Sportsworld. This is my twelfth summer coaching at Coach Wooden's overnight camp for boys, but this particular week will be different than any other, because it looks for sure as if this will be the final camp of Coach's career. Last summer everyone thought it would be Coach's last, but Sportsworld owner Max Shapiro recruited Coach for one more summer with a big mid-camp luncheon, where a bunch of us wore "Just Say Maybe" T-shirts and Dallas Cowboys head coach Tom Landry gave a motivational talk.

I started working for the legendary and brilliant Coach John Wooden as an excited, wide-eyed, and in-awe twenty-two-year old. Twelve summers later, I'm still in awe but also very comfortable and very grateful to be around Coach. He is still a legend, but he also feels to me like a beloved, wise, loving family member of wonderful spirit, great character, and playful personality.

I'm very excited to see Coach as well as the other coaches and counselors who are coming to staff this camp and who all share a wonderful camaraderie and a desire to learn rich basketball and life lessons from Coach. There is so much to learn and areas in which to grow but precious little time left to do so at camp. This will be a week to savor and to be fully alive and engaged.

As I pull up, coach Ed Tellez is taking his bags out of his car trunk. Ed has driven twenty hours from Fort Collins, Colorado, and dropped his family off at the Disneyland Hotel before joining hundreds of other cars driving to Thousand Oaks for what may be the last John Wooden basketball camp.

Coach Wooden's Camps

John Wooden, the great former UCLA basketball coach, is a celebrity in the minds of everyone except his own and those of his family. For nearly two decades Coach has held as many as ten camps per summer, and each of them has sold out, just as this summer's camps have. At this final camp of the summer, about three hundred boys ages seven to seventeen, along with camp directors, coaches, and counselors, are about to share a most memorable week together. This year, however, staff members feel a heightened excitement and perhaps a bit of nostalgia at that thought that this will likely be the last John Wooden Basketball Fundamentals Camp ever. If it is, however, Coach will not allow himself to be the focus of the camp.

California Lutheran College, with its plentiful dorm space, pleasant cafeteria, and contained and comforting environment, is an ideal location for camp. Cal Lu, as it is known, is a small, quiet college in a green, peaceful area bordered by rolling hills to the east and north and by houses on the other two sides. The weather is warm in the summer, and despite being forty minutes west of Los Angeles, the air is relatively clean. Cal Lu hosts a variety of sports, arts, and educational camps each summer, but none is more popular than John Wooden's basketball fundamentals camp run by Sportsworld.

The camps are highly organized and professionally managed through the personable and caring leadership of Sportsworld administrative directors Chris Smith and Pat Yount. Because precamp correspondence is done by mail, most new staff members assume that Pat is a male and are surprised, when they meet her in person, to find that she is a woman! Chris and Pat are a great team and have a gift for remembering each person's name. Pat's calligraphy skills make camp nametags a work of art.

Greg Newell, son of the legendary University of California coach Pete Newell, raves about these two. "I went to work for Converse," he relates, "and one of my first jobs was to try to get Converse to be the official shoe of the John Wooden camp. I succeeded because of both Pat Yount and Chris Smith. That was my first gold-star moment as a young buck working for Converse, and, happy to say, it allowed me the confidence to do other significant things for the company. Chris and Pat are great, great people, and it is heartwarming to work with them."

At every weeklong camp sixteen coaches work under Coach to help train the campers. Highly successful college, high-school, junior-high, and youth coaches come from all over the United States to staff Coach Wooden's camps—and to learn from Coach while doing it. Every coach will be responsible throughout the week for two teams of eight or nine players each. Eight coaches coach the younger "gold" division of campers, and the other eight have the older "blue" division. It is the coaches' job to carry out Coach Wooden's vision and to inspire and shape the campers under his care.

The campers and staff members are kept on schedule each week through the able leadership of camp directors Hector Macias and Hal Mitrovich, who have been with Coach since his first camp in 1971. Macias is fondly known as "Hector the Director." As a former camp coach and with his distinctive Honduran accent, he is the voice of the camp as well as the camp disciplinarian. The campers have a healthy fear of him, and he makes sure that the coaches and counselors do their job as well. Macias has a dry sense of humor that Coach enjoys, as does Pat Yount. Pat says, "I discovered shoulder pads to help me carry Hector throughout the summer." No one laughs harder at that than Hector, and no one appreciates Hector more than Pat. Hal Mitrovich, the other camp director, is a nurturing, considerate, understanding, and kind individual who is well-liked and appreciated by all.

Staff members feel a bit of nostalgia at the thought that this will likely be the last John Wooden Basketball Fundamentals Camp ever.

Counselors play a major role at each camp as well, living in the Cal Lu dorms with the campers. Counselors, along with coaches at times, act as temporary parents, especially to kids who are homesick. The sixteen regular counselors—one for each coach—also act as referees for the basketball games that will be played during the week.

The head counselors are Jack Currier and Steve Hawkins. Currier is affectionately known as "Jaws" because he loves the movie *Jaws* and has seen it many times. Hawkins is nicknamed "Hawk" and enjoys camp and the relationships he makes there so much that he says, "When camp ends on Friday, I can hardly wait to get back to camp the next Sunday." These two are more like assistant camp directors, handling numerous responsibilities and constantly being on call to assist the camp directors in whatever is needed. Along with the camp directors, the head counselors are the last to go to sleep every night and the first to wake up the next morning. If things go well, they may get five hours of sleep.

Ultimately, though, the camp's popularity reflects Coach Wooden's personal and basketball philosophy, which the Sportsworld staff and other staff members help him implement. He will not put his name to anything less than the high standards he is known for. Yet Coach is hands-on, unlike many other famous coaches who hold camps but make only an occasional appearance to the campers. Coach Wooden actively teaches the campers alongside the coaches and counselors who are hired to work the camp. He is accessible. He is the first person in line when the cafeteria opens for breakfast, and he eats the same food the campers eat. Coach is humble, down to earth, and personable with everyone he meets.

Coach's goal for his camps is to teach life lessons through basketball. In fact, he refers to himself as a teacher rather than a coach. His camps exist for the purpose of teaching the quick and proper execution of the simplest basketball fundamentals—things like dribbling, layups, and passing. These are not all-star camps for advanced players, nor are they designed for entertainment or for playing games all day.

Coach's main goals go beyond basketball. He has said many times, "What you are as a person is far more important than what you are as a basketball player."[1] He is most concerned with the campers' associations with other people in the camp and with the conduct, attitude, and attention to others shown by each person. He wants everyone to be courteous and polite and to show consideration for others at all times. He expects campers to develop new friendships, dress neatly, keep their dorm rooms in order, bus their dishes after meals, and listen attentively to their instructors.

Meeting Coach Wooden

By eleven in the morning, after attending church, as he does every Sunday, Coach Wooden is at camp, ready to meet his campers.

But one of the things most loved about Coach is that he invests not only in the campers but also in everyone he meets, including his camp staff. Before heading to check-in to greet the campers and their parents, Coach sees Wayne Carlson, the head women's coach and assistant men's coach at San Diego Mesa College, and Jim Nielsen, former UCLA player and graduate assistant coach for Coach Wooden, in the dorm lobby playing cribbage, and asks if he might join them. Nielsen has become a school principal, but he coaches at camps because he enjoys it and also in exchange for camp tuition for his son Jasen. Of course Carlson and Nielsen are thrilled to have Coach's company and not the least bit surprised when Coach proves to be a better player than either of them during their enjoyable thirty-five-minute game. After the game Coach makes the short walk with the two coaches to the cafeteria for a quick lunch before going to greet the campers and their parents.

After lunch, from twelve thirty to three, Coach Wooden, along with the camp directors and the counselors, greets parents and campers during check-in and registration in Pederson Hall.

Coach is accessible to and approachable by the parents and campers—not something one expects such a famous coach to be. A few are nervous around him since he is the great UCLA coach, but he makes them feel relaxed and comfortable. He is humble, genuine, level headed, and consistent in his demeanor, and he greets everyone with a smile and with personal interest in them. One gets the impression that he is accepting of all and non-judgmental toward everyone.

Many parents are thrilled and overwhelmed to be in the presence of Coach Wooden. Camper Alan Husted's mom excitedly greets Coach: "I'm so happy that my son gets to play under such a famous coach as you."

Coach answers politely and graciously: "Thank you, but I don't consider myself famous at all." Coach often uses the phrase "at all," in a slight Midwestern accent pronouncing it "atall," as if it were one word. "It is just the fact that I've been thrown into the public eye a little more, purely and simply because of having a lot of wonderful young men under my supervision. If they hadn't done well, I wouldn't be here," he adds with a smile.[2]

What a great opportunity this is for the campers! Six straight days of basketball, an all-you-can-eat cafeteria, and fun on campus and in the dorms. Campers are diverse in age, talent, background, experience, and personality, and their attention and motivation depend on many factors. Some are enthusiastic about being at camp, and they work hard to learn and improve. Some go on to play in college, and a few, like Jay Humphries, go on to play in the National Basketball Association (NBA). "What really helped my fundamentals at a young age was going to John Wooden's basketball camps," Humphries says. "That's where I got a good fundamental base."

Some campers are children of UCLA alumni or fans who want their kids to be around Coach Wooden—which they desire for themselves as well. Some parents, however, send their sons to camp so that the parents can enjoy a mini-vacation without the kids. One summer a father dropped his eighth-grade son off at Cal Lu and left him for six straight weeks of Sportsworld camps. After a few weeks, the boy knew the camp routine and how the camp ran so well that he became almost like another counselor.

Although this particular boy did well at camp, Coach Wooden does not like this approach on the part of the parents at all, as it often means that their son has no desire to be at camp. Coach sometimes asks the campers, "How many are here because mom and dad wanted you to be here? Just mom and dad? Ah, good—I don't see any. That's fine." He explains, "Sometimes at my camps I'll have parents leave a youngster at camp because they work, they want to go somewhere on vacation, sort of get rid of them for a week. The youngster doesn't really want to be here, and that's not good for him. I don't like that. I like campers to want to be here on their own. I think that it is much better that they really, really want to be here. The players have to be enthusiastic about it."[3] Fortunately, the majority of campers and their parents are very excited about camp.

No camper is treated as more special than the others, even if he has famous parents. Singers Christopher Cross and Natalie Cole both had sons at camp one summer; the boys played on the same team. Former NFL great Rosey Grier, actor Michael Landon, and actress Anne Archer have all sent their sons to camp. Both boys of actor and singer Ricky Nelson have attended camp, as have children of other celebrities. Coach's grandsons also participated in a few camps. Coach's son, Jim, sent his boy, Greg, who enjoyed the camps and was a good player, but another grandson did not quite enjoy camp as much as Greg did—"I don't like basketball, Papa," he would say. But all the campers, no matter who they are, are given the same attention and have the same wonderful opportunity to train under a legend like Coach Wooden.

The Coaches Arrive

The Sportsworld brochure advertising the John Wooden camps reads, "Learn to play better basketball the Coach Wooden way." Those of us who are coaches, however, want to learn to *coach* better basketball the Coach Wooden way. High-school basketball coach David Myers (not to be confused with former UCLA basketball player David Meyers) has brought his family from Texas. He states the feelings of all the coaches well: "We come to camp to be influenced by Coach's character and by his teaching."

It is a cherished privilege and honor to be asked to coach at Coach Wooden's camps and not something that any of us takes for granted. Camp is a renaissance week for coaches to recharge and rejuvenate and also a time for personal and professional reflection and growth. It is a chance for us to renew friendships with each other, get in shape, and exchange ideas and stories—and most of all to be around Coach Wooden.

It also requires a demanding schedule with high expectations, as is clearly stated in the coach's handbook: "A great deal of the camp's success will be due to the enthusiasm, willingness, and cooperation of you, the COACH. It is imperative that you are at your best at all times during the week." Each of us is responsible for passing Coach Wooden's high standards on to our two teams this week.

For many years Mike Thibault, nicknamed "Strawberry," coached camps all summer long. In more recent years he has no longer done so, because he moved up rapidly in the coaching world, becoming head scout for the Lakers and later for the Chicago Bulls, where he played a role in the drafting of Michael Jordan. Coaches love Strawberry and are happy for his success.

It is a cherished privilege and honor to be asked to coach at Coach Wooden's camps and not something that any of us takes for granted.

By one o'clock all the coaches have gathered, some tired from a long travel day and others still recovering from the previous week's camp. While the camp administrators and counselors are checking in the campers, the coaches enjoy their Sunday arrival time, when they can greet and catch up with coaching friends from past summers. Colorado coach Ed Tellez warmly greets local coaches and close friends Larry Lopez, Ray Tejada, and Bob Alaniz, three local coaches who, because of what they have learned from Coach Wooden, have elevated the level of basketball in nearby Ventura County. The quartet calls themselves the "four Mexicans."

Out-of-state coaches fly in a day to a week early, some even making the Wooden camp part of their family vacations each summer. Mike Kunstadt brings his family from Texas each year. His wife, Gerri, came with him the first two summers after they were married. During the second summer Gerri felt ill all week, and when Mike and Gerri returned the next summer with their four-month-old daughter, Karin, it became clear that the previous summer's illness had been due to pregnancy!

Each summer coach Don Showalter and his family drive from Iowa in their family van. The trip takes about a week as Don and Vicky and their kids, Melissa and Brent, stop at various national parks along the way, sleep in a tent, and enjoy camping together. Iowa is a landlocked state, so the end of their trip out West includes stops at beaches along the California coast. Their family road trips are a special bonding time and a source of wonderful family memories.

Coach Instructs His Coaches

At two thirty the coaches gather in Pederson Hall for our first formal meeting of the week. We are first officially greeted by camp directors Hector Macias and Hal Mitrovich. Hector the Director and Hal briefly instruct the coaches and assign us our duties for the week.

When they finish, Coach Wooden joins us. He is dressed in his white camp polo shirt, navy blue coaching shorts, UCLA game socks, and Converse shoes. It is always a pinch-me moment to realize that we are part of his coaching staff. Coach Mike Scarano, who has coached at the college level in both California and Alabama, savors the moment. "I am in the same room as John Wooden," he says, "the greatest coach ever and an inspirational man of faith and family, and I'm listening to him and get to coach for him!"

As Coach is getting older, those of us who are veterans wonder if he has lost any of his mental sharpness and physical condition. Once he begins speaking, though, it is obvious that he is as sharp and energetic as ever. The veterans have heard this talk many times before, but, as we do whenever Coach speaks, we listen as if hearing him for the first time, fully knowing that the more we hear Coach, the more his words and example make sense.

Coach begins his talk in a clear, calm, and patient manner, presenting the standard points that he makes at the beginning of each and every camp. He has incredible inner strength and character that come from a moral and ethical clarity, competitive greatness, personal discipline, godly faith, and careful family priorities. He speaks with clarity and wisdom and with the strength and authority of one who knows his subject well and has been highly successful with it. We are focused and listen intently.

> Our goal is not to make the campers into stars. The Lord makes them stars through the physical gifts they are given. What we can do is help someone make the junior-high or high-school team or become a starter on their team who might not be able to do it on their own. Those lacking God-given skills can never attain so-called star status in our camp. But we can help them bring about improvement at every level if they are attentive and industrious. And those who do have the physical ability to begin with and have the interest and desire, we might be able to help them.
>
> Emphasize quickness and balance in the execution of all fundamentals. Both are very important. But accuracy must not be sacrificed for quickness. Teach balance in all things—basketball and life. On the court be balanced and relaxed and make sure the head is not leaning too far forward. Always keep the ball close to the body, as the extremities throw balance off. Emphasize emotional balance, or self-control, and team play at all times. In all things show consideration of others.
>
> Remember that you are a teacher, and you must teach. Be positive and show great patience, and do not expect too much too soon. Do not neglect the less gifted for the more gifted, and especially remember that with the younger players this week. Remember that repetition is the secret of knowledge.

In games all players should get to play in at least half of the game and must participate in each half, even in the championship games, regardless of their ability. Emphasize doing their best rather than the score. Games are not important in terms of the score. Stress team balance—equal opportunities for all. At camp try to score from passing and cutting and not so much by dribbling. The players should be practicing what they've learned about proper body balance in the execution of the fundamentals and about balance, both offensively and defensively. And there will be no talking to or criticizing officials. Take all suggestions or complaints to the co-directors after the game. Put yourself in the officials' shoes.

Use no profanity, and permit none. This is very important. Do not allow campers to goof off. Be on guard about hurting the feelings of any player. Be careful and constructive in your criticism, and refrain from the use of sarcasm. Remember to be positive. Discipline to improve, help, prevent and not to punish.

Remind campers to pick trash up. At UCLA we wanted to leave the dressing/shower room neat and clean and nicer than we found it. I would get notes from custodians thanking me for that.

Each coach must be with his group to assist when I am leading the group fundamentals. The success of this camp will depend largely upon your efforts and cooperation. Together I hope we can make this a truly rewarding experience for every camper.[4]

Coach has one last powerful reminder for us: "Every one of you coaches, you are builders, you are pillars, and you are leaders. You should be setting an example. Everyone is a leader, a model, for someone. We all should try to be the type of leader that will bring a smile from all."[5]

Camp administrator Chris Smith wraps up the meeting. "We're sure that this is the way you would want your own children and players to be taught when they are away at a camp," he reminds us. "We want each camper to take home with him a better understanding of the fundamentals of the game, discipline, including self-discipline, and everything that goes into the making of a complete person and athlete. Thank you very much for your cooperation toward these standards."

Coach Welcomes the Campers and Parents

At three fifteen campers and their parents meet with the camp's staff in the gym. Camp directors Hector Macias and Hal Mitrovich are Coach's warm-up act. They introduce the coaches and counselors, briefly address the parents and campers, and then introduce Coach.

Coach Wooden welcomes the campers and parents and talks about his expectations for all his players:

> Be a gentleman at all times, and be a team player always. Be on time whenever time is involved. Be a good student in all subjects, not just basketball, by being enthusiastic, industrious, dependable, loyal, and cooperative. Work constantly to improve without being satisfied. Keep your emotions under control without losing fight or aggressiveness. Be in the best possible condition—physically, mentally, and morally. Earn the right to be proud and confident.
>
> It is very important that you show consideration for others at all times. Acquire peace of mind by becoming the best that you are capable of becoming. Never criticize, nag, or razz a teammate. Never be selfish, jealous, envious, or egotistical. Never expect favors, never waste time, never alibi or make excuses. Never require repeated criticism for

> the same mistake. Never grandstand, loaf, sulk, or boast, and never have reason to say sorry afterward.[6]
>
> Basketball is an experience in working together. At camp not only do we learn the game, but we learn some of the important aspects of life itself—living together, working together, being considerate of others, and maintaining good physical conditioning.[7]

Coach Wooden next talks to the campers about proper behavior in the dorms, cafeteria, and camp in general: "Discipline yourself so others don't have to," he says, delivering one of his famous John Wooden statements. This phrase is so powerful and impacting that campers remember it well into their adult lives. "Be polite in the gym, on campus, in the dorms, and in the cafeteria. Politeness is a small price to pay to get the goodwill and affection of others, and it will reap many benefits in the end," Coach continues.

He then talks briefly about basketball:

> In my opinion, the contribution of any athlete in a team sport is based on three things.
>
> The first is physical conditioning. This is attained and maintained by daily organized practices under the supervision of a coach and the proper mental and moral conduct of the individual players between practices.
>
> The second is proper and quick execution of the basic fundamentals. These can be acquired only by hard work in practice. It has been said that repetition is the secret of knowledge, and certainly proper habits can be acquired only by repeated execution of designed drills.
>
> The third is teamwork. This means an eagerness to sacrifice personal interests or glory for the welfare of the team. It is being considerate of others and realizing that it is the only way of ensuring consideration of others for you. It is also a great help toward the attainment of peace

of mind, because you must give to receive. Honor comes from giving.

Basketball is a game of habits, and it takes time and patience to develop the proper habits. You must never be satisfied, no matter how well you are doing. You'll never become perfect. I want my players to be working on something at all times while they are on the floor. If I catch them fooling around, I ask them, "Are you perfect? Do you think you are? If you don't think you need improvement in any parts of the game, I'll show you a few areas in which you do."

The player who gives his best is sure of success, while the player who gives less than his best is a failure. The cornerstones of success are industriousness and enthusiasm. There is no substitute for work, and when you find it hard to work, that is the time you should force yourself to work the hardest. It has been said that when you find it hardest to pray, pray hardest. Hard work is much the same way.

My personal definition of success is peace of mind, which can be attained only through self-satisfaction in knowing you did your best to become the very best you are capable of becoming.[8]

The tone and expectations have been set for the campers. For many of the parents in attendance, Coach Wooden's talk about such timeless values makes the camp worth every penny already. Parents, like their boys, have been instructed, inspired, and challenged. Their sons may not yet understand Coach's wisdom and greatness, but most of the parents surely do.

The Campers' First Lesson

Remarkably, the greatest coach ever now demonstrates a simple but powerful lesson that everyone will remember forever. Coach sits down on the floor, takes his shoes and socks off, and explains the proper way to put footwear on in order to prevent blisters and maintain proper shoe care. As a child of the Great Depression, Coach did not have the luxury of buying new, expensive, stylish shoes when he played. He needed to take good care of his shoes to make sure that they remained functional and lasted.

Many parents, especially women, are amused, while some of the men think it is odd to see Coach sitting on the ground demonstrating. His college players often had the same response on the first day of practice when Coach demonstrated this same lesson to them. It is a profound, humble lesson reflecting his desire for those under his supervision to be their best and also showing his attention to detail. My fellow coaches and I are riveted on Coach with a sense of awe and admiration.

Coach explains that when a player takes his shoes off at night, he should lean them up against a wall to allow a clear path for perspiration to evaporate so that the inside of the shoes dry out. "This prevents athlete's foot and helps out with shoe odors, because the inside of the shoe dries properly."

He then demonstrates the proper way to put socks on in order to prevent blisters: "With all the quick stops, turning, changes of direction, and changes of pace on a hard floor that you have in basketball, you can get blisters. Now when you pull on your socks, I want you to make sure there are no wrinkles or gaps as you put your socks on. Now pull it up in the back real good, real strong. Now put your hand around the little toe area. Make sure there are no wrinkles, and then pull it back up. Check the heel area. We don't want any signs of wrinkles."

Next he demonstrates the proper way to put a shoe on and tie it: "Now put your shoe on. Put it in wide, and now pull it up. Don't grab the shoelaces up by your ankles. Go down by the toes and pull each eyelet up, eyelet by eyelet, until it is snug. Then double tie it. This prevents ankle and foot injuries. Here at camp first put your room keys through the last eyelet on your left shoe and then double tie the knot."

With his shoes and socks back on, he comes to his feet. He wraps up his talk by reminding the campers that they are guests at Cal Lu. "It's a pretty campus. Let's keep it that way. Pick up trash even if it is not yours, and stay on the sidewalk and off the grass. On Friday let's leave Cal Lu a nicer place than we found it. It is difficult for you to do the right things when you see adults not doing them, but we expect politeness and decorum in the cafeteria, and there should not be teasing or harassment of others. Show consideration at all times for others."[9]

Coach demonstrates the proper way to put a shoe on and tie it. He understands that little things add up to big things.

Coach understands that little things add up to big things. Not all campers will understand the value of correctly putting on shoes and socks at first, but eventually they will. Former camper Leroy Smith played basketball at the University of California and is now successful in his career in the medical field. He has brought his nephew to camp, and he stops to chat with local coach Ken Morgan, a former assistant coach at Stanford. Leroy recalls to Ken, "At camp we were told that we need to understand the fundamental principles of success, and in basketball it begins with knowing how to tie your shoes. My first thought was, *How silly this is—I already know how to do this.* Eventually I began to understand that to reach any level of success, it starts with forming a solid foundation. That's what Coach is teaching these kids and what I have benefited from ever since I came to camp."

Actor Beau Bridges played briefly for Coach at UCLA before the championship years, saw Coach demonstrate to the team the proper way to put shoes and socks on, and appreciates the value of this lesson. He brings his son to this camp and quips after watching Coach put his shoes and socks back on, "All these years later, and Coach still hasn't learned a thing."

After Coach finishes on time at three thirty, Coach Macias directs the campers to their evaluation area, where teams for the week will be formed later tonight. He warns them not to walk on the grass and especially not barefoot since there are bees in the grass. Campers say goodbye to their parents and then are off to the courts, where they will play basketball until four thirty and then go to dinner.

Eleven-year-old camper Darren Ranck walks to the dorms with his friends and tells them, "You need to listen to what Coach Wooden said about how to put your shoes and socks on. I didn't listen my first year, and I got really bad blisters playing outside on the blacktop. Last year I did it like he says to, and I didn't get any blisters."

As the coaches walk out of the gym and Coach Wooden gets ready to go home, he asks coach Tom Gregory, a close friend of his who has been coaching Wooden camps for many years, how he is doing. Coach is aware that Gregory was unfairly criticized the past season. "Remember," Coach encourages him, "people who mind don't matter. People who matter don't mind." Gregory feels his spirits lift.

Eating in Lil Lopez's Cafeteria

Camp meals are served in the beautiful second-floor Cal Lu cafeteria, but in reality the cafeteria is Lil Lopez's. Lil, the director of food services at Cal Lu, is loved by all and is a special person to camp veterans such as camp director Hal Mitrovich, who says that "Lil is just a sweetheart." Lil, who always seems to have a big ring of keys in her hand, knows the way to everyone's hearts: through their stomachs and through her inner strength, charm, and love.

The younger campers, like eleven-year-old Jamey Power, are a bit intimidated on this first day of camp around the older teenage campers in the cafeteria. But it won't be long until most campers will feel more comfortable, as is evidenced by the pranks they pull on each other later in the week. Campers learn soon enough to be sure that the lids are twisted tightly on the salt and pepper shakers before seasoning their food; they also learn not to go to the bathroom during dinner lest they find their food tampered with when they return.

A loud crash of dishes followed by good-natured applause means that someone has dropped his food tray as he walks to a table. A fourteen-year-old camper has just become the first to do that, but everyone in camp, including the adults, knows that it can happen to them before the week is over.

Coach Wayne Carlson and I are extremely hungry, as are most in the camp after a day of travel and introductions and orientation meetings. Fortunately for us coaches and counselors, we are permitted to walk to the front of the line instead of having to wait outside with hundreds of campers. As we stand in line to get our food, Carlson points to a young woman serving food and boldly proclaims, "She's really cute. I think I'm going to ask her out." I look at him wide eyed, with a big smile, and say a bit incredulously, "Seriously? Do you know her?"

Carlson replies, "No, but I'm going to ask her out right now." Sure enough, when we get closer to the young woman, Carlson asks her out for ice cream on Wednesday night. She smiles and answers yes. I almost drop my tray right there.

As we sit down to eat, Carlson admits, "Okay, I do know her. I had a date with her roommate once, which is when I first met her, and she and I went out last Wednesday when I was coaching last week's camp. Her name is Laura Erwin. She goes to Cal Lu, and working in the cafeteria is her summer job." I laugh and gain new respect for my coaching friend.

Over dinner I tell Carlson a personal story involving Coach. Ed Powell, who played for Coach in high school back in Indiana and was also his longtime assistant coach at both Indiana State

Teacher's College and UCLA, had become the city manager of Placentia, a small town near Disneyland, and had arranged for a new neighborhood street in Placentia to be named Wooden Way. My mom, Patricia, who is a resident of Placentia, met Coach at the ceremony, and he spoke highly about me to her, as he does with everyone when he meets their relatives or friends. My mom loves each of her ten children as if every one of us is an only child, and her heart was touched by Coach's goodness, thoughtfulness, and humility. Many other camp coaches can tell similar stories about Coach having such a positive effect on their own loved ones.

The End of the First Day

After dinner the campers have free time for an hour or so; then they report back to the basketball courts, where the coaches evaluate the players' skill levels in order to assign them to teams. As we watch the players dribble, pass, and shoot, we balance teams by moving players up or down a division or from team to team based on the players' ability.

Thirty-two teams will be formed for the week, and the teams will be divided into divisions. For fun we use real names—the best players go into what we call the NBA, while the others are grouped into the Pac-10, the Southeast Conference (SEC), and the Big Ten. Each team will be named for a college team, such as the Lakers or Michigan or, of course, UCLA. The teams will spend the early part of the week drilling fundamentals in preparation for the highly anticipated team games to be played on Wednesday, Thursday, and Friday. Knowing that the success of our teams will depend heavily on the draw tonight, we observe and assign players carefully.

At seven thirty campers are given a brief free time before reporting to the gym for eight-fifteen roll call. The mandatory evening program includes UCLA championship team films shown under the stars on a big white sheet outside the gym.

Campers are in their rooms by nine thirty and given a short time for a quick call home, a shower, unpacking, and making their beds or getting their sleeping bags set up. It has been a full day. They need to become quiet and get to sleep quickly to be ready for an even fuller schedule on Monday. With only a few pay phones available at the end of the dorm hallways, not every camper who wants to is able to make the brief collect call home so that their parents can call right back to save money. Some campers talk for a long time, so by the nine-thirty "In your rooms" command, quite a few campers are unable to call home. It makes for a tough first night for some.

Lights are out at ten, and most are asleep by eleven thirty, although there are occasional late-night problems with campers who can get into all sorts of mischief and trouble if not monitored closely. Misbehaving campers are often awakened early the next morning for an extra workout. If the camper continues to misbehave after the first day, he has a private meeting with Hector the Director, which is not pleasant. The most feared punishment is consistent with Coach Wooden's philosophy—loss of the privilege of attending camp. A call home tells the parents to pick their youngster up from camp. This rarely happens, but it happens enough that campers know the seriousness of it.

Unless one specifically requests a friend, roommates are assigned by the luck of the draw, so campers may have a good roommate or a difficult one. Eleven-year-old Jamey Power's luck is good. Dodgers announcer Ross Porter's son, Ross Jr., who is a humble and polite kid, is Power's roommate. Jamey has been brought up in a home where it is understood that "to whom much is given, much is expected." Ross seems to have been similarly raised.

Hopefully each camper will have considerate roommates, quickly get used to being in a strange bed, and overcome any feelings of homesickness. Some are away from home for the first time ever. But from Monday on, the campers will stay busy playing basketball, which generally keeps their minds off their troubles. They will get to know their new teammates and find friends whom they enjoy being around. Soon most will feel comfortable with each other and with friendly, caring coaches and counselors, who become their parent figures away from home.

Coach Jeff Dunlap remembers being a nine-year-old camper away from home for the first time when his parents took a vacation to Las Vegas. He was homesick that first night and cried a lot. But he ended up having a great camp. He went two more times as a camper, and then, while a basketball player at UCLA, served as one of Coach Wooden's head counselors for three years. After that he became a camp coach and has served in that role ever since. Despite his dubious beginnings, Dunlap loves camp and thoroughly enjoys spending as much time with Coach as he can.

One thing has not changed since Dunlap first went to camp: the campers will need their sleep, as will the coaches and counselors. Early tomorrow morning, the hard work begins!

2

Focus on the Fundamentals

Up and at 'em. Everybody up, and let's get going." Today is the first full day of camp, and head counselors Jaws and Hawk, along with camp directors Hal and Hector the Director, are up early, banging on doors and waking up campers. Once awake, the campers dress in the "camp T-shirt and walk from the two main dorms by Mt. Clef Hall and then to the cafeteria." Hector made it clear the night before that campers were to "walk around Mt. Clef and not through the building." Breakfast is from six forty-five to seven thirty. A long line of hungry campers stretches along the sidewalk outside the cafeteria by the time the doors open.

Jaws is up at five each morning, leaving Cal Lu by five fifteen to pick Coach up at his condominium at 1111 Margate Street, unit 23, in Encino. They return five minutes before breakfast, which begins at a quarter of seven. On most mornings coaches and campers arrive in the cafeteria to see Coach Wooden already seated at his round table with his back to the area where campers and staff drop off their food trays after eating. But Coach Wooden is not there this morning. He is outside at "Madison Square Garden," on the Cal Lu tennis courts, where three courts have been lined for basketball and six baskets installed. He is there to teach the coaches the UCLA high-post offense and other fundamentals. Coach enjoys showing us coaches the precise way in which he wants things taught and has fun with us as well.

Coaches volunteer to run the offense as he puts us through the positioning and movements. This is an intense, focused time, but all of us enjoy being coached hands on by Coach Wooden. Coach puts his former player, Jim Nielsen, in the high-post spot to demonstrate. After a while Coach good-naturedly teases him. "Jim, you didn't know the offense when you played at UCLA, and you still don't."

Someone has told Coach that Tom Gregory is a great shooter, so Coach decides to put Gregory in the shooter spot in plays. Gregory comes off a screen but, instead of shooting, freezes when he is blinded by the bright morning sun.[1] Coach understands but has some fun with him as well. "Why didn't you shoot the ball?"

Coach offers us some simple reminders: "It isn't any one offense or defense that brings the most out of your players under your supervision. Your job is to get the most out of what you have. The more you worry about what the other teams have, the less you are going to do with what you have.

"It isn't this style or system you use that will get the job done," he goes on. "It's these three things: Get them in the best possible condition and keep them there. Teach them not only the proper fundamentals but to quickly execute them. Get them to play as a team, and keep in mind that balance is the most important thing."

Some of the veteran coaches have won a lot of games heeding this advice. Coach continues, "I want the shots to come from the offense, not from some individual dribbling around to get open, except in certain situations when the defense makes a mistake. On the shot from the offense, we want triangle rebounding power underneath, a long rebounder, and a protector. Never pass to a player standing still, and we must attack each side of the floor equally."

He follows this by a brief review of the offense. "Our center will start on one side or the other of the foul line," he instructs. "Our two guards will be just wider than the foul line extended to the top of the key. Both forwards should be one step in from the sideline, with the front foot even, with the foul line extended. The opposite forward must be alert to cut to the high post whenever he sees the defense on the off guard overplaying to deny a pass from guard to guard. As the guard passes to the forward, the guard cuts for the basket, and the forward has different options."

From there Coach further explains the famous UCLA cut, as it is now known, which is run by so many coaches in the country. This is when the guard passes to the wing player and then runs to the basket looking for a layup.[2]

As the coaches walk to breakfast, they marvel at how enthusiastic, wise, positive, and focused Coach is. He still gets so much pleasure out of teaching even the "big kids"—his coaches—and his teaching skills and attention to detail are exemplary.

Dining with Coach Wooden

The best part of camp for the coaches is the opportunity that we have to eat breakfast and lunch with Coach—for some of us every breakfast and lunch of every camp. Some of the coaches go to the nearby El Torito Mexican restaurant to socialize each night and get back to camp late, but those who do still get up early to have breakfast with Coach. Burning the candle at both ends, these coaches are more exhausted by the end of the week than anyone else, but breakfast with Coach is not to be missed.

Coach Jim Harrick, the head coach at UCLA and Coach Wooden's first camp director back in 1971, started the tradition of eating meals with Coach Wooden. He describes them as "Coach holding court with the coaches. It's like getting a doctorate degree in basketball," he says. "During those meals I had to blow my whistle after a while to break it up and get the coaches out of the cafeteria and back into the gym." Mealtimes are wonderful opportunities for coaches to learn a tremendous amount of basketball knowledge.

Coaches also enjoy hearing Coach talk about the morning sports section of the newspaper, especially when it comes to baseball and the Dodgers. But what is most lasting is the wisdom they gain from Coach on how to be better husbands, fathers, grandfathers, teachers, friends, and citizens. The discussions are enlightening, enjoyable, and impactful, and coaches remember what Coach Wooden says long after camp ends.

The more Coach talks about something, the more his listeners understand the wisdom behind it.

The newer coaches might ask questions that he has answered in previous years, but Coach always answers fully, honestly, patiently, with insight and great wisdom. The veteran coaches do not mind hearing the answers again, because the more Coach talks about something, the more they understand the wisdom behind it. Camp coach Lee Smelser, who gave Jim Harrick his first break when he hired him as his junior varsity coach at Morningside High School, says, "Coach never ducks a question. He can always relate a question to any subject of interest to us."

Coach is generous with his time and energy and genuinely enjoys talking basketball and life and just telling stories. Wayne Carlson of San Diego has sat in on a lot of these mealtime discussions. "Coach seems to have an aura of wisdom about him, and he speaks wisely with an economy of words," Carlson says. "He often quotes Shakespeare, especially the line 'To thine own self be true.' For Coach to be true to himself means that he will not gossip, criticize, or judge others nor complain. He is always gracious, dignified, respectful, and considerate toward others. And he has a great sense of humor."

It has become a friendly competition to try to sit next to Coach at mealtimes, but a rookie or a fairly new coach has little chance of sitting by him. It is an assumed rite of passage that the veterans get the seats next to Coach. The newer coaches and counselors and especially the rookies hope that they can just edge their chairs somewhere round the table, even if it means sitting behind another coach outside the inner circle.

I started as a camp counselor in 1977, but through the years I eventually made my way to sitting one or two seats away from Coach and even right next to him. I treasure these times and write down everything Coach says, so much so that a few veterans call me "Little Wooden." While there might be lighthearted teasing behind the nickname, I take it as a special compliment and consider the name a term of endearment.

But the coaches cannot compete with their children for a place in Coach's heart or a seat next to him—or on his lap. When David Myers' daughter Kelly was three years old, she wandered over to the coaches' breakfast table and climbed right up on Coach Wooden's lap. Myers was mortified as Kelly started eating bacon right off Coach's plate.

Coach asked her, "Do you like bacon?"

"Yes, it is crispy," replied Kelly. Coach loves bacon, and Lil makes sure that it is crispy and crunchy the way he likes it best. Coach's loving and gentle nature with Kelly made her father relax and enjoy the precious moment as the basketball discussion continued as normal.

Sage Coaching Advice

During breakfast Coach further explains to us the UCLA high-post offense, beginning with the correct play sequence and an emphasis on first teaching the fundamentals. "Guard backdoor is taught first, followed by hit the high post, guard cuts, guard handoff, and then forward reverse and pick-and-roll plays," Coach explains. "Only then should special plays be put in. From there teach the three passing options of every passer. Timing is key, as is moving after you pass. The most important part is player movement as you receive the pass and after you pass. There should never be anyone standing. Keep the ball moving. No one holds the ball more than two seconds except the high post. Emphasize floor balance and teamwork and that there should be equal opportunity for all.

"Which option is most effective depends on personnel and what will be difficult to defend," Coach continues. "You must have at least one intelligent guard to recognize these things. We never call the basic plays. If you execute well, you will get a good shot every time and hit a high percentage. If you have a small team, this is a good offense. My best high-school teams were small, and I put the smallest player at the high post. He was a good passer and could also drive from the high post."

It is an enlightening discussion, especially since so many of us coaches run this offense with our own teams during the regular season.

"Coach, which is more important, offense or defense?" asks coach Mike Scarano.

"I believe and have said multiple times that most of our championships were won on defense," answers Coach.

"How many of you coaches spend more time on defense than on offense?" he asks in return. "So while defense is key to winning championships, offense takes more time, because you must do things with the basketball. You have to learn to shoot, pass, dribble, protect, and stop and turn with the basketball. You don't have to do these on defense. There is no question in my mind that the coach who spends more time on defense is not using his time properly. Offense and defense are equally important, but it takes more time for offense than it does for defense."

Coach adds a quick point in a light tone: "I don't like players who say they like to play defense more than play offense. That's not natural, you know."

"People say that UCLA fans have become really spoiled," asks another. "What do you think?"

Coach has fun with this honest question. "When I was at UCLA, if you won all the games, you were considered reasonably successful, but not completely, because I found out that we had a number of years at UCLA in which we didn't lose a game—but it seemed that we didn't win each individual game by the margin that some of our alumni had predicted. Quite frankly, I really felt that they backed up their predictions in a more materialistic manner."[3]

As we all burst out laughing, Hector stops by the table. "Let's go, coaches. We need to get to the stadium for the camp picture."

Getting Underway: Day One

At eight o'clock on this Monday morning, coaches, counselors, and campers meet in Cal Lu's football stadium next to the gym for the group camp photo. Coach sits in the middle of the bottom row of the bleachers reading his newspaper, while coaches jockey for position next to him or as near to him as possible. Today it is Ken Morgan's and my lucky day. The younger campers' division takes their big group picture first. The bleachers are wet from the morning dew, so the older group appreciates the younger players drying the bleachers off for them. Coach Wooden sits on his newspaper to avoid the early morning dew.

Once the photos are taken, the campers head to the gym, while the coaches meet briefly with directors Hector and Hal outside the gym's front entrance to go over the day's activities. All of us know not to be late to these daily coaches' meetings.

Hector begins by reminding us that Coach Wooden insists on all shirts being tucked in—those of campers and coaches alike. We review the day's schedule: morning workouts for the campers led by Coach; training stations in which the coaches will sharpen their teams' skills; afternoon drills, also led by Coach; and evening practice and scrimmages. Hal talks briefly about Coach's high expectations of the coaches in teaching the first stations later this morning. As we finish up, Hal reminds us, "Hustle and work as hard during the teaching stations as if you were with your own team at home."

Coach enjoys these brief meetings each morning with the coaches. He is motivated to teach the campers, but he also really enjoys mentoring his coaches and interacting with them.

The campers assemble in the gym with the counselors as they wait for the coaches. Some play pickup games, some shoot, some sit and watch the others. The small gym reverberates with the noise bouncing off the walls and to the rafters as balls bounce and campers talk and laugh. Instant quiet reigns when Hal blows his whistle, and Hector commands attention from the microphone on the stage.

The two groups of campers—the younger gold division and the older blue division—will rotate between the gym and the theater from 8:20–8:50 and then from 8:50–9:20. While one group does morning workouts with Coach, the other group goes to the small, narrow theater next door, where on most mornings they watch instructional films shown on an old 16 mm projector that projects onto a portable standup screen. The counselors hope that the decrepit projector does not break since it is difficult to fix.

After a brief roll call, the younger group lines up for their first session with Coach Wooden, while the older group heads to the theater. On this first morning, instead of seeing a film, the groups attend an "Injuries and Conditioning" seminar put on by the Cal Lu sports medical staff. A qualified staff is on duty at all times, which shows that Sportsworld values camper safety and health. During the week some campers may take advantage of this camp perk and spend time being treated for injuries that normally would not require much attention, if any at all.

Fundamentals with Coach

Coach Wooden will put each group of campers through intense, energetic, and high-spirited fundamentals drills for half an hour each morning this week. Coach is at his best in these sessions as he stands on stage coaching 130 to 150 campers per session with the same sequential fundamental drills he used at UCLA. Fundamentals, discipline, hard work, intensity, and consideration of others formed the culture of his UCLA teams and now do so in his camps. Coach believes that the foundational learning strategy, the best teacher, is repetition to the point at which knowledge becomes automatic. For his UCLA teams that process went on throughout the season. For these campers it will consist of five intense and highly motivating morning workouts with Coach.

Many of the campers know of the glory days of UCLA basketball under Coach and still watch the Bruins play on television or in person at Pauley Pavilion, home of the UCLA men's and women's basketball teams. They are now eager and excited to be working directly under the famous coach, and they look forward to being able to brag about having been taught by Coach Wooden. Microphone in hand, Coach paces back and forth on stage, keenly observing each group of campers. On that stage he quickly transforms from the friendly grandfather figure to more of a drill sergeant, albeit a warm and caring one. With his whistle directing stops and starts, he instructs, corrects, and directs. A short whistle means that he wants the players to repeat a particular skill; a long whistle signifies that Coach wants to stop a drill, either to make a point or to move on to a new drill. The master teacher is in command of his classroom—the Cal Lu gymnasium.

"Okay, now I want you to spread your lines out along the court facing me. Double arm's length away from each other. Good. Alright now, I want you to get in a defensive stance. Be on balance. Every joint flexed and relaxed, head directly above the midpoint of your two feet, weight forward on the balls of your feet, hands in close."

Coach continues, "Now I want you to pick your left foot up and stand on your right foot. Now hold it there and stay on balance." He waits as all the campers stand on one leg and try not to fall over. Eleven-year-old Harvey Mason, right in front of Coach, does not want to fall. He manages to hold his balance, even as most around him fall onto two feet, and his legs start to shake.

Coach smiles. "Remember that balance is important in everything we do in basketball and in life. You must have good balance. Not just physical balance but also mental and emotional balance. Never get too high or too low emotionally." Harvey and the other campers who kept their balance on one leg feel pleased with themselves.

Now the session really gets going as players drill without a ball and focus on footwork, proper technique, and visualization. "Okay, position for the jump shot. Don't let any part of your body get out of whack. Good control. Try to do it together." At Coach's whistle the players shoot an imaginary ball at an imaginary basket six times. "Be on balance on the shot," Coach instructs. "You must look at the basket. See that imaginary basket, and keep your eyes right on it." At first the imaginary and visualization drills are hard for campers to picture, but the more they do it, the more they get the hang of it and do the drills with freedom, aggressiveness, precision, and real enjoyment.

"Ready?" Coach calls out. Whenever Coach says "Ready," it might be a statement or a question, but it is mainly a command to prepare to start a drill, and it is immediately followed by another whistle for the players to begin.

After several repetitions of each fundamental skill, Coach quickly moves on to the next drill. He continually shouts out instructions and information with the energy and sharpness of a young coach. He is specific with his information and often repeats the same command two or three times in a row, as he knows that this is necessary for learning to take place with so many youngsters at one time. He often commands with "You must" when insisting that a fundamental skill be done correctly, on balance, and quickly.

"Ready for the shot fake–drive and shoot," he calls. "Back up two steps. Alright, get the defense to raise up slightly, and as they're raising up, that's when you go by him. But if you don't go by quickly, you won't go by at all. Freeze the defense. Ready." Coach blows his whistle, and campers, with an imaginary ball and basket, fake a shot and then take a few dribbles toward the basket and shoot a layup.

Coach blows the whistle to stop them. He now has them practice offensive rebound tip-ins. "Hands above your shoulders, slightly crouched. Two offensive tips. Alternate the right- and left-hand tips." This drill, like so many others, builds off the previous drill. On the whistle the campers go hard forward to try to tip the ball into an imaginary basket. "Now come forward four or five steps as quickly as possible, then come to a halt and then go up for the tips. Ready." His long whistle ends the drill, and the campers clap rhythmically together as they often do when a drill ends.

Coach talks over their clapping, even as he appreciates their enthusiasm and has come to anticipate and expect it. There is no wasted time or standing around. Coach shouts instructions, while the campers drill over the echoing noise of shoes squeaking and balls bouncing. Coach Wooden rarely interrupts or stops drills to talk. If he does, it is for five to ten seconds; it's amazing that it takes so few moments for this nearly eighty-year-old coach to demonstrate the correct fundamental technique or to make a quick correction. Coach is quick, smart, and witty, and his old age does not slow him down even in the hustle and bustle of camp. He makes each fundamental drill transition quickly and efficiently.

The next drill involves the campers getting an offensive rebound, making a pump fake, and then scoring. "I want the two-hand rip and the pump fake to the power shot. Ready. Get the hands above the shoulders." On rebounds Coach wants players to assume that the shot has been missed, get their hands above their shoulders, and go hard after the ball with two hands. "Jerk the ball to your chest. Come fast for the rebound, but don't come and broad jump. You get there quickly to the position and then under control before you jump."

A lot of noise and energy fill the small Cal Lu gym as players work in small spaces. Coach's own intensity motivates the campers, as seen in their enthusiastic rhythmic group clapping. Their intensity rises in response to Coach Wooden's, and they are energized by him even as they fatigue. Coach is a great teacher and leader who motivates these young kids, despite his advanced age.

The campers feel good moving and working so intensely. Coach is not one to give a lot of verbal praise, and never false praise, but in his own way he gives much non-verbal encouragement and approval through tone of voice, facial expression, and gestures. His corrections are constructive and instructive, and the campers respond well to them. He directs corrections to the entire group so that everyone can hear and accept his teaching and message. Campers enjoy these corrective sessions, especially since Coach does not use physical punishment but rather positive motivation—in fact, many assert that this is one of the biggest success factors of his UCLA teams. The inspiration that drives the campers is internal—as Coach defines it, it is a peace that comes from knowing that they are their giving their best effort to be the best that they can be. Coach models this kind of inspiration himself. In fact, his very life is the strongest motivation that these campers need to achieve true success by working to be their best.

There is no pause between drills. "Take a defensive position," Coach instructs. "Ready? Move on the signal. Follow me." He points, and they slide a few steps in the direction in which he points. They move constantly by sliding in different directions as Coach points forward, backward, to the sides, and at angles. "Stay low. Be crouched. Be loose. Slide—don't jump. Good position. The head should stay relatively even as you slide. It shouldn't be bobbing up and down."

He continues. "Now straighten up your lines." Coach works with the campers on defensive rebounding block-outs and different ways to do them. "Face the other way. Face the far wall. Defensive position. No turning—no coming for the rebound. Just the step back." Coach is teaching very basically and making sure that the campers do the simple footwork in increments before adding the block-out and the imaginary rebound.

Now he adds the block-out. "Alright, hold it. Don't go for the rebound. Step back, cross over. Right foot forward. The next time you go out, have your left foot forward. Keep alternating. Ready." At the whistle the campers block out their "opponent" with a crossover step into the defender.

Coach has the players do the block-out again, but this time he has them do it using a reverse pivot. He is teaching them the two different ways to block out an opponent on a shot. "This time no crossover. Reverse turn. Go."

Coach's life is the strongest motivation that these campers need to achieve true success by working to be their best.

Counselor Howard Fisher won Coach Wooden's Pyramid of Success award—an award given to campers who exemplify Coach's principles of true success for basketball and for life—when he was a thirteen-year-old camper some years before. Before this morning's session began, he told his campers, "These repetitive fundamental drills had a big impact on me when I was a player. For two weeks after camp ended, I continued to do these simple fundamental drills on my own in my grandparents' driveway. Work hard. Don't take these workout opportunities with Coach Wooden for granted."

Finally the players add the imaginary rebound with the two types of block-outs. "Either foot forward," Coach continues. "Cross over, reverse pivot, take four to five steps, and go get a tough rebound. Come down on good balance. Don't be off balance." This is similar to what the campers did earlier with the offensive rebound, so it is simple for them to do. "Ready, go. Good balance. I want you there quicker. I want that rebound quicker. Come hard for the rebound and then hold it until I tell you to go back.

"Remember, cross over, and when the right foot hits the floor, you are coming hard to get the rebound. Ready?" The campers do about five repetitions of this drill. "Last one. Now let's have a real good one."

The campers make a focused and determined effort and then Coach directs the campers to the end of the court for the next drills. "Down here," he clarifies as he points to the end line by the wall. "Run. Look at your marker on the wall. Get in line."[4]

It has been a good start, with the campers working hard and enthusiastically. Coach is pleased with their good work and smiles as the campers form lines at the ends of the court. They work hard for another twenty minutes on a variety of simple fundamentals.

Coach always liked to end UCLA practices on a high note through little things such as a light comment, a smile, or a sign of approval or affection. He does the same now as he ends this workout before handing the microphone over to Hector. His action also calms the campers down so that they pay attention and respond to Coach Macias's directions. In doing this Coach Wooden demonstrates consideration for and team spirit toward Coach Macias. Coach is not one to hog the limelight. His consideration for others is humbling and enlightening.

The Coaches Get to Work

The hard work for the day is just beginning. From nine thirty until ten, the coaches work with their campers and evaluate each one's shot. Counselor Kevin Barbarick remembers this as being one of the most important and helpful parts of his own camp experience.

When the evaluations are finished, group stations begin. The coaches earn their pay most in these morning stations, which occur from ten to eleven thirty, Monday through Thursday. The stations are highly organized, but they require hard work, and they are tough on the coaches' vocal cords. The curriculum in the coach's notebook detailing the stations focuses on the fundamental drills needed to execute the UCLA high-post offense, an offensive strategy made famous by Coach Wooden. This fundamental skill contains precision in its details, and the coaches need to make sure the campers learn it.

Campers rotate through eight stations, each one focusing on a particular fundamental skill and manned by a different coach. Stations include layups, shooting, jump stops and pivots, passing, dribbling, pick-and-rolls, rebounding and defense, and UCLA high-post offense work. Each coach teaches sixteen to seventeen campers for ten minutes at each session.

Kevin Barbarick remembers as a camper working on the famous UCLA duck move—part of the UCLA high-post offense—and picturing himself as UCLA and NBA great Marques Johnson. It is a big deal to the campers to be doing these UCLA drills like the great ones did. This classic passing drill calls for a player to dribble out from the starting point three to four dribbles, jump-stop, reverse pivot with elbows out, pass to the next player in line, and then make a change-of-pace and change-of-direction cut to the end of the line.

Pick-and-rolls involve one player dribbling off a pick, or a screen, set outside the key by a teammate. Normally pick-and-rolls are simple to teach, but Coach Wooden insists that all screens be set as back picks to avoid offensive fouls—the screener is expected to step forward with the foot that is nearest the defender and then pivot so that his back is facing the defender. Coach Wooden demonstrated this morning, but newer coaches still struggle to teach it properly.

As the coaches work with the campers, the counselors often help. A strong counselor will even explain the station to the campers during a few of the rotations. Many counselors allow the coaches to be an overseer and mentor to them, while some actually help the coaches learn new things. I started as a camp counselor twelve years ago, and my coach, Joe Jennum, was so pleased with me that he praised me and even recommended that Sportsworld hire me as a coach. I have been a camp coach ever since and am extremely grateful for the opportunity I have had and for Coach Jennum's encouragement and kindness.

During stations, despite his arthritic knees, Coach Wooden takes a daily brisk five- or six-mile walk on campus, accompanied by a camp director and a head counselor. Coach Wooden picks up trash as he walks, which leaves an indelible impression on coaches, counselors, and campers. The coaches' children observe him do this as well whenever they walk for a short time with him. Coach loves these children and enjoys hearing what they have done since last summer.

Coach passes by the stations on his walk, and as he does, coach Don Showalter thinks, *Please let us run the high-post offense correctly just once when Coach walks by*. He is not the only one to think that. Coaches are eager to please and honor him by teaching things the way he wants them taught. No one wants to mess up or let Coach down; we feel a responsibility and pressure to coach perfectly for him. His picture and name are on the front of our shirts, and it matters greatly that we teach well for him—and, selfishly, that we be invited back to coach each year.

Coach might stop and make quick suggestions to coaches or campers, but he is considerate and never one to show the coaches up. He might say, "Have you tried it this way?" and then move on. On very rare occasions he will correct a drill that is not run correctly. "No. That is not how I want it. It should be done this way." But most of the time Coach just observes and gives coaches the opportunity to implement their own philosophy within the framework of the camp curriculum.

This morning, however, he stops by David Myers's shooting station. Myers's first thought is, *Uh oh, what am I doing wrong?* But Coach just wants to show the best way to do the drill for the betterment of both Myers and his campers.

Coaches are divided as to the best place to hold stations. The gym puts a strain on coaches' voices as whistles, bouncing balls, squeaking shoes, and people's voices echo throughout the gym and make it difficult to be heard. Still, some coaches choose to work in the gym, as it provides the campers more court space. If it is cool enough outside, however, some coaches choose to work there, where they can talk and be heard more easily, even though space can be a bit cramped, since they might end up on one of the smaller half courts.

On the outside courts, wise veteran coaches wear wide-brimmed hats, while the younger ones soak up the sun without protection. Jim Harrick wore one such a hat when he coached but once made the mistake of taking it off and leaving it on the ground for a while. Coach Wooden loves to tease Harrick, and he grabbed the hat and wrote something inside it. When Harrick picked it back up, he saw that Coach had written "This hat belongs to Nell Wooden."

Coach and Nell

Camp has always been special for Coach, but it was especially so when his wife, Nell, was alive. Coach was even better around Nell, if that was possible—it was almost as if he was not Coach Wooden but simply Mr. John Wooden, happily married husband, loving father, and doting grandfather. Nell was outgoing, funny, expressive, and gregarious. She always came to camp with Coach for the Sunday afternoon check-in, as did his children, Nan and Jim, and his grandchildren, including Nan's three beautiful daughters. In the earlier years of camp, Nell and Coach often stayed the entire week at camp, and Nell enjoyed tanning by the university pool or going shopping with coaches' wives. It seems that Coach was happiest when he was with Nell and his family on those Sunday afternoons at camp.

Coach and Nell made a great team. They were warm, friendly, and welcoming toward all. Parents in particular, especially those who had watched and cheered for Wooden's UCLA teams for years from afar, were excited to meet Coach and Nell in person. The Woodens made parents and campers feel at ease and comfortable, and they also treated the camp staff and their families well. Longtime successful Ventura High School coach, Mickey Perry, who coached in the early years of camp, remembers, "One camp I got a bad case of laryngitis, and Nell took care of me like she was my mother. They both treated us so well."

Coach always sees the best in people, but Nell read people well, especially those who might want to take advantage of Coach's kindness. She was a wonderful coach's wife who loved what her husband loved and was supportive of him and believed in him. Truthfully, he much preferred being with her at the Final Four—the national regional basketball championship—or at coaching conventions than being with other coaches.

Things changed as Nell became sick in the early eighties and found it difficult to come to camp. Coach was, of course, still wonderful with the campers and parents, but he missed her being there, and it was tough on him. When she passed on March 21, 1985, everyone wondered how it would affect him. Being the incredible man that he is, he continued to be considerate toward everyone and made an effort to be his best. But on the inside he suffered greatly, and his family and close friends worried deeply about him. They said that he pined for her, and they wondered at times if he would survive his loss. His son, Jim, and daughter, Nan, would stop by camp to see how he was doing, as would former players, coaches, trainers, and "adopted" family members, including famed female NBA player Ann Meyers Drysdale, who calls Coach "Papa."

Nell once told her husband, "Don't try to understand me—just love me," and Coach made that a daily focus of his life. Since her death Coach visits her crypt every month on the twenty-first; then he writes a love letter which he places on her pillow where she had slept. The letters have accumulated since. Coach and Nell's love for each other was as legendary as Coach's basketball success and the life-changing wisdom he passed on to his players.

The camp coaches were aware of the indescribable pain and loss that Coach was feeling. As a result, their admiration and love for him grew even greater that first summer after Nell's passing, when he returned to lead camps with the same industriousness and enthusiasm that he had always shown in the past. Still, the coaches were concerned that the camps might end after that summer. But Coach kept coming back, admirably getting stronger each day and year and thriving on his love of teaching and his love for the adults and children under his supervision.

3

Getting Acclimated

A highlight of the week for every camper is having an individual picture taken with Coach Wooden before lunch on Monday. The pictures are taken by Knight Photography in the white gazebo in Kingsmen Park between the gym and the cafeteria. Campers, counselors, and coaches alike stand in a quickly moving line, and when it is an individual's turn, he sits in a chair next to Coach to have the picture taken. It is exciting but also stressful, since everyone wants to look their very best in the photo that will be shown to family, friends, and others. Some look tense in the photo next to the relaxed and handsome Coach Wooden, who smiles easily and looks the same in every picture.

This morning there is an exception to Coach's normal seated pose. As Lil Lopez gets ready to sit down next to Coach, he stands up, gives her a big side embrace, and kisses her on the forehead as the picture is taken. This is a camp photo for the ages.

Coach interacts with each camper. As seventeen-year-old Robby Caulfield sits down, Coach asks him how camp is going. "I'm enjoying playing basketball so much," Robby says. Coach grabs his hand and says, "Take that same enjoyment and apply it to everything in life and to your family." This is the kind of personable moment with Coach that campers remember forever, and it is indeed special for Robby.

Eleven-year-old Harvey Mason, who stayed on one leg in front of Coach this morning in the balance drill, is one of the first in line. Coach recognizes him from the morning drills. "You did well this morning. You are a very good athlete and can become a good player." Harvey, knowing how many great athletes Coach has been around, takes it to heart and feels strong encouragement in that comment.

As he waits his turn, coach Gary Grayson, a UCLA graduate and Van Nuys High School coach, tells about taking pictures with coach Pat Riley, the LA Lakers coach who also runs popular basketball camps. "He is always so tan, and I was embarrassed last summer because I looked so pale in my camp picture next to Riley. So I coached at his camp last week, and to prepare, I sat out in the sun and got tanned. When I sat down next to him, I told him that I got a tan this year. Well, he kind of laughed and said, 'So you got a tan.' Then he said, 'Next.' He dissed me."

One of the last pictures of the day is of Coach with the Showalter family. Eleven-year-old Melissa has just returned from shopping and is excited to take her picture in a new dress. She gets a hug from Coach along with a smile and a compliment about how nice she looks.

Befriending Campers and Schooling Coaches

Coach Wooden has the shortest lunch break of anyone today, since he sits for pictures until the very last one is taken. When he finally gets to lunch, he sees one of the smallest campers, six-year-old Ken Ammann, sitting by himself. Coach invites him to sit with him and the other coaches.

Coach notices that Ken's pockets are full of items, and he says, "I'll bet I have more things in my pocket than you have in yours." They both empty their pockets, and soon each has a pile.

Ken empties papers, rocks, coins, paper clips, and other items from his pocket. Coach pulls from his a small silver cross, coins, papers, and more, and he builds a pile even bigger than Ken's. Coach wins the contest, but the young camper smiles and enjoys the special attention from Coach. Ken has little interest in basketball but has a new friend in Coach Wooden, whose genuine caring spirit has made another person feel cared for at camp.

Even as he eats a quick lunch, Coach patiently answers questions from coaches while campers and counselors head to free time until one.

"How do you develop confidence in players?"

"Confidence comes from being prepared and being successful every day in practice. Failing to prepare is preparing to fail. Don't be someone who whistles in the dark. Of course, ability itself leads to confidence, so build competitive greatness through teaching better skills. Richard Washington in the 1975 semifinals against Louisville made the shot at the end to win the game for us because he was confident and was not afraid. It was not going to ruin him if he missed that shot, because he was confident he wasn't going to peck the shot and shoot short.

"As a coach, the key is what is going on inside of me, such as wanting to win it for me. Players can pick up on that tenseness. The coach should convey a feeling of confidence. Teach them. Don't drive it into them."

"How do you coach underachievers?" a coach asks.

"All of us are underachievers," Coach answers. "There is no such thing as an overachiever. It implies we aren't capable of doing something. It is not possible to give more than 100 percent either. When Jim Harrick was an assistant at UCLA, David Greenwood was averaging twenty points and ten rebounds per game, and he was an All-American"—a title awarded those considered to be the best national players in a season. "Pretty good, you know," praised Coach. "Jim thought David could be doing even better and was tough on him. He asked me what I thought, and I said, 'Jim, would you rather have him or not have him?' Coach Harrick seemed to think that helped him appreciate David a little more," Coach says, smiling.

"Coach," says another, "what rules did you have for your teams?"

"Early in my career I had a lot of rules and a few suggestions. Later I learned to have a few rules and many suggestions, but I would stick to my three main rules: Use no profanity; if a player used profanity, it was an automatic dismissal from practice. Be on time to practice and everywhere else; if you were not on time and without a legitimate reason, you didn't practice. Never criticize a teammate; that is my job. If you do any of these three things, then you don't practice."

Coach has more to say about players' behavior. "Players shouldn't do anything to cause embarrassment to the school or team, in or out of season. Do what you think is right at the time and not to try to appease someone else, and don't be embarrassed by what you believe in. You will be challenged, but stand up for what you believe in. They'd lose respect if I backed down. You can enforce rules if you let them know in advance what the expectation and rules are. Then stand up to them.[1]

"Bill Walton challenged me a lot," Coach continues. "I would tell him to stick up for what you believe in; I'll stick up for what I believe in. He came to me on picture day with long hair and a beard, and he told me I didn't have the right to tell him how to wear his hair. I said, 'You're right, Bill. I don't have that right. However, I do have the right to determine who is going to play, and we're going to miss you, Bill.'" This gets a big laugh from the coaches. "He's been asked a number of times, 'Do you think Coach would have backed that up?' and he said, 'Well, I got fixed up in a hurry, didn't I?' But Bill Walton is a wonderful person.[2]

"Sidney Wicks and Steve Patterson challenged me by growing mutton chops. Children will test you, and my basketball players were my children in a way, like extended family. They'll get upset when they test you. Don't give in, or they've got you. Stand up for the things you think are right with tough discipline but with caring and flexibility. They'll end up one of your best boosters."

"How did you discipline?" a coach asks.

"I did not use physical punishment after my early years in coaching. Don't believe in it. Discipline through denial of privileges. Discipline to correct, to improve, but not to punish. The punishment they should fear most is the denial of practice. Then forgive. The next day is a new day. Don't allude to it. You must love your athletes, yet you may not like what they do.

"The bench is a coach's greatest ally. All players want to play. The biggest mistake coaches make is not using the bench. Even in practice, take a player out of five-on-five work. A coach can enforce things, because he has power over them. His job is to coach players, not court them. And remember to never punish one person for the actions of another. Once you do punish, don't hold it over them after that."

"How should a coach correct players in practice?"

"The good teachers correct without causing resentment. I might say, 'If you do this as well as you do that, we'll both be a lot happier.' Some teachers have great knowledge, but they lack people skills and maybe the ability to teach knowledge. Show patience with the goal of playing close to your ability level. Use constructive criticism, and be careful of feelings and use praise. You can't antagonize and expect to get positive results. Criticize—it is a law of learning—but be positive when you do. Stay away from sarcasm and from negatives. Do not tear down or embarrass players, and don't embarrass them before their peers. Command respect because of the way you are and not because of an authority to dictate. To test someone's character, give them power. You also can't demand more than what is possible."

"What did you look for in players when you recruited?"

"I looked for quick and big players. What separated Bill Walton and Kareem Abdul-Jabbar from other big players was their quickness under control. If I could not get both, then I looked for balance between the two. I would give up some size to get more quickness, but it must be under control. Quick players will be good usually no matter what they do, but if they learn the correct way and do it under control and balanced, they can become great. We also looked for jumping ability and especially quick jumpers. They must learn to be quick but not hurry, or you will have activity without achievement. And I don't like activity without achievement." Coach smiles, and the coaches laugh.

"Then, equally important," Coach goes on, "I wanted the type of players who I knew would be considerate of others and would be team players. I would study their transcripts to see if they had the grades to get in. I would find out about what faith they were, about their family, about their parents and siblings, and about their extracurricular activities. From all those things I would get a pretty good idea about them.[3]

"I relied a lot on the opinions of coaches who had coached against a particular high-school player that I was recruiting. I used to get about eight letters from opposing coaches about a player. I never saw Keith Wilkes play in high school but went off the feedback from opposing coaches."[4]

"Would you look for character?" someone asks.

"Absolutely," Coach replies. "Character is important in everything, and character is what you really are. You're the only one who knows your character. You know my reputation. It could be different. Reputation is what you are perceived to be by others. Your character is what you really are. That will determine to some extent if that individual will be a good team player or if he'll be a selfish player, thinking too much about himself.[5]

"Character will make you more consistent. Without character, regardless of ability, you will have more highs and lows. I never wanted to create an emotional peak for our teams, because for every artificial peak you create, there's a valley," continued Coach. "Character gives you the avenue necessary for success in whatever field you choose—in law, medicine, business, or whatever.

"If our aim in basketball was winning, I don't think we would have won all the championships we did. Winning comes as a result of something else: character. Reputation and character always need to be good, but you must always be more concerned with what you are than with what others think you are."[6]

"Is there anyone you recruited who didn't go to UCLA but whom you really wanted?"

"Yes, yes, there was. It was Paul Westphal. Paul wanted to go to USC, because he wanted to beat UCLA. And they never did." The coaches laugh at the story involving the NBA all-pro guard but also about Coach's competitive nature.[7]

"How do players show that they are getting away from a team game?"

"There are a number of ways," Coach answers. "They leave the boards too soon to get out on the break. Their weak-side defensive play is not good. Their off-ball play on offense is not good. Their shot selection shows it. For players who put self before the team, their ego might come from parents, associates, girlfriends, or friends."

"What about mandatory drug testing?"

"I'm 100 percent in favor of it. With drugs or alcohol the goal is prevention. The rule is clear, and it is a strong stand. No alcohol was permitted. The penalty was severe action, but I didn't decide what that action was. It depended on the circumstances, but usually it meant that you were gone from the team."[8]

Just then Lil brings Coach a banana split, which brings a big smile from Coach and an even bigger thank-you for her. "My favorite meal after games was a chili size [a chili burger] and a banana split. They wouldn't help me sleep well at night, but I sure enjoyed them."[9] The lunch talk ends with a laugh from the coaches.

Afternoon Amusement

After lunch Coach is asked to speak to a nine-year-old who has been in and out of the training room all morning with an assortment of problems. The son of a famous Beverly Hills lawyer, the boy does not want to be at camp and was pretty much pushed out of a limousine on Sunday. First he complained that he felt sick after eating breakfast. Then he needed to stop at the beginning of stations because he said he swallowed a bug. Now he is complaining that he cannot lift his right arm.

The boy says to Coach, "I can't raise my arm."

"Why not?" asks Coach.

"Because I hurt it this morning."

"Show me how high you could raise it before you hurt it." The boy easily raises it above his head. "This high."

"Okay, get going back in the gym." Coach smiles at the trainers as the boy runs into the gym for the next workout, knowing that Coach saw through his act.

All the campers are back in the gym at one for another half-hour workout with Coach. Those who ate too big of a lunch will soon learn not to make that mistake again, because they'll continue working with their own coaches for another hour and a half after Coach is done with them. They drill on the parts and fundamentals of the UCLA high-post offense, working to learn them for the official games that will begin on Wednesday afternoon.

Coach Wooden goes home each day in the midafternoon. At three Jaws drives Coach Wooden home, making his way south on the 101 freeway. "Coach, it's like clockwork," Jaws says. "As soon as we see your exit at White Oak, the traffic slows to a crawl."

Coach quickly responds, "All these people are driving to see my condo."

"Good one, Coach," says Jaws.

Camping with the Dallas Cowboys

The John Wooden Basketball Fundamentals Camp shares Cal Lu with another sports camp: the Dallas Cowboys preseason training camp. The Cowboys players are quite visible—eating in the cafeteria, walking to and from practice in full pads (trudging might be more accurate at the end of their day), driving on campus, and relaxing in town at night. Once in a while, they might stop in the gym to shoot during camp free time, and Ed "Too Tall" Jones might put on a dunk show to entertain campers. While campers swim in the Cal Lu pool during the hot afternoon free time, Cowboys players lift heavy weights in the workout area by the pool. All in all, the Cowboys players are kind to the campers.

Just as the campers are in awe of the Cowboys, the Dallas players themselves are more than a little in awe at seeing Coach Wooden.

Coach Mike Kunstadt and his wife, Gerri, are from the Cowboys' home of Irving, Texas, and Gerri has become comfortable around the players through the years. Mike tells a humorous story about her interaction with them. "Gerri was in the cafeteria taking pictures of Cowboys players holding our four-month-old daughter, Karin. Cowboys running back Tony Dorsett, who was working on eliminating a fumbling problem he'd had the prior year, stopped by and said, 'Hey, don't you want to take pictures of the baby with me?' Gerri quickly replied, 'Oh, no. You might drop her.'" That story surely has been retold numerous times in the Cowboys locker room.

Gerri did ask Cowboys' coach Tom Landry if she could take a picture of him with her infant daughter. "I made sure to change her before I asked to take the picture. He was so gracious and kind, and he didn't even react when after he handed her back to me he had a big wet spot on his shirt. He is a true gentleman."

Past campers once looked for the stars like quarterback Roger Staubach, also known as Captain America, and now in the late eighties they look for quarterback and punter Danny White.

Coach Jon Palarz, a California high-school coach who was once a camper, vividly remembers staring in awe at Cowboys wide receiver Bob Hayes, the world's fastest receiver.

Tony Dorsett is extremely popular and often leaves the cafeteria with his hands full of fruit to take back to his dorm. Campers are not allowed to bother the Cowboys players in the cafeteria, so they wait until the players leave the cafeteria to talk to them. Dorsett cannot sign autographs with his hands full of fruit, but he takes a lot of pictures with campers.

Coaches are well aware of the legendary Cowboys assistant coaches like Mike Ditka and Ernie Stautner. Stautner is a tough-looking man with a big heart. He and Coach on occasion take walks together. One summer coach Larry Lopez joined Coach and Stautner on a walk to the big "CLC" on the hill overlooking the Cowboys' practice facility. On the way back down, they realized that there was a steep stretch that would be hard on Coach and his knees. Stautner and Lopez half ran down that stretch before slide-stopping at a point where they could catch Coach if he got going too fast to stop. Sure enough, Coach's momentum got him going where he could not stop, and he crashed into Stautner and Lopez, sending a championship ring flying and bruising his left thigh. It took the men a while to find the ring in the brush, and Coach limped a bit for the rest of that week. Lopez got a laugh out of Coach this week at registration when he asked, "Coach, do you want to go for a walk with Ernie Stautner?"

Campers notice how big running back Robert Newhouse's thighs are, but they also talk about how strong and big Coach Tom Landry's calves are. Many of the linemen, of course, are huge and the biggest humans most of the campers have ever seen. Defensive ends Too Tall Jones and Harvey Martin and other Cowboys players are intimidating with their big beards, dark sunglasses, and short shorts. Counselor Chris Shelby still talks about how strong Roger Staubach was. "He was a quarterback, but he looked like he could play linebacker. He was just a stud." Walt Garrison is a similar type of athlete on this Dallas team and an impressive person as well.

Others notice that huge defensive tackle Randy White is sometimes so focused even in the cafeteria that his teammates often leave him by himself when he eats.

The campers probably do not notice Joe Fuca. He is a little-known wide receiver who is trying out with the Cowboys after having spent three weeks with the Los Angeles Rams. Fuca has seen camp from every angle. He was a camper at one of Coach Wooden's first camps in the early seventies; he later played football as a student at Cal Lu, and one of his summer jobs was to help the Cowboys staff; and now, in the late eighties, he is trying to make the Dallas team. One of his duties when he worked for the Cowboys was to pick up players like Drew Pearson and Tony Dorsett at the airport and drive them to camp. It is a thrill for him now to work out with Herschel Walker and the other Cowboys greats. Joe makes a great distinction about himself: "Who else can say that they have played for the similar calming, highly organized, and intensely focused leadership of both John Wooden and Tom Landry?"

Just as the campers are in awe of the Cowboys, the Dallas players themselves, as famous as they are as members of "America's Team," are more than a little in awe at seeing Coach Wooden in the cafeteria. Although they rarely visit with Coach, they often look over at him and perhaps exchange a nod or a brief hello. The exception is Thomas "Hollywood" Henderson, who is the only one anyone remembers calling Coach Wooden "John."

On the rare occasion when he has time, Coach Landry joins Coach Wooden at lunch, where the two coaching legends talk briefly about their families, faith, Cowboys football, and UCLA basketball.

Free-Time Fun

Free time occurs every day after each camper's last afternoon practice session or game and lasts until dinner at four thirty. Today four coaches are in the gym running optional skill clinics for campers who choose to use their free time this way. These run from 3:10–4:10 on Monday and Tuesday and usually draw the more motivated athletes. It is a good time for coaches to work on their own area of expertise and to have the freedom to run things the way they want to.

Some campers choose to stay in the gym during this time to work on individual skill development with a coach or counselor, play small pickup games, or just shoot. Others go swimming in the pool. Belly flops are forbidden and have been since Coach saw a camper puncture an eardrum doing one a few years ago.

The campers who are Dallas Cowboys fans watch the team practice and try to get a few autographs since they know to leave the players alone in the cafeteria. It is a thrill for them to watch such talented athletes practice. The biggest diehard fan among the campers is twelve-year-old Tony Strickland from nearby Simi Valley. He loves the Cowboys so much that he cries whenever they lose, which, fortunately for his parents, is not very often. Tony has a natural gift of being bold and comfortable talking with anyone and is not at all intimidated at the idea of talking to the Cowboys players and coaches. So, after their practice, he visits with a few of them and then carries Harvey Martin's helmet for him.

Many campers choose to hang out in the dorms and might even sneak in a nap. Naps are the top choice for some coaches, although they may not get them until they fall asleep reading. Those who burn the candle at both ends need the extra sleep to get them through the week.

Some coaches venture over to watch the Cowboys practice, while others find time for a run. A favorite run is to the cross on one of the hills overlooking the Cowboys' practice, about a quarter mile northwest of the "CLC." For the few who run early in the morning, this free-time run is their second run of the day. Coach Michael Scarano, nicknamed "Ski," is the most avid runner. He gets up early and runs to the "CLC" or the cross. At lunch he might play basketball, while afternoons mean another run, this time through the streets of Thousand Oaks. Today Scarano convinces me to run with him to the cross. To me it feels like a half marathon; to Scarano it feels like a warm-up lap.

Yutaka Shimizu, coach at John F. Kennedy High School in nearby Granada Hills, and Wayne Carlson make free time tee time. Shimizu is an avid golfer who brings his clubs with him to camp. As soon as their afternoon camp activity finishes, Shim and Carlson jump in the car to try to play nine holes. Since Coach Wooden has already gone home and won't be eating the evening meal at camp, they will miss dinner if necessary to get in nine holes before rushing back for their six o'clock activity.

Counselors love to use any free time to play basketball. Some of them are very talented college basketball players, like Eric Hughes out of Oakland, and they compete against each other. Some of the coaches join in the game as well, and it is a special time to build camaraderie.

Coaches Don Showalter, Mike Kunstadt, and David Myers join their families to play or swim. On some days they meet up with their families to find their kids playing tag with Coach Wooden, or "Papa," as the children call him.

Lil and the Cowboys

Dinner is from four thirty to five thirty. Campers lined up outside the cafeteria are entertained by Dallas all-pro lineman Randy White walking into the cafeteria with Kelly Myers hanging on his leg and Karin and Kerri Kunstadt hanging from his arms. The daughters of Texas coaches David Myers and Mike Kunstadt have been Cowboys fans from birth, but how many Cowboys fans are buddies with Randy White?

Lil has been in charge of the Cowboys meals for the past twenty-five years, and they love her for it. The Cowboys food line opens right after all the campers get their food, so the campers and Cowboys are often together in the cafeteria. The Cowboys, understandably, have better food than the campers, but the campers are happy to have simple meals like hamburgers, hot dogs, French fries, grilled cheese sandwiches, macaroni and cheese, and spaghetti. Coaches, though, sometimes linger at the food line, hoping to get some of the Cowboys' food after the Cowboys finish dishing up. Lil usually sends them away, politely reminding them that this food is for the football players. But being fond of some of the veteran coaches, once in a while she gives them a few leftover steaks.

Lil's big event every summer is the Cowboys fans dinner, when fans pay to eat dinner with the Cowboys players in the cafeteria. Lil and her staff always create a special and delicious meal, which further enhances her strong relationship with the team and Coach Landry.

The Coaches Reminisce

With Coach Wooden gone for the day, the coaches talk among themselves and bond with each other over dinner. Mike Scarano asks coach Tom Desotell about his long association with Coach Wooden. Tom coached his first John Wooden camp in the early seventies, when he was a young coach from Milwaukee; that started a friendship with Coach that continues. Desotell eventually became a highly successful coach at Sheboygan North High School in Wisconsin and each summer brings some of his players to camp as campers and counselors. He has been with Coach as long as anyone else and is a camp director of Coach Wooden's adult camps. Like Don Showalter, Tom Desotell is an excellent teacher and a humble person, and like Mike Kunstadt, he is a leader and mentor of basketball players in his state. These three coaches are so special to Coach that he mentions them in the second edition of his autobiography *They Call Me Coach*.

Desotell explains how he first got involved with camps. "In 1972 I saw an ad in the Sporting News for John Wooden's fundamentals camps. I wrote a letter to the sponsors, and they hired me to be a part of the camp. Just before I was to leave for camp, I was notified of staff expectations: hair was not to touch the ear, and sideburns were to be no longer than the earlobe. That was not the norm in the early seventies. Curfew for the staff members would be eleven thirty, and any profanity would result in termination.

"I was assigned two consecutive weeks, which paid enough to cover my flight and other expenses. Coach Wooden recognized right away that I, like him, was from the Midwest, and he went out of his way to make me feel comfortable.

"Later on, when I visited UCLA for the first time, Coach Wooden invited me to stop by his office. In addition to seeing Pauley Pavilion, I wanted to see where the UCLA players got those cool soft-toed Adidas Superstars shoes with the light blue stripes, because I wanted a pair for myself. When I found out that Ducky Drake, UCLA's equipment man (and famous track coach), was on vacation, I was disappointed, as he's the one who knew about the shoes. Coach's secretary heard about this somehow, and after my visit in his office, Coach Wooden took me to the coaches' locker room. 'What shoe size do you wear?' he asked me. 'Our team gets their shoes from Adidas, but I don't need mine except for when we take our team picture.' His shoes fit me perfectly, and he told me, 'I hope you enjoy them. I'm so happy that you took the time from your busy weekend to stop and visit.'

"'*My* busy weekend?' I said to myself.

"Early the next season I got a call from Coach Wooden asking if I could help him out. 'We play at Notre Dame in February,' he explained, 'and if you could somehow get to South Bend, I would feel a lot better having you sit with my wife, Nellie, during the game. She's not in good health, and the students are quite loud and rowdy. I have four good tickets, and Nell needs one, but I could give you the other three, and you could bring two of your players with you.' The opportunity became reality. A starry-eyed high-school coach with two of his athletes saw big-time college basketball in courtside seats before a national television audience.

Coach's folksy way and commonsense philosophy have made so many of us better people."

Coach Ken Barone, an assistant coach at UCLA, addresses coach Jim Nielsen. "You have one of the most unique perspectives, Jim, because you played on three UCLA NCAA title teams, you coached at UCLA, and then later you worked at camps for Coach. How different has each of those experiences been?"

"Coach is so genuine, humble, and patient with everyone. He's the real deal."

"Coach and I developed a totally different relationship once I started coaching at his camps," Jim replies. "I am so blessed to have had all this time with Coach, and I have such fond memories of camp. Coach loves to tease, tell funny stories, and play cribbage with us. We didn't see the fun, teasing side of him when we played for him or even much when I coached for him. But at camp he is fun to be around. I'm so impressed with the time that Coach takes to talk to the coaches, show us the right way to teach and to do things, and answer our questions. He is so genuine, humble, and patient with everyone. He's the real deal. He can teach, and he can teach his system."

Mike Kunstadt walks over with his tray and sits down. "Did you know that the first camp director for Coach Wooden's overnight camps was UCLA head coach Jim Harrick?" In 1970 Harrick had been the head coach at Morningside High School, where he had won a high-school national championship and coached future NBA player Stan Love. Kunstadt continues, "Dick Davies, the head coach at San Diego State University at the time, was recruiting Harrick's star player, and when Max Shapiro asked Davies to find a camp director for the overnight camp, Davies, perhaps looking for an edge in recruiting, suggested Jim Harrick. Harrick served in that role for four summers, observing Coach Wooden's precise fundamental teaching and learning the Wooden system. That ultimately led him to becoming the successful UCLA Bruins' coach. He embraces the legend of Coach Wooden."

Tom asks Mike Kunstadt to tell everyone how he became involved with camps. In his distinctive Texas drawl, Mike explains, "I had been coaching high school in Corpus Crispi for a few years, and our team finally made the playoffs. I was nervous about it, so out of the blue I decided to call Coach Wooden and ask for advice. He was still the coach at UCLA at the time."

"Was this after you started working camps?"

Mike laughs. "No. I had never met Coach before. I called expecting to get his secretary, but he answered. I stumbled around with my words, then got my poise and asked him for advice. He told me about his Pyramid, which I had never heard of before. He said, 'Fully prepare your team, make sure the players prepare themselves, and hopefully the outcome will be favorable. But if not, have peace that you did your best, that you did all you could.'

"He had given me permission to record the call, and I played it for my players—and my team went on to the Final Four. I wrote Coach a letter, thanking him and telling how his message had inspired my players, and then I asked if I could work at his camps. He sent a handwritten note back to me and put me in touch with Sportsworld. I came out to do one week but ended up doing three.

"Back then Coach and Nell sometimes stayed a few nights at camp," Mike reminisces, "so I got to know them well. Eventually I married Gerri, and she and Nell became good friends. Our kids eventually came as well. We are so blessed to be around Coach. He stayed with my family a few years ago when he was in Irving, where I now live, to receive the Theodore Roosevelt Award, which is one of the highest honors that a civilian can receive. Coach is so famous and successful, but he makes time for people. He is a great coach and an even better person."

Don Showalter speaks up next. "I wrote Coach a letter my senior year in college asking if I could coach at camp. I really had no idea that I would ever hear from him. Coach sent a handwritten note to me and gave me the name of Chris Smith and his address. He said I should write him and that they should be able to work me in a year or two. It happened, and now I bring my family every year. Coach has made it a family experience for me and the other out-of-state coaches."

Brad Barbarick tells his story next. "I grew up wanting to play at UCLA. I didn't get to, but I did go to Coach Wooden's camps several times as a camper. When I was sixteen, I attended Coach's advanced camp, and I knew I wanted to coach his camps in the future. My mom encouraged me to ask Coach about it, and he told me to write Sportsworld. I did, and I became a counselor, then a head counselor, and now I'm a coach. One of the best things about camp is the camaraderie and friendships, like when all of us talk over dinner. Most of my closest friends are those I work with at camp, and we stay in contact. Friendship is one of the best things in the world, and it is built here."

Coach Ken Morgan has been listening the whole time. "This is my fifty-second camp with Coach in the past eleven years."

"Fifty-two camps? You've spent an entire year of your life at his camps!" exclaims Ray Lokar.

"I've worked ninety-eight Sportsworld Camps, including a lot for Billie Moore," Morgan goes on, referring to the outstanding female UCLA and US Olympics women's basketball coach. "I look up to Coach more than anyone in my life except my parents. He is the smartest person I've met regarding how to live life. I've been extremely blessed. He treats everyone like they are important. Even when he needles you, he has a twinkle in his eye. I chuckle when he does that—unless, of course, he is correcting me."

Larry Lopez tries to top Morgan's story. "I've worked over seventy of Coach's camps."

Morgan playfully responds, "You work camp just so you can eat your mom's food."

The conversation is abruptly interrupted by the sight of a Cowboys rookie standing on his chair singing his college fight song. It is an NFL training-camp tradition, and the campers enjoy it as much as the Cowboys veterans.

Winding Down Day One

From six to seven, one group of campers meets in Pederson Hall to get a free pair of Converse camp shoes, while the other group practices and then half-court scrimmages another team. At seven the groups switch. It cools down quite a bit at night at Cal Lu, so coaches on the outside courts put on light jackets or sweatshirts as the sun starts to go down. At eight fifteen everyone is back in the gym for roll call, mail delivery, nightly films, buying candy at the canteen, or just hanging out with friends. Mail delivery is a highlight for some campers, although they might get some good-natured ribbing as they are called to come get a letter or package.

This time at the end of the day also offers the campers a chance to watch the counselors and coaches play high-quality basketball. It is easy to tell how long each staff member has been coaching at camp based on what camp T-shirt he is wearing. The longtime veterans wear shirts that younger coaches and counselors want to trade for, but usually the veterans are not willing to part with their personal piece of camp history. There are many talented counselors, including Butch Mettinger, a great shooter at Idaho State, who played in high school for me and at College of the Canyons in nearby Santa Clarita for coach Lee Smelser.

It is back to the dorms at nine thirty and lights out at ten. Fourteen-year-old John Brooks, like so many other campers, wants to learn how to dunk and gets excited watching guest speakers, coaches, and counselors show off their skill in this area. In his dorm room he tells his roommates about a camper who dunked in his afternoon game in the gym. "He's only five foot six and only going to be an eighth grader, but he can dunk!"

His coach, Jon Palarz, is impressed with John's positive attitude and hustle and because he is smart, hardnosed, and a great competitor. Palarz is an outstanding young coach who won the hustle award himself when he was a camper—an award given only to a few campers who work particularly hard at camp—and now he sees the same qualities he had in Brooks. Brooks is skilled and athletic, is projected to make varsity as a ninth grader, and has a high commitment to what Coach Wooden teaches. At night Brooks takes his shoes off and leans them against the wall to air out properly, as other serious-minded campers do with their own shoes. Many past campers have made that practice a lifetime habit and have to explain to their wives why their shoes are opened up and leaning against the bedroom wall.

Thirteen-year-old Jon Keller is away from home for the first time. As he walks to his dorm room, Coach Scarano asks him if he is homesick. "No. I'm having too much fun playing basketball all the time."

Don Showalter is tired after a long day. He kisses his children goodnight, but before he goes to sleep himself, he reviews the next day's schedule and prepares for his Tuesday stations assignments. He is down to earth, inquisitive, and purposeful in wanting to learn all he can from Coach and from the other coaches as well. He sincerely desires to be the best coach he can be for his players.

Once the campers are quiet in their rooms, some of the counselors head back to the gym. The counselors are a tightly knit group who bond with each other over their love for basketball, being around Coach Wooden and NBA players, and the chance to play quality basketball during free time. Many look forward to the coaches-versus-counselors game that will take place on Thursday night as well as to the one night off that each of them will have when they can relax with counselor friends.

While bed checks, refereeing, and stations can be challenging, the food is good and plentiful. Certainly the camp photo with Coach Wooden will be a cherished item for each of the counselors, no matter how many they have had taken before. Like the coaches, the veteran counselors can see by these pictures how they have changed through the years and how Coach never seems to age.

The counselors value the time to play until about midnight and then to hang out together at the nearby Carl's Jr. Some who have to be up early to drive Coach or to wake the campers don't get to bed until one thirty in the morning, but they do not mind. They thrive on the camp experience and have too much fun playing and being together to worry about sleep. Adrenaline and an occasional nap will get them through the week.

4

Tuesday Morning with Coach

The counselors have the best job at camp—driving Coach to and from camp. Coach can drive, but driving him has become a tradition over the years, and the camp staff considers it a great privilege to have the time with him. Even though they have to be up by five in order to go pick him up, whoever has the job relishes the opportunity to talk with Coach on the forty-minute drive between Encino and Thousand Oaks.

The head counselors, Jaws and Hawk, are too busy to pick Coach up this morning, so John Hayes (who happens to be my younger brother) gets to do the job today. John is driving our mom's old wine-red Grand Marquis, a boat of a car, but with its leather seats, it is quite a nice ride. In the early days Sportsworld provided an old blue Buick station wagon for the counselors to drive, but after too many engine troubles, smoky tailpipes, and emergency brakes coming out of the socket, it was decided that each driver would use his own car.

Hayes is excited to pick Coach Wooden up but underestimates the time it takes to get to his condo. He also cannot use the air conditioner, or the car will break down, so he is stressed when he finally gets to Coach Wooden's gate. By nature he is a bit shy, and although he has been a counselor a few times, this is really his first time being one-on-one with Coach. When he knocks on the door, Coach opens it in his stocking feet. Hayes and Coach spend the next ten minutes talking as Coach gathers his belongings and puts his shoes on. Coach never mentions anything about him being late and makes Hayes feel at ease. They have an enjoyable drive back to camp, converse freely the entire time, and get to the cafeteria in time for the doors to open at six forty-five.

Knowing about John's excitement about picking Coach up this morning, I reflect on the stories about driving Coach that other camp staff members have talked about. Jaws has been driving Coach for years, and he and Coach have always hit it off, easily engaging in conversation. In their first drives together, Coach and Jaws talked about UCLA basketball. But as the days and camps went on, the two have come to talk about family, faith, education, and so much more. One topic centers on Jaws's college education, which he has not found time to complete.

"Coach Wooden has a great sense of humor, and he is so easy to spend time with," Jaws likes to say. "He always makes me feel like I matter to him. He is down to earth, approachable, humble, and easygoing." Jaws has many of those same characteristics.

A treat for coaches and others is getting to ride in the backseat while the head counselor drives Coach. On one occasion Jaws's fiancée, Robin, went along to take Coach back to his condominium. It was just weeks before their wedding. "Of course Coach quizzed her about why she wanted to marry me," Jaws has told the other coaches fondly. "He loves Robin. He comes to our house for dinner once in a while and brings a bottle of non-alcoholic wine. One spring he visited and brought our kids Easter baskets."

High-school coach John Saintignon is normally a head counselor, but since those roles are filled this week by Jaws and Hawk, John has chosen, as many others have, to be a regular counselor this week so that he can be with Coach perhaps this one last time. "Our relationship blossomed in that car and in his condominium," I have heard him say. "What a privilege. He never critiques my old car or my driving. Even if I might be really nervous, he seems to enjoy every minute in the car. I have discovered, however, that Coach actually has one vice, and that is candy. We eat a lot of pieces of candy out of a glass bowl in the den of his condominium."

Counselor Chris Shalby has also driven Coach many times, and he gets up at four forty-five to make sure that he is never late. One day in the years when the station wagon was still being used but was in for repairs, Chris had to drive his own car. "I always enjoyed driving Coach and talking with him, but not this day. I had an old 1966 Karmann Ghia with no air conditioning and poor brakes, and I was afraid it would break down or that something worse would happen." But all went well.

Eric Hughes regularly drives Coach when he is head counselor. "A lot of times I'm really tired when I pick him up, but I see him out front moving around and warming his knees up for the day. We actually don't talk that much about basketball. We talk golf, family, the latest news, baseball, and life in general. A lot of people want to ride with me, but I like being alone with Coach. That is why I don't coach. We don't get paid much, but I value my alone time with Coach."

At times coaches drive Coach or ride along with the driver as a passenger just to spend more time with Coach. Tom Gregory rode along once with longtime popular head counselor Andrew Jones, known as A.J. Coach was weighing a lucrative offer from Lakers owner Jack Kent Cooke to coach the Lakers, and Gregory asked Coach, "Do you want to coach the Lakers?" Coach replied, "No, I don't want to do it. They are offering too much money. No one is worth that much money." This is an example of the many enlightening conversations that have been held in a variety of cars between Coach Wooden and different people.

One person who does not want to drive Coach Wooden is coach Gary Grayson. "I idolize Coach Wooden," he explains, "and I'm afraid I will get in a car accident, injure Coach, and be remembered forever as the guy who hurt him."

Camp director Steve "Hawk" Hawkins drives Coach often and has developed a special relationship with him. Coach Wooden has a way with words, and if Hawk drives over the speed limit, Coach might say, "Driving a little too fast, aren't you, Steve?" Hawk often has other passengers in the car with him. Detroit Tigers manager Sparky Anderson was at his home in Thousand Oaks during the All-Star break and rode along with Hawk to visit with Coach. Anderson sat in the backseat talking to Coach, and Hawk remembers it as being "nerve wracking driving them both." Another time Coach Landry sat in the backseat. Hawk remembers it well. "I thought to myself, *Please, God, don't let me crash this car and kill them both.*"

Coach Wayne Carlson drove Coach home one year at the end of camp. Director Hal Mitrovich said, "Wayne, the counselors are too busy driving campers to the airport and can't take Coach home. Since you are going that way, do you mind taking him home?" Carlson said yes, and then, echoing Grayson's fears, wished he had not, thinking, *What if I get in an accident and kill him?*

"I drove fifty-five miles an hour all the way in the slow lane and never moved my hands from the ten and two o'clock positions," Carlson says. "Got off on White Oak in Encino and took him to his condo.

"Coach talked and carried the conversation the whole time," Carlson continues. "Coach asked if I wanted to come in and have a Coke. I stayed just for about ten minutes because I didn't want to impose. But it is a special personal memory with Coach and another example of what a truly kind man he is. People ask me what makes him so special, and I just tell them that Coach Wooden is Coach Wooden. You just have to be around him to understand that."

Hal Mitrovich does not understand the stress about driving Coach. "I drove him home all the time from his first day camps in Pacific Palisades in the early seventies.[1] Of course, the drive was all downhill."

Even camp administrator Pat Yount has driven Coach and says that she is "the only staff member in camp history to be late picking up Coach." But counselor Steve Delaveaga has also been late and has his own horror story about it. "I set two alarms whenever I picked Coach up in the morning. The day of the 'Just Say Maybe' program in 1987 when we were trying to convince Coach to keep doing camps with Sportsworld, I hit my snooze button at five o'clock so I could sleep nine more minutes. But we had a power outage, and I woke up in a panic at six forty-five. I raced to the cafeteria and saw Coach sitting with the campers and counselors. I felt two feet tall and apologized. Coach just said, 'It's okay; I drove myself. It's no problem.' I sulked for the next few days. My fellow counselors waited until I got over it and then gave me a hard time about it."[2]

Coach Brad Barbarick drove Coach when he was a counselor and has great memories of those times. "Once in a while coaches would tag along," he remembers. "When I got back, all the other counselors wanted to know what we had talked about in the car. Coach probably thought I was silly because I talked with him so much. It was so important to me to write down the questions each morning that I wanted to ask him. Coach is so humble. We talked about religion, baseball, and basketball, which is what I wanted to talk about most. It was a wonderful experience."

Coach Jeff Dunlap drove Coach as a head counselor and also wrote down questions that he wanted to ask Coach the first time he went to pick him up. "That first drive, I never got to ask him about anything," Jeff says. "He said, 'Good morning, Jeff,' and then asked me where I grew up, where I went to school, and everything else about my life for the next forty minutes. He showed such interest in me, and I didn't ask him one question."

Coach Ken Morgan has driven Coach four times. "I wish now I had done it every day. We work hard, and we work long hours, so it is tough, but it is so special to get up early and be in the car with him. It's kind of intimidating but just a blessing."

Sportsworld director Chris Smith started as a camp director and always enjoyed driving Coach as well, at least after his first time picking up Coach. "It was 1973, and he was still head coach at UCLA. I was embarrassed because I was picking him up in an old, beat-up tan Volkswagen bug. I was as nervous as I could possibly be, but as we sat shoulder to shoulder on the drive to camp, he was just so pleasant and easy to talk to. A lifelong friendship began in that car.

"Years later I picked him up at the airport after he had been away speaking. There he was standing on the curb as I pulled up in my brand-new black Cadillac Seville. Coach looked at the car, looked in at me, and got in. He asked me to wait a second, and then he laid the seat back, put on his sunglasses, and lay all the way back on the seat. 'Okay, let's go,' he said."

Chris continues, "Then there was the time when Coach and Nell drove my bride, Mae, and me from the church to the reception the day of our wedding. It is a wonderful memory."

Don Showalter got up occasionally and sat in the backseat when Brad Barbarick or Dunlap drove. "The drives with Coach are tremendous opportunities. Coach is always so upbeat. He quit coaching UCLA so many years ago, but he is so positive and motivated to start the morning with the campers. I'm sure that there are days when he doesn't feel it, but you can't tell. He'll mention what a beautiful morning it is and how he is looking forward to the day. It just shows how Coach lives in the moment. He is going to make today a masterpiece. He's always prepared, but he enjoys the moment."

There is another long line waiting to get into breakfast this morning but not as long as the one on Monday. Tuesday is starting out to be a hot and humid day, but it will be an exciting, full day as well. Today the campers will play their first full-court scrimmage, listen to the first guest speaker, and hear Coach Wooden's Pyramid of Success talk.

Coach and Lil

To save his knees, Coach takes the service elevator up to the cafeteria. Lil has his standard oatmeal ready for him—the breakfast he has eaten since he was a boy on his father's farm in Indiana. Lil also brings him a banana, since she knows that bananas are one of his favorite foods. Coach treasures beginning each morning this way.

Lil loves Coach Wooden. She is very comfortable around him and treats him like a family member. She and Coach's wife, Nell, were close. Lil lost her husband years before Nell passed away, so she is understanding of Coach's deep sense of loss and takes great care of him. She often comes out of her kitchen to check on Coach, give him a hug, and occasionally give him a little something special to eat. Coach has a sweet tooth, and Lil makes it her goal to satisfy it.

Lil oversees a staff of fifty and enjoys it when Coach's eldest granddaughter, Cathleen, volunteers to help. Lil's top chef is Frank Pace, from Italy, who is assisted by Lil's son, Robert, and Brian Tellez, son of Ed Tellez, the very successful coach from Colorado. Lil met Ed many years earlier, and through a simple polite discussion discovered that they were second cousins. They have treated each other like the family they are ever since.

Coach remembers all the cafeteria workers' names, such as Gladys and Shirley, and asks about their families and their lives, just as he did with the janitors when he coached at UCLA. Cal Lu head coach Larry Lopez is impressed by this. "I can't imagine another coach or celebrity remembering the names of cooks, servers, and dishwashers," Lopez says. "But that is Coach's character. He sincerely cares about everyone."

Questioning Coach

Most of the coaches are seated around Coach, except for Ray Lokar, who is leading an optional shooting clinic on the front courts. The talk among the coaches centers on baseball for a while this morning. Coach talks about his great respect for former longtime Dodgers manager Walt Alston and then tells the story about an offer he received to manage the Pittsburgh Pirates. "The Pirates' general manager, Joe Brown, was a UCLA graduate," Coach tells us. "When a manager's vacancy occurred in Pittsburgh, he called to ask if I had any interest in becoming their field manager. He said if I had even the slightest interest, he would be on an early plane to L.A. to offer me a long-term contract. It was very flattering, and of course I stayed at UCLA. It seems like I made a pretty good decision." Coach enjoys telling that story. Coaches are astonished by this but at the same time know that Coach Wooden would have been an outstanding manager.

Coach asks if anyone wants to talk basketball.[3]

"How did you use your assistant coaches?" someone begins by asking him.

"Denny Crum and Gary Cunningham were the best assistant coaches," Coach replies. "Crum was in charge of recruiting. Cunningham was in charge of academics.

"The biggest difference between the head coach and the assistant coaches is that the head coach makes decisions and the assistant coaches make suggestions. You don't want yes-men who are afraid to make suggestions. Before you make decisions, listen to your assistants. They should hold no grievance if you don't use their advice. If you use it and it works, then give them credit for it. If you use it and it doesn't, then take the blame. Never blame. You must have loyalty. It is the same with the team.

"It is amazing how much can be accomplished if no one cares who gets the credit," Coach goes on. "Jerry Norman is the one who came up with the idea of using a box-and-one against Houston and Elvin Hayes in the 1968 NCAA semifinals after they had beaten us in the Astrodome," he says, crediting his longtime assistant coach. "Although I don't normally like this type of defense, Jerry convinced me to use it. I didn't like that it would be a box-and-one, because it would take Lewis [Alcindor, later Kareem Abdul-Jabbar] away from the basket, so I changed it to a diamond-and-one, and of course it worked quite well."

"What did your assistants do during games?"

"Each assistant coach had a role. Denny Crum would watch and talk about the press before the game at timeouts and at halftime and would chart it during the game. Gary Cunningham might do the same with the set offense. They would also focus on those areas in practice and during individual attention. At timeouts I wanted concise, pertinent info. If you had nothing to say, then you should say nothing at all."

> "It is amazing how much can be accomplished if no one cares who gets the credit," Coach instructs the coaches.

Cowboys coach Tom Landry, wearing his standard white baseball hat with a blue "D" for Dallas on it, comes by. He apologizes for interrupting and says hello to Coach. It is amazing to see the leaders of two of the greatest sports dynasties of all time talking together. The coaches nearest Coach move away from him and bring a chair over for Coach Landry. Coaches sit quietly with admiration for these two men and their collective wisdom. The two share so many of the same great qualities of faith, humility, inner strength, character, competitive greatness, and concern for their fellow man. The mutual respect, admiration, and affection they have for each other are apparent to all.

They ask about each other's families, and then Coach Wooden asks about the Cowboys. Coach Landry brings up leadership and talks about what a great leader Roger Staubach was. "I could step back some, because Roger set the standard so high himself and made the other players better."

Coach Wooden says, "Eddie Sheldrake, Mike Warren, and David Meyers were the best leaders I had at UCLA." He then talks about how relationships grow through the years. "When you coach them, you aren't as close with them, but after they graduate you become much closer."

After Coach Landry leaves to join his staff, the coaches continue their questions.

"How did you pick captains, and what were their roles?"

"Leaders naturally emerge and develop. I did appoint game captains. Captains need to set a good example in games, practices, trips, and in every other area. The point guard should be the leader on the court, but Bill Walton [a center] was the leader of his teams. The point guards must make good decisions on the break and in the set offense. If they don't, it affects and can upset the others. In the set defense, the back line players are more the leaders."[4] With that, the coaches get up, bus their trays, and move to the gym.

More Advice from the Master Coach

Coach Mike Scarano and I leave the cafeteria with Coach Wooden for the coaches' meeting, walking to the gym through Kingsmen Park, an open green area lined with shade trees. Scarano has a question for Coach. "If your best player is constantly late to practice, what do you do? I bench my other players for that."

Coach answers with a guiding principle instead of specific advice. "You can't treat all your players alike, because treating all alike is a sure way to show partiality. Players don't all earn the same treatment nor deserve the same treatment. You have to be the judge. You won't always be right, and if you find out you are wrong, then change."[5] This is an example of Coach's wisdom; he causes a coach to think rather than telling a coach what to do. Scarano realizes that his benching rule penalizes players disproportionally. It might have little effect on the player who doesn't play much but a big effect on a starter. Instead he must think individually and case by case. He turns to me and quietly says of Coach's advice, "That is profound."

While in front of the gym waiting for the other coaches to arrive for our morning meeting, I get up the nerve to ask Coach a personal question. Knowing that Coach had a minor heart attack during the 1973 season, I ask, "How is your heart doing?" It is a question that I never dared to ask for the longest time, but I feel comfortable with Coach now.

"It is good, but my doctors have me keep a couple of nitroglycerin tablets with me just in case," says Coach, showing the tablets to Scarano and me. "Haven't had to use them," he says, smiling. I feel a special closeness with Coach because of his honesty and vulnerability.

At the beginning of our ten-minute coaches' meeting, Coach has some fun with coach Ken Stanley, a USC graduate. Coach smiles as he announces to all the coaches, "You know, I would like all of you to wear UCLA colors"—blue and gold. "What color stripes did you have on your socks yesterday, Coach Stanley?" he asks pointedly.

"Red and yellow, Coach." Ken smiles a bit sheepishly as he admits to wearing USC colors. He knows that the needle is directed at him.

"Here, put these on," Coach says as he hands Ken a pair of official UCLA basketball socks.

On a more serious note, Coach reminds the coaches to be positive. "It is amazing how the youngsters' hearing improves when they hear praise and encouragement from their teachers."

Hector then gives us several details about the day. He asks us to have our campers in the gym by eleven for the Pyramid of Success talk. Also, every Tuesday and Thursday after lunch, the camp hosts a guest speaker, and Hector tells us that former American Basketball Association (ABA) player George Lehmann will be speaking later today.

Coach Wooden speaks again, reminding the coaches of fundamentals details. "The off guard needs to stay a step behind the ball-handling guard, and the forward needs to take one step further than normal before cutting backdoor to the basket," Coach clarifies. "He should throw the hand through as he cuts."[6]

Coach Wooden, who is very aware of all that goes on at camp, walks with Ray Tejada after the meeting. "Ray, I hear that you have a young man on your team who has been difficult to work with."

"Yes, Coach, he is very challenging. He's a great shooter and a really good player, but he is cocky and doesn't listen."

"Just do the best you can with him, and if you have any more problems, let the directors know."

"Thanks, Coach. I'll do that."

Tuesday Morning Workout with Coach

In the theater one group of campers watches the classic black-and-white ball-handling film with Pete Maravich and Press Maravich, Pete's LSU coach and father. The two Maraviches explain and demonstrate Pete's world-famous ball-handling skills and drills.

The other group of campers is ready to go for the morning workout, and Coach moves them through the imaginary ball drills. Coach is intense but relaxed, and the campers are energetic and enthusiastic in spite of being tired after their first full day of camp. In each session with Coach, a different team stands at the front of the group nearest him, as the teams rotate one line toward the front.

This morning Coach stresses change of pace and change of direction. "Only one round unless I tell you more. Change of direction, change of pace, go. Now I really want to see you working on this change of direction, change of pace. Really work at it. I want good movement on this now. Quick change of direction, change of pace. You are not to cross the center of the floor. Go. Keep on balance." Campers clap in rhythm as they wait their turn to go and then stop on his whistle. "Never forget balance. It is the attainment and maintaining, or regaining, of good balance."

Individual coaches focus on each player as the campers fly by. They know by Coach's example that players must do things right the first time and not let little things slip by, for those then turn into big things. Quickly Coach directs the campers to defensive sliding. They slide two to three steps at an angle, like a zigzag, as they slide down the floor. "Defensive slide. Go. Stay low, stay low, stay low."

Now Coach adds defensive sliding and then a quick run so that the defender can get back in front of the offensive player if he's been beat. "Defensive sliding, turn and catch up. Go. Balance, balance, balance. If you don't do it, you'll never catch up."

It is time for jump stops. Players run a short zigzag and then jump-stop. "Zigzag, jump-stop. Zigzag. Go." Coach often repeats things two to three times for emphasis and so that the campers will hear him as they are moving. "Now I want the jump stop from the zigzag. Get balanced, get that tail down, and get your feet spread. Feet wide, don't pound the floor. Get the head up. Tail down. Get the tail down."

The drill ends. Now it is a zigzag drill with an offensive player moving side to side, without a ball, and the defense staying in front of the offensive player. This drill combines what the campers have just worked on. "I want you to really work. Head up. On the whistle, offense goes to defense, and defense runs to the end of the line. Really working when the whistle blows."

Coach doesn't talk to anyone while he is on stage. He is watching and observing the players intently and alertly. The same drill is run again, except now the offensive player dribbles the ball. It is another example of Coach Wooden's wise skill-development progression. "Defense stay. First offensive player get a ball. Now do it with a ball. Keep the ball close to your body. Don't let it come up higher than your waist. Up and down quickly, maneuvering, quick stop and quick pass." This drill goes for a long time without Coach saying anything. His silent, intent observation is a sign that the campers as a whole are doing the drill correctly and that the coaches are teaching it well.[7]

As during all drills, the floor squeaks, and the campers clap. These are Coach's players today, and he drills them as if they are his own team.

A Little Slower at Stations

When the morning workout ends at 9:25, campers either stay in the gym or move outside for stations. As the week goes on, the walk outside is slower each day. But once at their stations, most campers pick up their energy and relish the chance to work hard, learn, and improve.

Not all do, however. For the third straight day, a ten-year-old pays little attention and does not try hard. The coaches have tried but failed to motivate him since Sunday afternoon. In the morning meeting they talked to the camp directors about him as Coach listened.

During the drill the campers clap. These are Coach's players today, and he drills them as if they are his own team.

During his daily walk and with Hector alongside, Coach stops by the rebounding station, where the two of them observe the boy's poor effort and concentration. Coach politely asks the camper to join him on his walk around campus, and off they go. A mile into the strenuous walk, the boy is tired out and asks if he can take a break and get a drink. Coach Macias returns him to his station drills, where his attitude and effort are suddenly much improved. Stations do not seem so hard anymore after trying to keep up with Coach.

The biggest challenge coaches face in conducting the stations is motivating the campers to fully pay attention and give their best effort. The motivated players improve a lot in the stations. Other campers try only in some stations, distract other campers in line, ask when the next water break is, or look around at other stations that seem to be more fun. Coach Tom Gregory uses the Dallas Cowboys to motivate his own campers, pointing out to his campers how hard they work and the skill repetition to which they dedicate themselves.

The post-player station is run by College of the Canyons head coach Lee Smelser, and as always, he runs it very well. Coach Brad Barbarick still talks about how much he learned from Coach Smelser as a camper and how he has used that same teaching to instruct his own players. Coach Smelser began as a successful coach at Morningside High School, next to the Forum, where the Lakers play. His junior varsity coach was Jim Harrick, and Smelser and Harrick would often go together to watch UCLA practice, where they got to know Coach personally.

After completing the stations, the coaches direct the campers on the outside courts to get a drink and then hustle to the gym for Coach Wooden's Pyramid of Success. It is a talk that will impact them for the rest of their lives.

5

Coach Wooden's Pyramid of Success

At eleven o'clock three hundred tired campers sit on the court in the hot gym. Coach Wooden is about to share with them his famous Pyramid of Success—fifteen principles that form his philosophy of basketball and of life.

"I know that many of you have heard Coach Wooden talk about his Pyramid of Success," Hal Mitrovich begins, holding up the plaque that Coach will reference during his talk. "I have heard Coach give this talk many times too—probably more times than any of you have. Each time I pick up something new that I find very valuable in my life.

"It is particularly gratifying for Coach to be able to offer this talk to you young men in the hopes that it might help you in some way. It is my pleasure to introduce to you Coach Wooden and his Pyramid of Success."

Seated on a chair on stage, using only a plaque of the Pyramid as a visual prop, Coach begins to explain his renowned building blocks for true success both in basketball and in life:

> I sometimes have thought that the Pyramid of Success is the only truly original thing I have ever done. The reason

> for this is because I was not satisfied, when I entered the teaching profession back in the thirties, with the general perception that people had toward success as far as their youngsters were concerned in my English classes. An A or B was successful, and anything less than that seemed to be unsuccessful. I didn't like that, because I think that the Good Lord in His infinite wisdom did not create us equal as far as intelligence any more than we are equal in size or appearance.
>
> We are not born into the same environment, we do not all have the same opportunities, and not everybody can earn an A or B. Not every team can win all their games, and you're not necessarily unsuccessful because you are outscored in a game. You are unsuccessful even when you outscore an opponent when you didn't play to your ability level. That's failure—when you fail to do what you are capable of doing. It isn't failure when the other fellow is more capable than you are.
>
> So I wanted to come up with something that I thought could help me to become a better teacher, whether it would be in my English classes, or at the time I was coaching baseball and basketball teams, and I wanted to come up with a different idea. I started in 1934 and completed this in 1948. I wasn't obviously working on it the whole time, because I had a job, trying to feed my family, and so on.

Coach understood that his UCLA players were not that interested in his Pyramid of Success while they played for him. Many years after leaving UCLA, however, it made much more sense to them, and they found great meaning and practical application in it. Similarly, Coach understands now that the campers will sit politely and listen but that some might not have much interest in what he is telling them. But Coach knows that he is planting seeds that may produce fruit later in these boys' lives.

He continues confidently,

> I came up with my own definition of success, something to which I was going to aspire to and to which I was going to try to get the youngsters under my supervision to aspire. And I think perhaps the influence of something that my father had tried to get across to myself and my brothers—we were brought up and raised on a farm in southern Indiana. I remember him always trying to get across that we should never try to be better than someone else but never cease to try to be the very best that we can be. And I think that possibly had some influence on my arrival at this particular definition of success.
>
> I define success as "peace of mind" that can be attained only through the self-satisfaction in knowing you made the effort to become the best that you're capable of becoming. That is success, and only you individually will ever know that. Just like the camp here. There are some of you who may have made every effort to improve yourself all the time. There are others who haven't made that effort. We can't be sure, but you know whether or not you've made that constant effort.
>
> The coaches know whether they've made the constant effort to try to improve themselves as coaches; others can't. The barber doesn't. He thinks he does. The butcher and everybody else think they know more about it than the coach. Sometimes I suspect the coach thinks he knows more about the butcher than the butcher does, but it doesn't work that way.
>
> So my point of view is that you just must try to be the very best that you can be, and you're the only one who can determine that or know that. And you're failing to some degree unless you try that.

Two young campers, Luke and Nate Walton, know the Pyramid and UCLA fundamentals well because they are the sons of UCLA great Bill Walton, who played for Coach from 1971–1974. The Walton boys are smart, fundamentally sound, hardworking players with coachable attitudes.

Coach continues, introducing the first two of the fifteen characteristics that make up his Pyramid of Success:

> If any structure, mythical or other, is going to have any real strength and solidarity, it must have a strong foundation. And the foundation is anchored by the cornerstones. I have two cornerstones in the Pyramid of Success: one is industriousness, and the other is enthusiasm. I think you are all enthusiastic about basketball, or you wouldn't be here. Some of you are not as industrious as others, but you are all enthusiastic.
>
> You need both industriousness and enthusiasm. Grantland Rice, a great sports writer, one of the greatest of all time, wrote many things in verse. I enjoy poetry. My master's thesis was on poetry. I'm working on a book of poems now. I love it. I enjoy it very much, and I enjoy verses that make a point. He wrote one time, which I sort of apply to industriousness, something he called "How to Be a Champion." And he said in part,
>
> You wonder how they do it, and you look to see the knack,
> You watch the foot in action or the shoulder or the back.
> But when you spot the answer where the higher glamours lurk,
> You'll find in moving higher up the laurel-covered spire,
> That most of it is practice, and the rest of it is work.
>
> There is no substitute for work. Don't try to get by with the shortcut. Don't try to get by with the easy way out.

Don't try to get by with a trick. Work, and you'll get the best results.

The other cornerstone is enthusiasm. You have to like what you're doing. You can't do well unless you like what you're doing. In other words, you might be gifted with an enormous ability, and you might appear to be doing well in the eyes of others. But unless you are enthusiastic about it, you're not going to do as well as you're capable of doing. Enthusiasm definitely brushes off upon those with whom you come in contact. The coach must be enthusiastic. The teacher must be enthusiastic if they expect those under their supervision to be enthusiastic. I could give you many examples of that. So you must have industriousness and enthusiasm as the cornerstones.

Between the cornerstones, forming the foundation, I have three blocks that are strong, because each block includes others. And when we include others, we are adding strength. There is no question. One is friendship, one is loyalty, and one is cooperation.

Friendship, young men, you must work at. Often you take friendship for granted. There are many who have made no effort here to make new friends. There are others who have. There are those who are content with the old friends, and an old friend must never be cast aside or discarded for a new one. But you should always be looking for new friends and making new friends.

And then after making new friends, you must work to keep them. You must not take friendship for granted. It isn't friendship when someone is doing something nice for you all the time. That's a nice person. But it isn't friendship until you do for each other. Both sides must work at it for it to be friendship, just like marriage. There is no marriage unless both sides are working at it. With only one side, it is not successful and cannot be. You have to give in friendship as you must give in marriage.

Another block, in addition to friendship, is loyalty. You have to have something to which you must be loyal. And you have to have someone to whom you must be loyal if you are going to be able to make the most of the abilities the good Lord has given you. You must have loyalty. No way can you become the best of which you are capable unless there is loyalty within you.

And then we must have cooperation. It's a small world in which we live today. We don't realize it, young men, how small it is. When I was your age, I would never have dreamed of someone being on the moon. Would never have dreamed of jet travel, where we get places so quickly. We would never have dreamed of so many of the things we have today, the advances that have been made even in television, the telephone, the telegraph, and so on. We never would have dreamed of a lot of those things. And the more sciences have developed, the smaller the world becomes, because we get to places more quickly. We see things as they are happening on the other side of the world today. We didn't see those things when I was your age. Sometimes we might see a still picture, sometimes later as a moving picture, but not as it was happening, as we see someone landing on the moon today. Imagine that. It is almost impossible.

We need cooperation. Try to think of something that you need that is essential in your life, and try to think of anything for which others are not responsible. How about the food you eat? How about the clothes you wear? How about the means of transportation to get you from one spot to another? How about the homes in which you live? How about the schools in which you attend, and so on? We need cooperation of others to make the most of our own particular abilities.

Having explained the five qualities that make up the bottom tier of his Pyramid, Coach moves up to the next level:

> On the second tier I have four blocks: one is self-control, the second is alertness, the third is initiative, and the fourth is intentness.
>
> Self-control you must maintain. You cannot play basketball well if you lose your temper. A coach cannot coach to the best of his ability if he loses his temper. A golfer is not going to be in the fairway too much if he loses his temper. When you make a mental decision that must be made, like maybe your parents do in disciplining you—and you need discipline at times, we all do—but if they lose their control, if they discipline you to punish and not to help, not to improve, not to prevent, not to correct—if they do it just for punishment, I don't think it can bring productive and desirable results. It must be done with self-control and within reason. Emotion we must have; we must empathize. We must have sympathy, but we must act through reason, under self-control.
>
> And then we must be alert and alive. There is something going on around about us all the time from which we can learn if we are just observant. Too often we get lost in our own selves, in our selfish narrow way, and we don't see the things that are happening around us from which we can learn all the time. You can learn something not to do, as Mr. Lincoln did—the greatest of all Americans, in my opinion. He once said, "I never met a person from whom I didn't learn something, although most of the time it was something not to do." But if you are not observant, if you're not alive, you are not going to learn many things. So we must have alertness to develop our own potential.
>
> We must have initiative. Are some of you afraid to shoot at times for fear you might miss? Some of you are

The Pyramid of Success

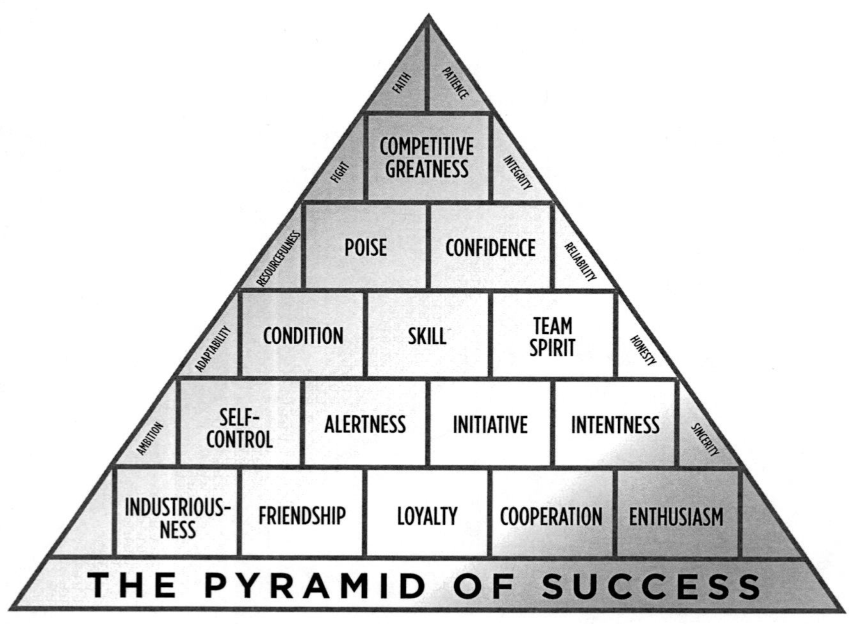

"Success is peace of mind
that is a direct result of self-satisfaction
in knowing that you made the effort to become
the best you are capable of becoming."

John Wooden

Competitive greatness: being at your best when your best is needed; enjoyment of a difficult challenge

Poise: just being yourself; being at ease in any situation; never fighting yourself

Confidence: respect without fear; may come from being prepared and keeping all things in proper perspective

Condition: mental-moral-physical; considering rest, exercise, and diet; practicing moderation; eliminating dissipation

Skill: a knowledge of and the ability to properly and quickly execute the fundamentals; being prepared and covering every little detail

Team spirit: a genuine consideration for others; an eagerness to sacrifice personal interests of glory for the welfare of all

Self-control: practicing self-discipline and keeping emotions under control; good judgment and common sense essential

Alertness: constantly observing; staying open-minded; being eager to learn and improve

Initiative: cultivating the ability to make decisions and think alone; not being afraid of failure but learning from it

Intentness: setting a realistic goal; concentrating on its achievement by resisting all temptations and being determined and persistent

Industriousness: recognizing that there is no substitute for work, that worthwhile results come from hard work and careful planning

Friendship: comes from mutual esteem, respect, and devotion; like marriage, must not be taken for granted but requires a joint effort

Loyalty: to yourself and to all those depending upon you

Cooperation: with all levels of your co-workers; listening in order to be heard; being interested in finding the best way, not in having your own way

Enthusiasm: brushes off upon those with whom you come in contact; truly enjoying what you are doing

Faith: through prayer

Fight: determined effort

Resourcefulness: proper judgment

Adaptability: to any situation

Ambition: for noble goals

Patience: knowing that good things take time

Integrity: purity of intentions

Reliability: creating respect

Honesty: in thought and action

Sincerity: keeping friends

afraid to do things because of your fear of failure. You must have initiative to act when action is needed. When action is needed, act without fear of failure. You're going to fail at times, because you are not perfect. Don't fail by making the same mistake all the time. Learn from the mistakes you make, but don't be afraid to act because you are afraid of failure. Just act with reason. Act with self-control. Act with the experiences you have and according to the knowledge you have acquired in regard to the particular situation. But act without fear of failure.

The fourth block on the second tier is intentness. You must have goals, but make your goals realistic, young men. Don't make your goals so idealistic that they are unattainable. Too often we do that, and the time comes when it becomes apparent that the goal is unattainable, and then it becomes counterproductive. I believe in idealism. I definitely do. But I don't believe in goals that are so idealistic that they are unattainable. I think goals should be difficult to achieve, because if they're easily acquired or achieved or attained, they aren't very meaningful. They don't amount to much, and they won't be very lasting. They must be difficult. Goals should be difficult but should be within the realm of possibility. We must be intent on reaching them and not worrying about the obstacles we're going to hit along the way.

We're going to have adversity. Of course we're going to have adversity. We need adversity to get strength. To gain physical strength, weights are used. To gain mental strength, we tackle increasingly difficult mental problems. We don't start with calculus. We start with arithmetic and work up to algebra, geometry, trigonometry, and so on. We need increasingly difficult things in order to strengthen ourselves mentally. We need to strengthen ourselves emotionally. We learn through that, but we do not let adversity deter us from our course. It may slow us down, it may cause us to change our method, and it may cause us to back up, use a different style. But we must not quit. We must have the intentness, the persistence, the determination to go onward.

Coach moves up another level to the middle tier:

And then on the next tier I have three blocks. One is condition, one is skill, and one is team spirit, which is nothing more than consideration for others.

You must be in condition for what you are doing. You must be in condition to play basketball. You must be in condition to play different positions in basketball, just as in football wide receivers aren't conditioned the same as linebackers. You have to be conditioned for what you are doing, as a surgeon has to be conditioned differently than a salesman, a salesman has to be conditioned differently from an attorney, and so on.

You must be conditioned for whatever you are doing, and that is something within your power. That's not something over which you have no control. That's something over which you have control. And it's within your power to attain and maintain if you will do it. And it's not making a sacrifice to have yourself in good condition for what you do. That's no sacrifice at all. But you must have it.

And in addition to being conditioned, you must be skilled. You must have knowledge, or know-how, to shoot a basketball. And you'd better be able to do it quickly, or you may not be able to do it at all. I have had players who could really get shots, oh, they could get shots, but they couldn't shoot, and that didn't help us any.

The campers laugh at this. Coach continues,

I had others who could really shoot, but they weren't quick and couldn't get shots, and that didn't help us either. You have to be able to do it and to do it quickly. A surgeon may have to react quickly to save a patient, regardless of his knowledge or ability. If you can't react quickly, you lose the patient. An attorney will lose the case. You can lose your life in many situations unless you can react quickly. So you must have the skills. The skill is the knowledge of and the ability to not only properly but also quickly execute.

The third block is team spirit. And that's nothing more than consideration for others. We must have consideration for others to make the most of what we have. It is a sad commentary on the history of our civilization—many wars have been fought and millions of lives lost because heads of state did not have the consideration for others. Wars came about because of differences in religion. Wars because of differences in race. You know that is true, and it is a sad commentary that has to be, or must have been, I should say. It doesn't have to be, but it has been.

We must have consideration for others; we must have teamwork to have success as a basketball team. There is no such thing, in my opinion, as individual success on a basketball team. It's the combination of people's roles that may be quite different, but each is important, just as the nut holes of a wheel on a machine are important to the machine itself, just as the wheel on an automobile is just as important as the engine itself, because the engine is no good if one wheel is missing.

There are parts to be played, there are roles to be played, and they must all work together toward the achievement of some common objective, or goal. We must have teamwork.

Coach, almost to the top of the Pyramid, now moves up to cover his second-to-last tier:

And then above that I have two blocks. One is poise, and one is confidence. I also made up my own definition for

> poise. Poise is a very simple thing, in my opinion. Poise is just being yourself. That is my definition of poise. Just being yourself. You're not acting; you're not trying to be something you're not. Therefore, in my opinion, you'll be functioning near your own particular level of competency. Don't permit the things over which you have no control to adversely affect you. Because you are within yourself, you're going to function near your own ability level.
>
> Then you must have confidence. You must have confidence that is real, that is not false. Not whistling in the dark. That isn't confidence at all. That's false. You must have real confidence. Can you have poise and confidence that's real? I think it's difficult, but you can have poise and confidence by being industrious, enthusiastic, friendly, loyal, and cooperative; by maintaining your self-control, by being alert and alive, by observing all the time, having initiative without being afraid to fail; by having consideration for others, real team spirit, by being conditioned for whatever you are doing; by being skilled in whatever you are doing and by being imbued with consideration for others, you are going to have poise and confidence that are real.

The campers are feeling ready for lunch, but they listen as Coach winds up with the final block at the top of his Pyramid of Success and then shares two final characteristics that make all the blocks possible:

> Just above the blocks is the last block of the structure called competitive greatness—being at your best when your best is needed, enjoying it when it is most difficult. There is no true pleasure, no true joy, no true satisfaction in doing something that anybody else can do. And yet most of the tasks we have to do, each and every one of us every day, are simple tasks. They are tasks that others can do without any

particular difficulty. And whatever we are doing, it should be done to the very best of our ability.

Grantland Rice again said when he wrote "The Great Competitor":

Beyond the winning and the goal,
Beyond the glory and the fame,
He feels a flame within his soul,
Born of the spirit of the game.

And where the barriers may wait,
Built by the opposing gods,
He finds a thrill in bucking fate
And riding down the endless odds.

Where others wither in the fire
Or fall below some raw mishap,
Where others lag behind and tire
Or break beneath the handicap,

He finds a new and deeper thrill
To take him on the uphill spin,
Because the test is greater still
And something he can revel in.

The great competitor revels in it when it is difficult and enjoys it, gets satisfaction and pleasure from it. That's the last of the blocks.

But leading up to success on the apex, according to my definition, leading up to the last block, on the one side is patience, and on the other side is faith. You must have faith that things will turn out as they should—not necessarily the way you want them to but the way they should. You must have patience. Good things take time, and that's exactly the way it should be.

Those are the blocks that make up the Pyramid of Success. I don't want to tell you I have lived up to this Pyramid. I merely want to say to you that I've tried. And that's what I'd like all of you to do—to try. And if you do, then you can hold your head up always and have peace. Try to be the very best that you can do. Don't be satisfied. Don't try to be better than someone else. Just be the best that you can be. No matter how accomplished you may be, don't let it go to your head.

One of my favorite poems is called "God's Hall of Fame," and part of it goes like this:

This crowd on Earth, they soon forget
The heroes of the past.
They cheer like mad until you fall,
And that's how long you'll last.

But God, He never does forget,
And in His Hall of Fame,
By just believing in His Son,
Inscribed you'll find your name.

I tell you, my friends, I would not trade
My name, however small,
Inscribed up there beyond the stars
In that celestial hall

For any famous name on Earth
Or glory that they share;
I'd rather be an unknown here
And have my name up there.

I think we would all agree, if we just admit it to ourselves. What we are is far more important than what others think

> we are. And individually we're the only ones who truly know what we are.

"Okay," Coach says, switching gears as he finishes his talk, "I see Coach Mitrovich walking up here, and that usually means that it's time for me to stop talking. Okay now, let's all listen to Coach Mitrovich."[1]

Holding Coach's Pyramid of Success plaque in his hands, Hal tells the campers, "By the way, a plaque like this one will be awarded to one person on each team who best personifies and exemplifies what Coach Wooden is looking for at camp. This won't necessarily mean the best player or the most valuable player," he clarifies, "but rather the individual who understands team play and really embodies the philosophy of Coach Wooden.

"Alright, fellas," Coach Mitrovich finally says, switching to the subject the campers are most interested in at the moment. "Let's go to lunch. Don't run!" Hungry campers walk—very quickly—out of the gym!

Coach visiting with UCLA cheerleaders on the flight to Portland, Oregon, for the 1975 NCAA West Regionals

Coach speaking to the campers with UCLA greats Kiki Vandeweghe, Jack Hirsch, and Bill Walton

Official Sportsworld camp photo of Coach

Coach on the stage in the Cal Lu gym teaching the campers

Coach with camper Harvey Mason

Coach with me as a twenty-two-year-old camp counselor

Coach with coach Wayne Carlson

Coach with coach Michael Scarano

Coach with head counselor Steve "Hawk" Hawkins

Head counselor Jack "Jaws" Currier, camp visitor coach Steve Tucker, Coach, and me

Coach with Tom Desotell, camp director for Coach's adult camps

Lil Lopez and her son, coach Larry Lopez, with Coach

Coach Mike Kundstadt, his wife, Gerri, and his daughters, Karin and Kerri, with Coach

Coach Don Showalter, his wife, Vicky, and his children,
Melissa and Brent, with Coach

Coach David Myers and daughter, Kelly, with Coach

A group camp photo from 1986

Me with my daughters, Megan and Kara, at Pauley Pavilion
as the girls meet Coach for the first time

6

Coach and Friends

Many people visit camp to talk to Coach Wooden, who is patient, gracious, kind, and considerate toward all. Some are relatives of campers, while others are just admirers of Coach Wooden. But if you want to talk to Coach, you'd better be prepared to join him on his brisk morning walk around campus. Knowing this, some people join Coach in sweats and warm-ups and try their best to keep up with him. Other less active visitors hope to talk to Coach between his morning activities, after he has finished his walk, or when Coach is free from activities after lunch.

One of the favorite visitors among campers and staff members is actor Al Lewis, who played Grandpa on the hit sixties TV series *The Munsters*. He is here again this year to watch his grandkids at camp. He is kind, friendly, unassuming, and stays out of the way. He loves basketball and loves his grandkids.

Steve Tucker, a college coach from Sam Houston State University in Huntsville, Texas, is also here today. Tucker feels incredible anticipation to meet Coach Wooden. As Tucker talks with another coach, he realizes that Coach Wooden is standing by, waiting patiently and politely to greet him. Tucker is amazed that Coach would show such respect and consideration to him. Coach Wooden immediately puts Tucker at ease as they talk about basketball and life. At one point

Tucker mentions that he has a fear of flying, and Coach tells him that for the longest time he too did not like to fly. He shares with Tucker a few harrowing flights he's been on as well as some fortunate circumstances that kept him off flights that did not end well.

Tucker is an admirer of legendary Alabama football coach Paul "Bear" Bryant and Indiana basketball coach Bob Knight, and he has patterned his coaching after such men. His meeting with Coach Wooden changes that. Tucker elevates Coach above the other two legends, not only because of Coach Wooden's coaching greatness, but also because of his personal humility, character, wisdom, and generosity. Many camp coaches who have worked for other great coaches echo Tucker's thoughts.

As he is about to leave, Tucker tells a coaching friend, "Coach's insights on life are just as intriguing as what he and I talked about concerning basketball. He is a fascinating person. I don't believe I've ever met anyone directly who was more impressive to be around. Every word seems to be in place and to fit so eloquently, and you can tell that comes from his days of teaching high-school English. I'm just so in awe. Meeting him today makes this the most incredible day of my life."

Tucker takes a tangible gift home with him as well. During Coach Wooden's Pyramid of Success talk, Tucker was present, and when Coach finished, he walked off stage and handed Tucker the plaque of the Pyramid. "He told me that it was a pleasure to spend time with me. That is Coach Wooden—so humble. This is going up on my office wall, and it is always going to stay there. I know I don't measure up to its standards, but I'm going to strive to." Tucker is just one of many visitors profoundly affected by Coach throughout his many years of camps.

Coach has another special visitor today. Debbie Willie, a member of both the 1978 UCLA women's basketball team and the softball national championship team, is the head women's coach at Biola University. During the past season Coach gave a powerful Pyramid presentation to her Biola squad. Debbie, who attended

Coach's girls' camp as a fifteen-year-old, has brought her shy nine-year-old nephew, Zach, to meet Coach. Coach says hello to him and then tells the boy, "Turn around for me." Upon Zach's compliance, Coach says, "This is a fine young man, a fine young man." Zach instantly lights up with a big smile and newfound confidence and has fun talking with Coach.

Rehashing the Pyramid of Success

About this time the Showalter, Kunstadt, and Myers kids all run from the pool to eat lunch, and seeing a long line of sweaty campers, they run to the front of the line. "Hey, you can't cut in line!" yell a few older campers.

Kelly Myers tells them, "Yes, we can. We're the coaches' kids."

"No, you can't! Who's your dad?"

Kelly tells them, "My dad is Coach Myers."

"Mine is Coach Kunstadt," says Karin.

Melissa proudly says, "My dad is Coach Showalter."

Their dads have obviously impressed the campers, because they all agree, "Yeah, they can cut in."

At lunch the coaches' questions for Coach naturally center on the Pyramid as it relates to his definition of success and the remarkable success he has had.

"A coach can only do his best, nothing more," Coach explains, "but he does owe that not only to himself but also to the people who employ him and to the youngsters under his supervision. If you truly do your best, and only you really know, then you are successful, and the actual score is immaterial, whether it is favorable or unfavorable. However, when you fail to do your best, you have failed, even though the score might have been to your liking.[1]

"This does not mean that you should not coach to win," he goes on. "You must teach the players to play and to win everything in their power that is ethical and honest to win. I want to be able to feel—and I want my players to sincerely feel—that doing the best that they are capable of doing is victory in itself and less than that is defeat."[2]

The coaches listen, some of them taking notes. "I continually stressed to my players that all I expected was their best effort at practice and in the games," Coach Wooden tells his listeners. "They must be eager to become the very best they were capable of becoming. I told them that although I wanted them to be pleased over victory and personal accomplishment, I wanted them to get the most satisfaction from knowing that both they and the team had done their best. I hoped that their actions or conduct following a game would not indicate victory or defeat.[3]

"The score can't make you a loser when you know you do your best, nor can it make you a winner if you do less," Coach instructs.

"Winning and losing take care of themselves. If you get beat, be realistic. If the other team is better, admit it. If you play your best and lose, the other team is better than you. There is no shame in that. If you're going to lose, lose because the other team played well, not because you didn't play to your level of ability or competency. The score can't make you a loser when you know you do your best, nor can it make you a winner if you do less. I came to understand that losing is only temporary and not all-encompassing. You must simply study it, learn from it, and try hard not to lose the same way again. So try your hardest. Do your best. And only you will know whether you did it or not.[4]

"All are not equal," Coach concludes, "but all have equal opportunity to make the effort. That's what really matters in the long run. If you're good enough, you'll eventually outscore the other team. I didn't want our teams to be better than someone else. I wanted them to be the best they could be."[5]

"Coach, what was the key to UCLA's consistency?" someone asks. "You won year after year with different players, had a lot of long winning streaks, even as everyone focused on beating you."

"I believe it is because we played nearer to our level of competency than other teams did," Coach replies. "It is not that we did things differently than other teams. I praised my players if they played close to their ability level. Convey to players that you play as close to your level of competency as possible. You will have peace that you did all you could. Be upset when you don't play to your level of competency, win or lose. Have peace when you do play to your level of competency, win or lose.

"We wanted to avoid peaks and valleys. For every peak there is a valley. Don't get too high in victory, get overly excited. Don't get too low in defeat, get depressed. No need for excessive exaltation or dejection unless perhaps you failed to play your hardest. It's just a game. Do not be afraid to fail. We are all going to fail. Learn from it,"[6] Coach encourages.

"Just do the best with what the good Lord in His infinite wisdom gave each of us. Success is realizing the maximum potential for each person. Don't compare. Don't worry that it's not the best. Just do your best."

Coach recalls, "Two players that gave me great satisfaction and came closest to reaching their full potential, one was Conrad Burke, and one was Doug Macintosh. When I saw each one of them on our freshman team—now they were years apart—I thought, *Oh gracious, if he ever makes the varsity, the varsity must be pretty miserable, if he's good enough to make it.* Conrad started for a season and a half. And Doug played thirty-two minutes in our 1964 championship game and did tremendously for us, and the next season he was a starter on our national championship team. So those are the things that give you great joy and satisfaction. I consider them to be as successful as Lew Alcindor [Kareem Abdul-Jabbar], Bill Walton, and many of the other outstanding players we had."[7]

"Why were your teams so good in the tournament?" another coach asks.

"Our UCLA teams almost always played near our competency level, not up and down—and that is a real key in tournaments. I didn't emphasize 'This is it—one loss, and you are out.' Some make the games bigger than they should be. Don't make the mistake of making games bigger than they should be.

"I emphasized doing what you do well and adjusting to the other team. And don't mention mystiques [psychological challenges]. Prepare for a hostile environment, but don't mention it. The more you worry about it, the more excuses the players will make, the more complaining the players will do.

"When I coached, non-league games didn't matter. Winning your conference was everything. But I would do it differently today, because the non-conference does matter. As the season goes along, there should be less and less physical contact so you don't take away their competitive edge as the season goes on. It is not games that wear out a team mentally and physically during the season. It is practice. It is important to ease the emotional and mental aspect of practice after a while. In my early years I overworked my teams. I quit overworking them, and this helped in tournament time. In later years the better condition we were in, the better we did in tournament. In my earlier years I also put new things in at tournament time, and that hurt us. So I stopped putting new things in. We did the old things better and well. I learned to do the same thing with the second half of conference."

"What about game coaching?"

"I wanted a businesslike, non-emotional approach to the game for coach and player," Coach answers. "You will have emotions, but have them be purposeful and under control. I wanted calm analytic coaching, not emotional, including at halftime and timeouts as well, not ranting or raving. Emotions, especially anger or frustration, destroy analytical thinking. If you do that, you will get out-coached, and players will get out-played. Maintain mental and emotional balance. You can't brood over mistakes. You will make mistakes. You can't change the past. Forget it and learn from it, but you must forget."

"What about halftime?"

"Be prepared for halftime. I might fire up an individual if he seems down but not the team. If the team is flat, the coach could be at fault. The players might be mentally fatigued. They might be overconfident or not respecting the opponent. There is more over-coaching than under-coaching. As a coach, there is not much to do in the game if your team is prepared."

"What is the key to winning close games?" a coach asks.

Coach Wooden has a ready answer, as always. "Execution is the key to any game. When you are not executing, it is often because of emotions or lack of conditioning. Be in better condition than your opponent, and if you are not, at least believe that you are. As a coach, I wanted to be concerned with our execution to the standard of our competency. Good teams will probably play close games. Don't talk about your opponent; don't worry about your opponent. Play your game, and control your emotions. I didn't want my team showing emotion in response to bad calls, especially in close games, and I didn't want to either. I felt my players would be more under control if I seemed under control. How can I tell them if they lose their self-control they are going to be outplayed if I am losing my self-control on the bench? I once heard something said: 'No written word, no spoken plea can teach our youth what they should be, or all the books on all the shelves. It is what the teachers are themselves.'"[8]

A coach decides to tease Coach Wooden a bit. "What did you think after you lost to Houston in the Astrodome?" The question is about the 1968 "Game of the Century," when the top-ranked Bruins, on a forty-seven-game winning streak, lost to number-two team Houston 71–69 before more than 52,000 people in the Astrodome in the first ever nationally televised regular season college basketball game.

Coach's mood suddenly changes, and his competitive but playful side comes out. "It is sort of interesting you bring up that game," Coach says with a touch of humorous indignation in his expression. "Of all the games in which I was involved, that is the one you bring up. You didn't ask about the return game in the NCAA tournament, the one that counted, when we led by over forty points before I called them off a little. Why don't you talk about that one?" The coaches are busting up, and Coach continues.

"And next you will want to know what I said after we lost at Notre Dame to break our eighty-eight-game winning streak. 'What do you think about that game?' Well, it's another game. Why don't you bring up the game when we won our sixty-first in a row and broke the old record? That was at Notre Dame, and we beat Notre Dame five times during the streak. Why do you want to talk about that one loss all the time?" Coaches are laughing so loud that the entire cafeteria looks over at the table. "Seems like people only want to remember the games we lost," Coach finishes, with his trademark smile and a twinkle in his eye.[9]

Guest Speakers

A guest speaker addresses the campers on Tuesdays and Thursdays after lunch, and today is no exception. Campers are always excited to see and learn from a former UCLA player, an NBA player, or a specialty speaker such as a ball-handling specialist or shooting expert. The speakers are paid $500–$1,000 to give an hour-long talk. Many speak at other camps, but it is special to speak at Coach Wooden's camp and to see him.

The speakers are generous and caring toward the campers, and everyone at camp—coaches, counselors, and campers—comes away with at least one or two memorable points from each one. No matter what the speakers talk about, however, the campers are thrilled simply to have the chance to touch, talk to, and have a picture taken with a famous player.

Bill Walton is, arguably, the most notable speaker who speaks at camp, and when he comes, he teaches and demonstrates post moves. He explains that when he was growing up, he was a guard. After a big growth spurt, the guard skills he learned as a kid helped him to be successful as a bigger player, since larger players often never develop the kind of dribbling, passing, and shooting skills that the smaller guards do. He also demonstrates his famous outlet pass, one of the best in the history of basketball, in which he turns in the air and delivers a strike to a guard on the run down the court. Walton and Wes Unseld, who was first a player and later a coach for the Baltimore/Washington Bullets, are generally regarded as the best two outlet passers ever in the NBA. Coach Lee Smelser remembers Unseld speaking at one of Coach's camps and seeing him demonstrate his outlet pass. "He threw the ball up on the backboard, ripped it down, turned in midair, and while still in the air, fired a pass that hit the net on the opposite end of the floor."

Occasionally Walton's buddy and former UCLA teammate, Greg Lee, himself once a camper, shares the speaking platform with Bill. They might also play basketball with talented campers in two-on-two games. A future University of Kentucky player once dunked on Walton in one of those games and made a show of it. That woke Walton up, and he absolutely dominated and schooled the hotshot high-school kid after that.

Many camp stories include Walton, such as one involving Hawk. It is the head counselor's job to set out a table for the guest speaker to sit at after his talk where he can sign autographs and have his picture taken with campers and others. It was a hundred degrees one day when Walton came to speak, so Hawk made sure to put the table in the shade for Walton and his co-speaker Lee, both of whom he had gotten to know well from driving them to and from camp. The fair-skinned Walton looked at the table in the shade and said, "Hawk, you're killing me. I need to work on my tan." Hawk moved the table out into the sun, where Lee and Walton took off their shirts and signed autographs and had pictures taken.

Walton is an excellent speaker who is personable and caring toward the campers. The first time he spoke, he was so intent on doing a good job that he went thirty minutes over his allotted time. Coaches appreciate his enthusiasm and natural teaching ability. He is also gracious toward the staff at Cal Lu. Chef Robert Lopez loves Walton, so Coach brought Walton by one day to meet Lopez. Walton was very friendly, and Robert says, "Meeting him is one of the greatest things to ever happen to me."

Three-time NBA rebound leader Swen Nater, another former Bruin who speaks at camp, teaches rebounding fundamentals. Swen often reaches up and, while flat footed, grabs the net as he talks, which the campers get a kick out of. Coach loves Swen and might even put him though rebounding drills. Coach enjoys putting his hand on Swen's head as Swen sits on the floor (since Swen is seven feet tall and Coach is five foot ten!) in a show of affection while he praises him in front of the campers. Coach and Swen share an appreciation for poetry.

Swen quotes Coach Wooden's three rebounding keys: "Assume that the shot is missed; get your hands above your shoulders; and go get the basketball with two hands." He also demonstrates imaginary rebounding, which the campers practice every morning with Coach Wooden. Swen tells the campers, "The great offensive rebounder is one who loves to rebound, goes for the rebound every time, and makes it a priority in his game." Coach Wooden used to chart where the ball hit the rim and where it would most likely bounce, and Swen became a student of this. Swen emphasizes to the campers that they should learn where their own teammates' missed shots tend to go.

NBA scoring champion Kiki Vandeweghe inspires campers and gives them hope to believe that they can find a way, an edge, to make their high-school squad. He demonstrates his rocker steps—offensive moves—and explains that he is actually not a great shooter but has learned to be a "marksman at his position." By this he means that he asks his coaches where he will get his shots and then practices just those shots, which might be at the top of the key, the wings, or the corners. He also inspires campers when he tells them that he was doubted at every level and told that he would never be athletic enough to play in high school, then at UCLA, and then in the NBA. Through hard work and determination, he became an elite player on all three levels.

David Greenwood, former UCLA All-American and later NBA player for several teams, is a limber athlete who tells campers that they can gain three to four inches on their vertical leap by stretching well. After his talk many of the campers work on their stretching so that they can jump and dunk like him. The fact that Greenwood is such a great leaper reinforces his message.

Beloved Lakers announcer Chick Hearn was a guest speaker one session. He enthralled the campers with stories of the Showtime Lakers—the 1980s era in which the Lakers sought to make basketball games more entertaining - and expressed tremendous admiration for Coach Wooden.

A former player for the Los Angeles Lakers, Pat Riley was a motivating and inspiring speaker in the early days of Coach's camps who talked about his dad and the work ethic his dad instilled in him. Pat taught some of the same drills he had learned as a college player from his legendary University of Kentucky coach Adolph Rupp. Pat impressed the camp coaches with his coaching ability, and no one is surprised that he has become a great coach for the Lakers.

Kareem Abdul-Jabbar has spoken a few times; former Bruin and Laker Keith Erickson always does well with the campers as well. Perennial All-Star Marques Johnson of the Milwaukee Bucks gives his popular demonstration of one-on-one moves and dunks. Walt Hazzard, Gail Goodrich, Mike Warren, John Vallely, Brad Holland, Roy Hamilton, James Wilkes, Richard Washington, Dave Meyers, Pete Trgovich, Andre McCarter, and former camper Ralph Drollinger are among the many former Bruins to speak at camp. NBA All-Stars Walter Davis and former camper Paul Westphal have also been guest speakers.

Before he began running his own camps in the late seventies, former Bruin and later UCLA head coach Larry Farmer was a guest speaker. Farmer is an excellent coach whose help and encouragement built my confidence and coaching ability as well as the ability of other young camp coaches who heard him speak. Farmer once told Hawk that the camp coaches are in some ways closer to Coach than the Bruins players were when they played for him. "The camp coaches get to see the fun part of him and his sense of humor. We didn't really see that side until after we played for him."

All speakers end their talks with a question-and-answer segment. Invariably, the first question any camper asks a guest speaker is "Will you dunk for us?" which is followed by cheering from the other campers. After a brief leg stretch, the speaker will make a simple dunk, which pleases the campers momentarily but also elicits a request for a more sophisticated dunk. At this point the speaker will smile, politely decline, and ask for other questions.

Coach introduces today's speaker, George Lehmann, after thanking counselor John Hayes for a pleasant morning ride to camp. Hayes is humbled by this unexpected public encouragement from Coach, who seems to know that John could use a pat on the back. Lehmann, who played in the heyday of the ABA with its red, white, and blue ball and experimental three-point shot, will not be asked to dunk. At first glance most campers are disappointed to see an average-looking athlete walk into the gym with a ball on his hip. But it is not long before they are enthralled with Lehmann, who proves to be a dynamic and inspirational speaker.

For forty-five minutes Lehmann talks about shooting and keeping it simple using the acronym BEEF—balance, eyes on the target, elbow keeps the basketball straight, and follow-through. He talks about his one-piece shot, muscle memory, quality over quantity in practice time, and the cycle for success: "Practice leads to success, which leads to confidence, which leads to more practice, and the cycle repeats itself." He mesmerizes the campers as well as the counselors and coaches, talking non-stop, moving non-stop, shooting non-stop, and usually swishing the ball non-stop. The rare miss brings a reaction from the campers, some of whom start quietly counting his next streak of baskets made in a row. Lehmann is one of the Wooden camp's most memorable guest speakers ever.

One More Special Visitor

Ann Meyers Drysdale, the only woman ever to play on an NBA team, has developed her own special bond with Coach and stops by this afternoon to give Coach a hug and visit with him.

Ann first met Coach when her older brother, Dave Meyers, was the leader of UCLA's improbable 1975 NCAA title team, Coach's last team and one that he loves and cherishes, and their friendship has deepened over the years. Ann's younger brother, Jeff Meyers, was himself a special success story on the UCLA JV team. He had been a little-used, pudgy high school player at Sonora High School, where his older brother Dave had starred on a California Interscholastic Federation (CIF) title team. At UCLA Jeff worked hard and became a key contributor on an outstanding crowd-pleasing JV team coached by Coach's future grandson-in-law Craig Impelman. That team included future All-Pro Seattle Seahawks safety Ken Easley. In one game Jeff went up against future Utah Jazz and NBA block record holder seven-foot-four Mark Eaton and scored on him a few times.

Ann helps coach at some of Coach Wooden's adult camps. Adults from all walks of life attend these camps to be trained by Coach and to interact with players from UCLA's 1964 and 1965 NCAA title teams. True to her competitive nature, Ann once jumped into a camp game involving a former NFL football player. Camp legend has it that at one point in that game, Ann, who was four months pregnant at the time, took a charge on the NFL player. Anyone who knows Ann can believe that story and would assume that she was the best player there.

Ann has become very special to Coach over the years, and she is one of many loving and devoted family members and friends who have helped Coach through the loss of Nell, a pain so great that only those who have profoundly loved a spouse for many years could ever begin to imagine it. Coach appreciates Ann's visit today and the continuing support and encouragement that she brings him.

Tuesday Afternoon

After George Lehmann's motivating talk, the campers have one more hour of drills with their coaches to prepare for the camp games, which will begin tomorrow. Anticipation runs high, and the players work hard to master the fundamentals that they are learning.

Free time follows, with four coaches running three-on-three tournaments in the gym. These tend to be highly competitive, with most of the best players in camp participating as campers pick their own teams.

The counselors trade off driving Coach this week, since so many past head counselors are at camp. John Saintignon will drive Coach home today, but first the two of them stop briefly to watch the Cowboys practice. They notice defensive back Charlie Waters's intensity and hard work; he looks as if he will run through anyone and anything to make a play. As Coach Landry and Coach Wooden briefly talk, Saintignon savors the opportunity to observe the two legends. Both are calm, quiet, thoroughly prepared, and intense teachers. Coach stays only for a short time, not wanting to upstage anyone or be a distraction.

Camper Tony Strickland runs out to watch his beloved Cowboys practice again. Today he not only carries Harvey Martin's helmet but also wears Martin's huge shoulder pads. What appears to be a really good deal for Martin is really a caring act to benefit Tony.

Swapping Camp Stories

Tonight coach Ray Lokar almost gets the opportunity to eat the Cowboys' desired food. He walks in wearing a white Converse T-shirt with its big trademark blue star on the front of the shirt. The attendant mistakes the shirt for a Dallas shirt and directs

Lokar to the Cowboys' food line. Lokar's mouth waters as he gives his fellow coaches a quick smirk and walks to the other food line. But he does not have the nerve to stay there. He humbly takes his tray and joins his coaching friends in their own line.

Over dinner counselor Kevin Barbarick tells the other coaches a story about Cowboys player Thomas "Hollywood" Henderson from when Kevin was a camper years ago. "At lunch one day Hollywood Henderson got in line, pointed at the Cowboys' food, and said, 'I don't want any of that junk—I want some of what these guys are eating.' He got in line with us coaches, was served the campers' food, and sat down with about five or six of us. Just really cool. When I got older, I realized that it had been his way of showing respect to Coach Wooden and having fun with us."

We laugh. "I can't top that story," I jump in, "but I have a good one. One of our friends, Troy Dueker made the team at San Fernando Valley College, which is now Cal State University Northridge, but was given only a partial-scholarship."

"I know Troy," says Lokar. "His dad was a great coach at Los Angeles Lutheran High School."

"Yes, that's him," I reply. "Well, Troy's dad got smart, got out of coaching, and is now making big money selling financial plans to teachers. Anyway, Troy was not happy about not getting a full-scholarship, plus he had to get a job now to get through college. So he was hired as a waiter at a local Marie Callender's, where he met his future wife."

Lokar jumps in. "I've seen her. She is gorgeous. Tell him he needs to thank Coach Cassidy for giving him only a partial-scholarship.

I laugh. "He sure does. So Coach Wooden went into that Marie Callender's for dinner one night. Troy paid the waiter in charge of Coach's station so that he could wait on Coach. Coach must have really liked the restaurant and Troy, because he kept coming back and requesting to be seated in Troy's area. Eventually he brought his son, daughter, and grandchildren with him. It was a tough time for Coach, since it was right after Nell's death, but he was really gracious to Troy, and they talked a lot. Troy talked basketball with Coach, but Coach was more interested in talking to Troy about his education. It is still a great memory for Troy, and he loves Coach for it. He must have learned about competitive greatness from Coach too because Troy became a three-year starter at CSUN, one of Coach Cassidy's favorite players ever, and a fan favorite"

It was a tough time for Coach, since it was right after Nell's death, but he was really gracious to the young waiter. The waiter loves Coach for it.

Coach Ken Barone and coach Frank Carbajal, who had coached high school and then college basketball at Santa Barbara City College, remember back to the free-throw shooting contest against Cowboys star quarterback Roger Staubach that they used to hold at night in front of the campers. "The campers loved it, because the loser had to buy pizza for all the campers," remembers Barone fondly. Barone and Carbajal were two of the nation's best free-throw shooters when they played in college, and Staubach was a great shooter as well. Sportsworld didn't like this competition, so they only did it for a few years, but it was great fun. "Sometimes Staubach won, and sometimes Carbajal or I would win," recalls Barone. "But win or lose, Staubach always bought the pizza, even though the campers didn't know that. He is just that generous of a person."

Mike Scarano starts entertaining his fellow coaches with camp stories. The best story involves a Caucasian counselor a few years back from Angelina College in Texas. "Some black counselors were giving him a hard time about whites not being able to jump. The counselor decided that he'd had enough of it, and on the walk to the gym, he stopped behind a car, took a run, and leaped from the back of the car over the front bumper."

Coach Wayne Carlson does not believe the story. "Come on. There's no way."

"People saw him do it."

True or not, it is typical of the camp stories that have been retold throughout the years.

Playing Basketball—and Playing Around

From six to seven, one group of campers practices and then plays a full-court scrimmage against another team, while the other group has free time. The groups switch activities from seven to eight. Everyone can feel the energy in the gym at the eight-fifteen roll call as campers talk and boast in anticipation of tomorrow's first official games.

Kevin Tamura, a sixteen-year-old five-foot-ten guard from nearby Taft High School, is having a great camp experience. Kevin is working hard and loves everything about camp. For the first time he is away from home and on his own with his friends, and he is finding it fun to be in the dorms. Besides, he enjoys meeting many new kids from all over the country and seeing different styles of basketball.

He has played basketball almost non-stop from morning to bedtime. He particularly enjoys stations because he is learning new skills and developing his weaker left hand. He is mature enough to value the repetitive drills under Coach Wooden's direction. After stations today he told his coach, Wayne Carlson, "I'm learning so much, and I feel like I'm improving." Coach Carlson asks what he is learning specifically. "I realize that I can't just take the ball and drive through two or three players to get a layup. And I'm learning to be more disciplined in basketball and in life."

But in an afternoon pickup game in the gym, his camp experience takes a dramatic turn when he comes down on an opponent's foot and badly sprains his left ankle. The counselors take him to the doctor, and Kevin finally returns three hours later on crutches and with a cast on his foot. His basketball playing is done for four to six weeks.

Coach Carlson is disappointed to hear that his best player will not be able to play anymore and asks him, "Are you going to go home or stay at camp?" Kevin was initially discouraged by the injury, but he has picked his spirits up and displays determination and maturity to make the best out of his tough break. "I talked to my parents, and they told me that I can stay the rest of camp if I want to. I'm having a great time and having fun with my friends, so I'm going to stay. I know that I'm not going to play after high school, but I can still learn basketball by watching, and I can also learn valuable lessons that will help me later in life. So I want to be around Coach Wooden as much as possible."

Two really good kids, ten- and eleven-year-old brothers John and Joe Caruso, are also having a great time at camp, but too good of a time tonight. They have worked hard in workouts with Coach, in stations, and in their team practices. They also have had a great time playing water polo during afternoon break time. Tonight, though, they have been sneaking in and out of their rooms and into friends' rooms. At eleven thirty the counselors catch them running out of their room again. Wearing only their T-shirts, boxers, and shoes, they are marched out to the front courts to run a few very unpleasant sprints called suicides. It is doubtful that they will cause any trouble the rest of the week.

7

Rainy-Day Adjustments

It is raining this morning! Wednesday is called Hump Day at camp, and appropriately so today, as the rain is a major bump in the camp. It is said that it never rains in Southern California—and definitely not in mid-summer.

Sportsworld camps are highly organized and efficient, but they do not have much experience with rainy days. Campers are certainly not prepared. Cal Lu provides a unique camp experience with three hundred or more campers and only a small indoor gym with two courts side by side, which is why the camp leadership offers so many outdoor activities. But the rain has taken away the outside court options, leaving staff with only the gym to conduct basketball activities.

Lil and Coach Wooden come to the rescue. Lil offers to serve breakfast earlier and lunch later than normal so that the camp has a longer morning in which to stagger stations in the gym, and Coach agrees to give a special talk to campers while others rotate through abbreviated stations. Camp directors Hector and Hal are grateful for the help, and they devise a plan for the day.

Soaking Up More Time with Coach

A smaller than normal number of campers waits at the doors under the overhang outside the cafeteria and eagerly comes in for breakfast as soon as the doors open.

As coach Tom Williams takes his tray to sit with Coach, he notices a nine-year-old who has been affectionately nicknamed "Lunch Bucket." For the past two days, it has looked as if the boy was always about to fall asleep, and his camp T-shirt has had food stains all over the front of it. But this morning Tom notices that the camper is wearing a new, clean camp T-shirt. Hal explains to Tom that Coach Wooden gave the camper a new shirt and asked him to try to keep food off it. Coach will take his dirty shirt home with him and wash it for the youngster. So far so good—this morning all the food is going in the boy's mouth or staying on his tray.

The coaches this morning are discussing the great game Orel Hershiser of the Dodgers pitched the night before. Hershiser is Coach's type of player—humble, with excellent character and determination, and fundamentally strong. After wondering if tonight's Dodgers game will actually be rained out, the coaches turn the breakfast discussion to basketball.

"What do you miss most about coaching?" someone asks Coach.

"I miss teaching," he replies. "I don't miss the games. I don't miss the tournament. I miss the daily practices."

"Coach, so many of the veteran camp coaches remember watching your UCLA teams practice so well," a seasoned camp coach asks. "Can you tell the younger ones about your practices and philosophy?"

"There is no difference between a classroom teacher and a coach, so you must follow the laws of learning. The last of those, repetition, may be the most important. The best teacher of all is the good Lord. My dad was a great teacher. He would say, 'You are as good as anyone, but not better than anyone.' My own coaches were great teachers. My wife was a great teacher.

"The goal of practice is to get the fullest out of every player," Coach continues. "Individual improvement is in direct proportion to what you put into it. Every player and coach must have hard work and enthusiasm. I tell my players that in practice you are mostly a basketball player. When practice is over, you are hardly a basketball player. I would tell the team that once the game starts, I have done most all I can, and now it is up to them. Practice is homework. The game is the test. Practice is where the coach does most of his work. The poet Cervantes said that the journey is better than the end, and I liked that.[1] It is the getting there that is the fun, and when you get there, it can almost be a letdown. At UCLA I liked the practices to be the journey, and the game would be the end result.

"Analyze each day's practice while it is still fresh in your mind before you leave workout that day. I would meet with my assistants for two hours each morning to plan and go over practice. Once you plan it well, don't cut out drills because you spent too much time on a previous drill.

"Stay on schedule," Coach continues, "and if something isn't going well, move on, and come back to it another day. Teach new things early in practice, when players are still fresh mentally and physically. Start and end practice on time.[2] Don't run practices late, because you will go home in a bad mood, and that's not good for a young married man to go home in a bad mood." The younger coaches don't understand his meaning, but the older veterans laugh, probably because they've learned this the hard way with their own wives. "When you get older," Coach adds, "it doesn't make any difference." The older coaches laugh harder, but the younger coaches still do not seem to get it.[3]

"This is something that was a learning process for me," Coach explains. "When I got older and wiser, I learned to end practice on a positive note so you feel good and so do your players. Never be mad, so that you and your players look forward to coming back the next day. It was different every day, such as a spirit drill, shooting contests, team fast break drills, or relay races. It might just be something that is said or a pat on the back, but go home in a good frame of mind, in a good mood. It is especially important for the married coaches."

"Were your practices open or closed?"

"It depended on the facility," Coach answers. "In the men's gym they were not open. In Pauley Pavilion they were usually open to sit in the upper part. The players might work harder if people are watching. There would be no talking with people or looking up in the stands, though—100 percent attention to practice. UCLA practiced best in open practices because of the ego aspect. Players felt the recognition of what they did from those who watched practice."

"How long did you practice?"

"In the preseason we practiced for two hours. Practice was rarely more than one and a half hours in conference play."

"What did you do to condition your teams into the great shape they were always in?" someone asks. "Would you make them run drills like suicides?"

As always, Coach has a ready answer. "Believe you are in better condition. The players had their own responsibility through proper rest, healthy eating, no smoking, alcohol, or drugs. The coach's responsibility is to see that you work hard in practice. The players must work hard and pay attention off the court.

"I didn't believe in doing fundamental drills and then separate conditioning drills. Condition through drills. We would run our three-on-two conditioner fast-break drill for ten minutes every day. Our shooting drills included movement for conditioning. Our three-man-lane fast-break drills were for conditioning as well. Our early season scrimmages were mainly for conditioning. Also, six times per day the players did five fingertip pushups together. I would say 'On your stomachs' any time during practice."

"How would you handle it or respond if your team had a bad practice?"

"If we had a bad practice, it could be the coach's fault, and you must admit it." Coach's answer shows his standard unassuming attitude. "If it's the group as a whole that is having a bad practice, it is probably the coach's fault. If the team or individual is not practicing hard, something is wrong. Be nice about it, and find out why. Now I rarely got angry. Disappointed? Yes, but rarely angry. If there was a poor attitude or effort in practice, I would send them home. I first give the players a chance to rally each other and say, 'No. We want to practice. Let's get going.' Usually they will.[4]

"You have to work hard in practice," Coach urges the coaches. "Good things shouldn't come easy, and usually they don't. The things that come easy get away from you anyway. An ancient Chinese philosopher said that 'happiness comes from the things that cannot be taken away from you,' and that is true. You have to work for them. It is not easy, not at all; but then, life is not easy. If you are looking for the easy way, you're not much good, whether you're a coach or a player or anything else. Did I make that strong enough?" There is complete silence among the coaches as Coach Wooden finishes that point.

Planning for a Rainy Day

Breakfast over, the coaches move out to the gym for the coaches' meeting. Of course, Coach is prepared and has an umbrella. The rest of the coaches duck under covering as much as possible and sprint to the gym.

Before the meeting Coach Scarano raves about Andy Milner, the counselor working with him this week. Andy is a former camper and the son of Marty Milner, one of the stars of the hit television police series *Adam-12*. "I had Andy as a twelve-year-old camper at Point Loma," he says, speaking of the earlier years when the camps were held at various universities. "Even then he had the mindset of a sixteen-year-old. He works really hard and is enthusiastic. He is a huge help to me."

The rain makes things more unusual and exciting. The coaches' meeting focuses on the rainy-day schedule. The coaches will meet again after lunch if the rain does not clear up in case another revised schedule is needed. Coach Wooden reminds the coaches about being patient with the younger and inexperienced campers. In addition, he emphasizes precise fundamental details, such as how to create a lead, make a V-cut, step to the basket to set up the duck move, do correct post pivot footwork, and use the target hand to block and tuck on the catch. The coaches absorb it all with deep appreciation for the brilliant simplicity in all Coach's teaching.

Each morning the counselors meet as well, usually to discuss any problems in the dorm the night before. This week the camp boasts a superstar group of counselors, with so many former head counselors working as regular counselors in case it is Coach's last camp. Still, Jaws and Hawk remind them of counselor standards and expectations: "Be on time to your activities, and be sure to work hard and hustle when you referee. Remind the campers to stay off the grass, not to litter, and to bus their own trays." But this morning they mainly talk about the revised rainy-day schedule.

Drilling Despite Distraction

Today's color instructional film is the 1970s' Pro-Keds classic *Individual Offensive Techniques with Lou Hudson, Ed Macauley, and Pistol Pete Maravich*. Through the years many coaches have learned individual offensive moves and how to teach them from this film, especially from watching the Atlanta Hawks' "Sweet Lou" Hudson demonstrate the skills. In the gym on this rainy hump day, campers, counselors, and coaches have to work extra hard to focus. Coach puts campers through imaginary ball drills and then the good offensive change-of-pace and change-of-direction footwork with defensive zigzag sliding.

The campers are a bit distracted by the rain, and Coach reminds them that a good player has to "earn the right to be successful."[5] He asks a coach to volunteer to demonstrate the correct change of pace and change of direction. Some coaches were really good players in their day and are still in good shape. Gary Grayson is not one of them, but he volunteers, and since he is right in front of Coach, he is selected. Grayson demonstrates but not well. Coach refrains from criticizing Grayson and says, "Okay, next time maybe a little lower, and slow down a little." Grayson walks over to me and says, "The look he gave me says, 'Don't volunteer again. You are not Greg Lee.'" Grayson makes me laugh just as he used to when he was my assistant coach and loosening me up in the midst of tense games.

The drills have evolved to more catch, pass, and cut action. Each camper runs to the coach, catches a pass from him with a jump stop, passes back to the coach, cuts around him, and runs back to line, one after another. As with all the drills, movement is continuous and flowing. Corrections are made while the drills go on, either by Coach Wooden on the microphone or by the coaches and counselors on the floor. Eleven-year-old camper Darren Ranck continues to impress coaches with his focus in these sessions and stations. He is an average athlete but so fundamentally sound and industrious that he has become a very skilled player. He has taken to heart Coach's teaching.

"Hit that coach in the chest. Chest-high pass, chest-high pass, chest-high pass. Really move. Keep that ball in the air." Coach Wooden talks over the campers, carefully observing all the lines.

"Be quick but don't hurry." This is one of Coach's signature maxims and one that is remembered for a lifetime by practically everyone he has ever coached or taught. Coach calls out to Coach Palarz, "Jon, make sure that player is doing it correctly." Jon gives the boy special attention.

Now Coach has the campers execute the overhead pass correctly. "Overhead pass back to the coach. I want you to work on just this one pass. Receive that ball from the coach. Bring it to your chest, raise it immediately about your head, and wrist-and-finger snap it overhead. I do not want you to rock. I don't want the ball behind your head. Now, coaches, in reference to the age of some of you, you do not have to bring it above your head to pass an overhead pass. But, campers, you must make the overhead two-hand pass, wrist-and-finger snap, wrist-and-finger snap. Pass to the chest. Pass to the chest. Receive it at your chest. Go."

The older coaches smile. His joke about their age is taken by them as a sign of Coach enjoying himself, being pleased with the campers' activity and achievement, and as a sign of affection toward the coaches. For coaches this camp is a basketball laboratory for learning to teach the fundamentals through repetition and with attention to detail. But it can also be intimidating, because from up on that stage, Coach sees everyone and everything, including how the coaches are teaching.

"Come and meet the ball, come and meet the ball." Coach talks over the coaches as they drill. "Catch, pass, and move. Come up to meet the ball. Always meet the ball. Don't try to pass too hard. Don't try to pass too easy. I want a crisp pass, crisp and accurate. You never want to sacrifice accuracy. We want it quickly as possible, but it must be accurate." Hector comes up and sits on the stage. The campers know that the session is more than halfway over when they see the camp director on stage. Coach is really verbal on this drill. "Jump-stop. Catch it at the chest and move. Catch it and keep it close to the body, not in the front."

Coach seems pleased with the progress, and within five seconds of finishing the drill moves to the next one. Each player passes to the coach, runs to him, catches the pass, reverse pivots, and passes to the next person in line, who does the same thing. This is a classic UCLA team warm-up drill that incorporates many different fundamentals.

"Meet the ball across the double line, then make a reverse turn," Coach instructs. "Make a complete low turn facing your line, tuck the ball in, and make a good pass to your coach. Reverse turn. I don't want a front turn. Bring your heel back. Don't rise up. Get as low as you can. Good balance."

Coach quickly changes the drill. "First two in each line have a ball now. Hold them up. Pass to the coach; now meet your passer the same way. Head-fake up, drive around the coach and close to the coach, low-bounce dribble hard and fast, and then back to your lines. Two-foot jump-stop, down, good possession, look both ways, and then short pass-off. Quick, move down there. Move. Drive low, low around the coach."[6]

The players are sharp, and the drill goes smoothly with constant moving and squeaking of shoes on the court. The passing and stop-and-go drills have gone well. Coach is in his element.

A Rainy-Day Talk with Coach—Maxims and Creeds

Due to this morning's revised schedule, Coach Wooden meets with some of the campers in a side room off the gym to give them a spontaneously planned talk. He is holding a copy of his autobiography.

Coach begins to talk, turning the pages of his book.

> I thought I would talk a little about what is mentioned at the front of the chapters of my autobiography, *They Call Me Coach*. I have been a collector of little principles, mottos, and maxims, whatever you want to call them. My co-author Jack Tobin put one in front of each chapter. I've been asked to talk about some of these.
>
> Here is the first one: "Who can ask for more of a man than giving all within his span? Giving all, it seems to me, is not so far from victory." In other words, making the most of what you have is what I try to get across in the Pyramid, and you can't do more than that. We try to compare ourselves with others, and in doing so, we get concerned with things over which we have no control, and therefore we lose control over the things we have control over, and we don't do as well as we should. So we should have been trying to do what makes the most of what we

have. And only you will really know that, because you can fool everyone else.

The next one is,

A careful man I want to be;
A little fellow follows me.
I do not dare to go astray
For fear he'll go the self-same way.

In a sense, every single one of you in all probability has someone following you, and it is just asking to be a good example, and that is exactly what parents should be for their youngsters.

Chapter 3 begins with,

Worm or beetle, drought or tempest
on a farmer's land may fall.
Each is loaded full o' ruin,
But a mortgage beats 'em all.

Hard times sometimes come. Farmers in the Midwest and various areas are now having hard times. Their mortgages are being taken over, and they are losing their farms and whatnot. The important thing is that you get stronger through adversity when you have hard times; you don't give up. The road to accomplishing something is hard. You may have to change your methods, and sometimes you have to go around, under, over. But you don't quit. You continue to move forward toward accomplishing your objective.

Let's see. How about this one? "Stubbornness we deprecate, firmness we condone. The former is our neighbor's trait, the latter is our own." Do you feel that way about others? They are stubborn. Others are stubborn, but you're not. You're just firm. But of course we can be stubborn too without realizing it.

"Learn as if you were going to live forever. Live as if you were to die tomorrow." Those are pretty good things to go by. Keep learning. It will always be good for you. Be careful how you live, because you can go tomorrow. There was a fellow who was going into a cemetery one time, and he was looking at the epitaphs you find on tombstones at the cemetery. Most of you are probably too young and haven't done that. Most epitaphs say nice things about you after you are gone, oh, very nice things. The very same people who write these very nice things while you are living may be giving you your due with those nice things. And on this one tombstone this was written: "As you are now, so once was I. As I am now, you are sure to be, and may I say as here I lie, 'Prepare yourself to follow me.'" And someone had scratched under that epitaph, "To follow I'm not content until I find out which way you went."

Coach smiles, and the adults laugh. "That's pretty good," Coach chuckles. He is pleased to be instructed by his own maxims. He moves on to the next one:

"The true athlete should have character, not be a character." Character is what you are; reputation is what others think you are. You should definitely be more concerned with your character, what you think you are, more than what others think you are. Do not let what you can do interfere with what you can't do. That's getting back to that earlier thought: Don't let the things over which you have no control take over, because they will; they will take over things over which you have control and be very hurtful.

I like this one too: "You cannot live a perfect day without doing something for someone who will never be able

> to repay you." I daresay that every one of you, now stop and think, your first thought will not be that. When you stop and think, the very happiest moment that you have is when you do something for somebody else and make them happy. That is better than getting a gift or anything else, because when you do for others, you receive. That is what this is saying. You cannot live a perfect day.
>
> Now if you are doing something for someone else with the thought of what you are going to get from them, it's sort of lost. It's like those who go to church just so people will know they go to church. They go to church just to impress other people. That's not church. It's like the widow with just one mite who gave all she had. The widow gave a lot more than someone else who gave hundreds of dollars because they had a lot.

He flips through the book. "I'm going to pass that one up," he says, wrinkling his forehead at a maxim. "I don't understand it." The campers laugh.

> "Things turn out best for those who make the best of the way things turn out." Some, a lot of us, always complain about that or this or that. It's always something we didn't do that we should have, but we do a lot of complaining. Abraham Lincoln is my favorite American, and he said, "Things turn out best for those who make the best of the way things turn out."
>
> This one says, "The worst thing parents can do for their children"—or anyone can do for those they love—"are the things that they could, and should, do for themselves." That's the worst thing your parents can do for you—the things you could and should do for yourself. You have to learn to have intentness and accept responsibility to do the things that must be done.

I love poetry. My master's thesis was on poetry. I dabble in writing poetry. I'm not very good, but I like to write down verses of different poems that make an impression on me. Here's one:

Remember this your lifetime through—
Tomorrow there will be more to do,
And failure waits for all who stay
With some success made yesterday.
Tomorrow you must try once more
And even harder than before.

"Tomorrow you must try once more and even harder than the day before." That merely says, don't get satisfied; don't get all pleased with yourself so that you don't think you have to work anymore. It always becomes more and more difficult. There's always more and more to do.

Oh, you know there are a lot of these. I don't think I'll go any further. "No one cares how much you know until they know how much you care." That's good too. These are just little things that I picked up. I have a book with maybe a thousand things that I picked up.

Coach continues his talk by sharing some advice that his father gave him when he was a young man:

When I graduated from a small country grade school, and just think how long ago this was, 1924, my father gave me two things. He gave me a two-dollar bill, and he said, "As long as you keep this, you'll never be broke." And there were many, many times in the years since then when that's all I had, but I would never spend that two-dollar bill. It is frayed and worn and not in very good shape now, but I still have the pieces of it anyway. And I've carried that in my pocket since that time.

> I also carry a creed he gave me, seven points he gave me. I want you to just go with me through each point. The first one you'll notice is "Be true to yourself." What do you think that means?

Coach points to a camper, who answers, "Don't lie to yourself?"

"Don't lie to yourself—that's good, you shouldn't. Yes, that's a part of it. It is many things. Somebody else. Yes?"

"Don't be overconfident."

"Don't be overconfident. Yes. Very good, very good." He points to another child. "Yes?"

"Doing the things you should be doing."

Coach goes on to explain the statement:

> There was a great writer, one of the greatest writers of all time. His name was William Shakespeare. A character in one of his books was a man by the name of Polonius. Polonius wasn't the nicest person in the world, but he was partial about his children, and he wanted to advise his children, wanted them to behave properly. And one time his son was leaving home, like maybe we all do in life. His son was going out in the world on his own, and Polonius wanted to give him some good advice, father to son, and he said to his son, "Neither a borrower nor a lender be; for loan oft loses both itself and friend, and borrowing dulls the edge of husbandry. This above all: to thine own self be true, and it must follow, as the night the day, thou canst not then be false to any man."
>
> Where he says "Neither a borrower nor a lender be; for loan oft loses both itself and friend," these words are so true. Be true to yourself, and you're going to be true to everyone else. Sometimes you loan to a friend, he doesn't pay it back, and what do you lose? You lose the friend as well. You don't like him. So it is not good—neither a borrower nor a lender be. But the main point is to be true to yourself.

> The second is "Make each day your masterpiece." That should be very simple. Just do the best you can. Don't worry about how others are doing. Be the best you can be. You have control over that. So just make each day your masterpiece.
>
> The third is "Help others." Just help others. That maybe composes most of the others, like love for your fellow man.
>
> Fourth, "Drink deeply from good books." You should read something every day, and make sure that they are good books. Don't read trash. There is much of that today too. Read about the great people of history. Read biographies. Read great authors. Read great poets. Most of all, read something from the Bible every day. Every day try to read something from it. On every page you'll find something that will be helpful.
>
> The fifth is "Make friendship a fine art." How many youngsters here during this week have made a new friend?

Hands go up. "Oh, good. I like that you all have." Coach bites his index finger and smiles as he looks at the campers. Coach Wooden expects those who come with a friend to reach out and make new friends.

> Now maybe some of you, when you come to a camp, you come with someone else. If that's the only one you want to be with while you are there, then you don't take advantage of the opportunity you have to make new friends. In situations like this, take the opportunity to make new friends. Then follow up when the camp is over. Friendship—you have to work at. If you don't work at it, it doesn't work out. Not one side—both sides have to work at it. So make friendship a fine art. Very, very important.
>
> Next is "Build a shelter against a rainy day." Don't just deal with the present, although you can't do anything

about what's passed. You can help the future by what you do right now. It is making each day your masterpiece, and it is also building a shelter against a rainy day. And that doesn't just mean a material shelter. It means something far more important than just building a material shelter.

And then the last one is "Pray for guidance, and give thanks for your blessings." How many of you pray? How many of you do not? I think you all should. I don't care what religion you have. You should have one, and need to pray. We all need help, and we need to give thanks for the blessings we have, because we all have many blessings, and I think we need to give thanks for the things that we have. Very important.

These are the seven things of the creed. Well, those are just a few little things that I think are important. And you are an exceptional group. You sat there very quietly, and at least some of you, most of you, pretended to listen.

The campers laugh.

Whether you did or not, it is important that you did show a lot of consideration. You were very patient, and I hope somewhere, something I said might be of help to you, some way, and some little way. If we could help one person each day a little bit, we've had a pretty good day. And that's what we should all try to do in our own personal ways.[7]

The campers clap appreciatively and then, as directed by Hal, move on to their next activity.

After Coach Wooden's talk, coach Ken Stanley, the one USC grad among us, brings a young camper up to Coach. "Tell Coach who you wrote your school project about."

"I wrote it about you," the boy tells Coach proudly.

Coach Wooden smiles, thanks the boy, and asks him two questions: "Did you get a good grade? And is your teacher a USC fan?"

"I got an A, and she likes UCLA."

"Oh, good. That would be a terrible thing to have a teacher from USC."

Stanley takes the good-natured ribbing with a smile. "By the way, Ken, I do speak twice a month to a group downtown, and the person who introduces me is from USC, and he does so in a very flowery way."

Ken replies, "You know, most of the coaches here have a relationship with and follow UCLA basketball, and they come to camp because they naturally love all things UCLA related. Now I'm a USC guy, but I still come to camp, which means that I care more about the purpose of the camps than they do."

Coach hands Ken a Pyramid of Success plaque. "Yes, Ken, I know that you and your family understand the values in the Pyramid. But try to pass this along to your people at USC, will you?"

Ken gives Coach a big smile and says thank you. All coaches at some point learn that you cannot beat this great competitor at much, and especially not at out-needling him.

Lunch Clinic with Coach Wooden

On Wednesdays, whenever one of us asks him, Coach puts on a special lunch clinic for the coaches. It is another pinch-me moment for us. The first time we ever asked him, several years earlier, the other coaches volunteered me to approach Coach with the request. Coach enthusiastically agreed to do it, and the Wednesday lunch clinic is now a tradition.

Whenever we hold one, Coach Wooden and the coaches eat a quick lunch and then move to the dorm lobby, where Coach answers basketball questions and draws diagrams on a chalkboard or a dry-erase board. It is another memorable and rich time for the coaches as Coach Wooden generously gives us his time and expertise. Coach enjoys it, and the coaches focus intently on him just as we do in the morning meetings, teaching sessions, and mealtime talks.

Coach pauses with that twinkle in his eye that coaches know means that he is going to say something special.

Because we were distracted by the rain this morning, no one asked Coach early in the day about having a clinic. At the end of breakfast, however, Coach smiled and asked me, "Are we going to have a clinic at lunch today?"

I replied, "Yes, I'll be there!"

"Okay, if it's just you and me, let's eat quickly and get over there." At that the other coaches signaled excited RSVPs that they would be there as well.

Today's clinic focuses primarily on the famous UCLA full-court press. It was a weapon for many of Coach Wooden's title teams and especially the '64 and '65 teams. Coach has set up a mini court complete with a trashcan as the basket. The coaches jockey for a front-row seat and then eagerly listen with admiration as Coach explains the press with the energy and intensity of a twenty-five-year-old. Coach makes clear the roles for each position and then explains the precise footwork, basic defensive fundamentals, orchestrated shifts, fine details, how to read an opponent's eyes and feet to anticipate a steal or a rotation or a movement, and why the back player is the key. He says that Keith Erickson was his best ever back player in the press.

"It is important to stick with the press," he teaches. "Be patient with it, and remember, sometimes you have to go backward to go forward. If a team is shooting well early in the game, most likely they will cool off later. If they are not attacking your press, keep pressing. Stay with the press. It is easier for you to adjust to what their plan is than it is for them to readjust their plan to your adjustments."[8]

Coach then shows the shifts for both the one-two-one-one and two-two-one presses. When he finishes, the coaches are motivated to teach these points to their own teams at home.

As they are about to leave, David Myers has a question for Coach. "I've always wanted to ask you–is there one principle of coaching that is above, more important than anything else?"

Coach pauses with that twinkle in his eye that coaches know means that he is going to say something special. With complete silence in the room, he says, "It is the principle of transferability."

A long silence ensues as Coach playfully looks at the coaches. Myers finally breaks the silence. "What is that?" The other coaches silently thank him for asking.

"A teacher should ask, does what I am teaching on the practice floor transfer to the game? David, tomorrow morning I want you to tell me what you would change in your practices that will transfer to the game." Coach has made a brilliant point that makes each coach think about his own answer. These men marvel once again at the greatness of Coach Wooden and are thankful to be one of his coaches, about whom he cares so deeply.

Dampened Spirits and Clearing Rain

After lunch counselor Howard Fisher returns to the dorms to find that his brand-new and very expensive Nike shoes have been stolen. The camp directors constantly emphasize locking dorm rooms, but thieves still find ways in. It angers Fisher that someone would steal his shoes, but it also angers him that it has happened at Coach Wooden's camp. Coach often quotes his father: "Never lie, never cheat, never steal." You never lie, cheat, or steal and especially not at Coach Wooden's camps.

The camp directors give Fisher a new pair of Betas, the shoe Coach Wooden helped design and sponsor. Fisher continues to work just as hard without complaining, even as he feels the loss and sting of the theft.

Fortunately the rain stops before lunch, and the courts dry with the help of counselors sweeping them free of puddles. The campers meet one more time with Coach Wooden from one to one thirty, and then they are off to their respective courts for a final shooting evaluation session before the official camp games begin.

8

Let the Games Begin!

Finally, to the delight of the campers, it is game time! The first official camp games will be held today in the afternoon and then again after dinner. Campers love competing, so the games are a highlight of camp. Each team will play two games today, two on Thursday, and one on Friday morning in the hopes of winning all five of their games—and the camp championship.

Counselors referee four games per day. Some counselors are eager and diligent, but others are unmotivated, to the chagrin of some coaches, who are not allowed to say anything to them. But the head counselors expect the best effort from the regular counselors and get after the ones who lean against a pole, stand around, or never get past half court. But highly motivated and hardworking counselors like Howard Fisher love to referee and do so with enthusiasm and effort, which gives them the added benefit of seeing the game from a new perspective.

There are great coaches at every Wooden camp—men like Yutaka Shimizu, Nash Rivera, Ed Tellez, Don Showalter, Bill Fleming, Tom Desotell, and Mike Kunstadt, each of whom has had consistent championship success in their careers. They coach four games a day, which can be an up-and-down experience based on how each team plays and how each counselor referees. It feels a lot better to win than to lose, of course. Dinner tastes better after an afternoon win, and sleep is better after an evening win. Most coaches know that their fate is largely determined by the team draw that was held Sunday night. Those who got the best players will usually win the championship and be able to smile as their team receives recognition at the closing ceremony that will be held on Friday. Coaches dread having a poor team assigned to them that might cause them to go winless all week. The good coaches remain positive and encouraging, but losing can still take a toll on their morale.

Games are forty minutes long, consisting of two twenty-minute halves. The clock stops in the last two minutes of the game, and at that point only half-court man-to-man defense with no double teaming is allowed. Each team has to try to run the UCLA high-post offense, at least for a pass or two. Teams might score on the guard cut, the duck move, or a low post play. Veteran coaches learn to put in special plays, cheat on defense (since everyone knows the opponent's plays), and let good athletes roam a bit on defense.

Coach Wooden expects the games to be instructive for campers. He also expects players to exhibit good sportsmanship; for example, those who score should acknowledge the player who passed the ball to them. Coach wants campers to play quality organized team basketball. The coach's handbook is clear: "The purpose of the competition is to allow campers an opportunity to put into practice what they are learning throughout the day and to learn to play together on a team. Winning at the cost of swearing, losing your temper, or otherwise setting a poor example for your players will not be tolerated!"

Counselor Kevin Barbarick found out firsthand when he was a camper that Coach has high expectations for camper play and behavior. Stan Morrison, coach at USC at the time, had sent his son Eric to camp. Coach Wooden wanted this to be a great experience for Eric, so he asked Kevin, who Coach had been impressed with in the several camps he'd been to, to be Eric's roommate and teammate. Coach Larry Lopez encouraged Kevin to be a good friend to Eric during the week. During an afternoon camp game, Kevin made a perfect pass to Eric on a two-on-one fast break, but when Eric missed the layup, Kevin yelled at him. Coach Lopez immediately took Kevin out of the game. Coach Wooden just happened to be courtside. "Goodness gracious, Kevin!" said Coach, stopping just short of adding "sakes alive" and making it a full-on Coach Wooden rebuke. Coach reminded Kevin that he expected him to be a more positive and supportive teammate and to help Eric have a good experience.

A regimented numeric "sub system" was developed at some point to ensure equal playing time for all campers, and it works quite well. Each player is given a number, with a team's two best players given numbers to ensure that one of them is on the floor at all times. Because there is a talent gap, this helps make for better matchups and also helps some players enjoy more the challenge of playing against better players. Coaches learn to strategically number their players to ensure a balanced lineup.

Legend has it that the sub system was developed to counter the coaches' highly competitive spirits. Longtime camp coach Mickey Perry is a bit of a camp historian and recalls, "Jim Harrick and Frank Carbajal were so intent on beating each other one time that they only played their best players the majority of the game. The campers all pay the same money and deserve to play equal time. So the sub system was developed, and it has been successful since."

Coaches take different approaches to the games. Some sit quietly, while others are passionate and spirited. I tend to be enthusiastic and energetic when I coach, which annoys some coaches, amuses others, and encourages still others to follow suit. Some coaches are more reserved and analytical, and coaches like me learn from their approach. Coaches have different approaches to calling timeouts as well. Coach Shimizu, known as Shim to the coaches (although he says, "My players may never call me Shim!"), does not like timeouts. He might bark, "What did you call a timeout for?!" at an opposing coach. Shim is funny, but he is also an intense coach who is well respected as the high-school coach of Sidney Wicks, who later went on to be a great player for UCLA and then in the NBA.

When coach Brad Barbarick was a camper, he played on Shim's team and missed a breakaway layup off the front of the rim. Shim called a rare timeout and told the six-foot-four fifteen-year-old to "either dunk it or use the backboard." Brad has remembered that since, and that timeout was the beginning of a special relationship between the two.

In general the Wooden camp coaches are skilled teachers with highly competitive spirits. During the games one coach keeps score, while the opposing team's coach keeps time. The reason for this is that years earlier, coach Jim Nielsen, a former Bruin, angrily accused Larry Lopez of cheating on the clock late in a tight game. Lopez fired back, "Fine! You keep the time, and I'll keep the score!" The next summer Nielsen became the principal at Frontier High School, and one of his first hires was Larry Lopez.

A few coaches want to win badly for their own reputation. When they win, they act as if they have out-coached their opposing coach. Ken Barone and other veterans jokingly tell the new coaches that camp records will go on their résumés. Most new coaches know to laugh at that, but a few think that the veterans are serious and feel the pressure to do all that they can to win. These coaches might be part of camp coaching stories for years to come.

Overall, however, the coaches enjoy the friendly competition. Mark Coffman, another Texas high coach, told me a story about when he coached his first camp game. "We were playing outside on Madison Square Garden against Steve Hawkins' team. I was so pumped up I was pacing up and down the sidelines. Just as the game started I saw Hawk sitting in a chair with his shirt off. I could tell right then that the games were a little more laid back than I had anticipated." Camaraderie grows, and games make for some enjoyable El Torito, Baskin Robbins, or dorm-lobby post-game talks. Mike Kunstadt and Coach Shim are an example of such camaraderie and friendship when they room together at the Final Four every year.

Those who play on the larger indoor courts can rely more on outside shooting, as they have more open space. Three-point field goals are not allowed, however, even though the three-point shot has recently been approved for high-school competition. Games on the outdoor courts are often the most intense, the courts being small and the rims tight. It is more difficult to make outside shots, and thus scoring tends to come from drives, post-ups, offensive rebounds, and steals. Coaches enjoy the special challenge of adapting to these unique conditions, which include playing slightly uphill for one half on the front courts. There is little if any complaining—not that any would be tolerated. Campers play hard, and tough-nosed players really shine on the outdoor courts, even though the heat and hot asphalt of the afternoon games challenge even the toughest of players.

Some games have exciting finishes. Often the outdoor night-time games might finish just as it gets dark. One of the classic all-time Wooden Camp games occurred at Pepperdine University in 1980. It involved two twelve-year-olds—future UCLA star Don MacLean and future University of Pennsylvania player Jerry Simon. The game came down to the end, and as MacLean drove to the basket, Simon fouled him hard and got a piece of MacLean's head. Simon's team ended up winning the game and the camp championship, but the camp directors later awarded MacLean's team with a co-championship, because they determined it was an unsportsmanlike foul by Simon.

Since Coach missed his morning walk today due to the rain, he walks now and observes the games. The rain this morning was warm, which makes for a hot and humid afternoon. Coach has his shirt off and tucked in the back of his blue Bike coaching shorts as he walks and observes. Coach's strong presence makes everyone aware when he is near and observing.

Today camper Tony Strickland's team loses its first game, but Tony gets over the loss quickly as he races to the Cowboys' practice field. Harvey Martin will have to find someone else to carry his pads and helmet today, though, because Tony is throwing the football around with All-Pro wide receivers Tony Hill and Drew Pearson after their practice. On the way to the cafeteria, Tony asks Too Tall Jones if he can have his wristbands and headband. Jones says yes and tosses the muddy, sweaty items to him. With an exuberant thank-you, Tony hurries to show his friends in the cafeteria.

Coach's Cocktail

Hawk drives Coach home today, and they talk about Nell. When they get to the condo, Coach asks Hawk if he has time to come inside to finish talking. "If they ask why you are late getting back, tell them it is my fault," he assures him.

As they walk inside, Coach asks Hawk if he would like a cocktail, and without waiting for an answer, he walks into the kitchen to fix it. Hawk does not know what to think. He was certain that Coach doesn't drink, but now he is not so sure. Plus he has to drive home soon.

Coach walks back into the den where Hawk is waiting and hands him the drink. "I hope you like it. Nell and I really enjoyed this drink—Welch's grape juice and 7-Up," he says with a smile and a sparkle in his eye. Hawk breathes a sigh of relief and enjoys the drink as he and Coach finish their conversation.

Back at camp he tells Eric Hughes about the cocktail. Eric tells him, "Grape juice and 7-Up. I've had it a few times with Coach. It's really good. First time I had it, Coach gave me a tour of the condo and showed me his bedroom. Nell's side of the bed is the same as when she was alive. He sleeps on his half of the bed and leaves her side untouched except for the love notes he leaves her. It is really touching to see that."

Dinner Break

At dinner Tony Strickland excitedly tells his friends about talking to the players and coaches and throwing the football around with Pearson and Hill. They jump all over him and accuse him of lying. Before he can defend himself, Coach Landry walks by their table, puts his hand on Tony's shoulder, and says, "Hi, Tony. I hope you gave our receivers some tips on catching the ball today." Tony's friends stare at him dumfounded, wide eyed and open mouthed, while an extremely pleased Tony just smiles at them.

Nobody is quite sure why, but two of the Cowboys players are in the campers' line for dinner. The main entrée is Cornish game hen. Laura Erwin, serving dinner, asks one of the Cowboys, "What may I serve you?"

He replies, "I want some of those little chickens."

Of course when she asks the next young camper in line what he would like, he also asks for "one of those little chickens."

Evening Games and Inspiration from the Whitsitts

Good friends Ray Tejada and Ed Tellez face off that evening, their teams playing on the outdoor courts. They enjoy the friendly competition until Tejada's Stanford team scores three perfect backdoor layups using the guard backdoor play, or "the pig," as some call it. Tellez calls a timeout and quickly changes from a relaxed camp coach to an in-season, intense, fiery coach. He grabs his clipboard, vigorously starts drawing, and emphatically confronts his team as Tejada observes with amusement. Tellez's Oregon Ducks team returns to the court and goes on a big spurt, aided by a favorable sub rotation. Tellez's team wins, and Tejada congratulates Tellez afterward with respect and a big grin.

Following the evening games the gym is filled with energy as campers talk about their competitions. It is also a special program night, as Novian and Damon Whitsitt and their dad, Luther, present a skills-training session for the campers. The three started training when Novian was seven and Damon was four. They would get up at six every morning to shoot before school at a nearby park, even on cold mornings. It was not until Novian was in ninth grade that they found an inside court to shoot on.

When they were little, the boys hated getting up so early to shoot and were not too happy with their father for putting them through it. But they later came to value the discipline and hard work that produced success for them in basketball and in education. Their mom is the glue to the family; she has been supportive of her husband and also understanding toward her boys throughout the many years of their workout regimen.

The campers benefit tonight from observing challenging jump roping, foot speed, quickness, agility, strength, and endurance drills. This is followed by intense layup, ball handling, and shooting drills. Novian and Damon are not performing, nor is this a glamorous event for them. Even as they teach the campers, they are working hard at their daily workout under the demanding and relentless coaching of their father.

Their workout demonstrates a skills-development game plan that campers can use to raise their own skill aptitude. It gives them hope that they can improve and make a bigger impact on their own teams at home.

Coaches also benefit from the presentation by learning new drills, such as the two-two-two half-court game. This game is played two on two or three on three, and to win a team has to make two swished shots, two bank shots, and two driving or cutting layups. It provides an engaging, challenging, and highly competitive twist on the normal half-court game.

When the workout presentation ends, the Whitsitts play full court in front of the campers, along with counselors led by Eric Hughes. It is an enjoyable way for the campers to end their night before heading back to the dorms for bed check.

Coach Bill Fleming, the motivating, enthusiastic, and innovative coach from Iowa, returns to his room. As he does so, slippery bars of soap are being dropped on shower floors throughout camp. This morning at his ball-handling station, he told campers to throw a slippery bar of soap up in the shower and try to catch it in order to develop quicker hands. In showers tonight campers are realizing that they need a lot of practice to catch slippery soap.

One fourth-grader in particular needs to use the soap on himself and his clothes. He is affectionately known as Crazy Joe. When the counselors picked him up from the airport on Sunday, he was wearing a white shirt, white shorts, and basketball shoes, and he had no other clothes with him except underwear and socks. Tonight no one can stand the dirt and smell on him any longer. The counselors drag him into the shower, clothes and all, for a thorough cleaning.

But everyone loves him. He is a tireless, hardworking, spirited, determined player, mentally and physically tough. Tuesday night he got slammed into the basket-support pole on a layup on the front courts. It was a scary collision, and coaches and counselors alike ran to him for fear that he had been badly hurt. He jumped up, said some inappropriate words (which were ignored), and said, "I'm okay. Let's go." Most likely he will talk about this mishap fondly for years to come.

It has been a memorable and successful rainy hump day. With lights out at ten, tired campers try to sleep.

Coaches' Companionship

Once the eight-fifteen roll call is over, coaches have free time. Some go out to eat, some to the movies, and others for ice cream. Wayne Carlson meets Laura, the cafeteria worker he "boldly" asked out our first day at camp, at Baskin Robbins, and while there, they see Dallas Cowboys special team star Bill Bates ordering ice cream.

Two French Canadian coaches from Quebec are observing camp this week, and they hear that Cowboys great running back Herschel Walker likes to go to the nearby Carl's Jr. to get a late-night snack. Being big Cowboys fans, the two coaches drive there with the hopes of seeing him. Sure enough, Herschel Walker is in line ordering food. The former Heisman Trophy winner is known for building strength through pushups and sit-ups. As he waits for his food, Walker finds an empty space in the restaurant and does pushups.

Some coaches head out to their regular nighttime destination, El Torito restaurant. Coach Gary Grayson, one of the regulars with this group, is an exceptionally funny guy. "Thousand Oaks is the land of a thousand jokes, and El Torito is the place to tell them," he likes to say. Grayson is single and reminds the married guys to keep their wedding-ring hand on the table at all times.

Quite a few coaches are in Michael Scarano's room talking when Ray Lokar tells them about a comment made by a visiting coach after he observed the morning workout with Coach. Lokar is really fired up about it, and he gets the other coaches riled up as well. "That high-school coach told one of his players that Coach Wooden was great in his day, but now he is old. 'What does he know now?' the guy told his player. 'The game has changed, and what Coach Wooden is telling you doesn't work now.'"

I kept thinking, *Okay, Coach, now give us the good stuff.* My third year I finally realized this *is* the good stuff. Coach's simplicity is part of his genius.

I respond to that. "That coach is so wrong. He's trying to make himself look smart, but his campers know how good Coach is," I defend Coach Wooden. "My first few years at camp, I watched and listened as Coach emphasized the fundamentals, team spirit and play, conditioning, and the ideas in the Pyramid. It was all very good and interesting, but I kept thinking, *Okay, Coach, now give us the good stuff.* My third year I finally realized this *is* the good stuff. He is a great teacher and person, and his simplicity is part of his genius. The campers love working hard for him and show great improvement from what he teaches them."

Coach Bill Fleming tells of his first encounter with Coach Wooden. "I would tell this story to that proud, visiting coach and to anyone else who doubts Coach," he says determinedly. "It was late spring 1964, and I was getting ready to graduate from Iowa State and then get married that June. I knew absolutely everything that anyone could ever possibly want to know about coaching basketball, but I had seen an article in the Des Moines Register advertising a coaching clinic, and I decided to sign up and attend. A middle-aged coach walked quickly to the front and began speaking. As usual, I was slouched down in my chair, arms crossed, notebook on the floor, daring to be taught anything that I didn't already know. But after listening thirty seconds to John Wooden, I knew that I was in the presence of the greatest, smartest, most genuine human being I had ever come across in my life. Suddenly I was sitting straight upright at attention, writing furiously, tears streaming down my face, and discovering in that instant that I knew nothing at all about basketball. Ever since, I have seldom missed an opportunity to go anywhere to see, listen, or talk to Coach Wooden."

"Okay, he is a great coach, but he also had great players," says one of the newer coaches who is too young to have remembered much about Coach when he coached at UCLA.

Michael Scarano jumps into the discussion. "He did, but not always. Coach agrees that he had some great talent on his teams, but he says that while no coach can win without talent, some coaches don't win *with* talent. UCLA was terrible when Coach first took over, and they played in the small, hot, dusty "BO gym," as they called it. And yet they still won the conference championship that first year. Coach won his first two NCAA titles playing off campus before Pauley Pavilion was built. Plus he kept winning NCAA titles even after his superstars graduated and with different talent and styles."

David Myers adds to this. "Every summer Coach would focus on one area of improvement, and he would study about it and try to learn from other successful coaches. He was always learning, always improving. How many times have we heard him say, 'It is what you learn after you know it all that counts,' and, 'Be most interested in finding the best way, not in having your own way'?"[1]

Lokar adds, "Coach was amazing. Everyone knows he won eighty-eight in a row, and NCAA tournament games were included in that streak. But he also won forty-seven in a row another time, and forty-one in a row another time. That's 176 wins in 178 games!" Guys laugh at his reasoning, but it also makes the point.

Mike Kunstadt knows Coach very well and adds, "Coach wouldn't say that he won any games. He would say that his players did. He never talked about winning—just his players playing their best. He doesn't even talk about all the games and titles he won, all this time after he has retired."

"Unless we ask him about it, since he won't bring it up himself or flash his awards," says Scarano. "This might be more impressive: he won thirty-eight NCAA tournament games in a row. That's unbelievable. UCLA actually won forty-three out of forty-four NCAA tournament games in one stretch."

"It just seems that he had it really good." The newer coach is about to get playfully jumped on as he says this. The normally easygoing Tom Desotell has been quietly listening to the entire conversation, but this last comment brings an intense and direct response from him. "That is just not true. I understand the perception, but it is so wrong. It is disappointing to hear people fail to give Coach the credit that he deserves and then to judge and criticize him. Some folks are just plain jealous and envious of him."

"But he coached Walton and Abdul-Jabbar," says the newer coach, echoing what he has read somewhere.

"Sure, but with that came so much pressure. He won so much that UCLA fans got upset if he didn't win by enough points. The college boosters told him that he had let them down when they lost to North Carolina State in the 1974 semifinals in double overtime—after he had won seven straight titles! He once told me, 'For my best friend I wish one NCAA title. For my worst enemy I wish two NCAA titles.' His success created unreal expectations."

"I wouldn't mind that kind of pressure," responds the new coach.

"Yes, you would. His focus was on doing his best, but fans focused on winning, and it got to the point where they felt entitled," answers Desotell.

"The fans loved him, though," I chime in from my perspective as a former trumpet player in the UCLA Band. "Our UCLA Band would play the *Tonight Show* theme song, 'Here's Johnny' when Coach walked onto the court before games, and the crowd would give him a standing ovation every time."

"There's no way they'd win that many in a row now with so many more teams in the NCAA," responds the new coach.

Lokar looks at him and answers patiently, "Back then you only got in the NCAA tournaments if you won your conference title. You had to be good for months to win the title back then. Now you can play poorly and struggle but get hot for a few weeks and win the title. It was much harder back then to win a title. Do you know that Coach's ten NCAA title teams lost a total of ten games? And back then everyone was focused on beating UCLA, yet they still couldn't."

The new coach was starting to get it. "Good point. It was an incredible accomplishment. But do you really think that Coach Wooden could have been as successful today?"

Ken Morgan answers that. "Coach would have been great in any era, and that includes today and also however the game will change in the future. Coach Wooden is the only person who has been inducted into the Basketball Hall of Fame as both a player and a coach. He won as a player and a coach on the high-school and college levels, and he was also a great pro player. He once made 138 free throws in a row. He would have been a good player today too because he was so tenacious, smart, in incredible condition, and a tremendous competitor. Great competitors adapt to whatever the competition is, and Coach would have been like John Stockton is today."

Lokar agrees. "That's so true. Maybe that is why Stockton is one of the few pros whom Coach really enjoys watching play."

Desotell nods. "Coach always adapted, and his principles are timeless," he adds, "so he would have been very successful as a coach today. Coach wondered a few years ago if he should stop having his camps because fewer and fewer people know who he is. We told him that there was still no one better than he was at teaching these young players the fundamentals and the principles of true success. The proof is in how well these kids respond to Coach, how much they improve and thrive under his coaching, and how much spirit they show at the opportunity to learn from him."

David Myers passionately makes the case about how great Coach Wooden still is. "He can still coach! He is a great teacher and tactician; he is the best at adapting to his personnel. He could still win NCAA titles today!"

A new coach, Chad Phillips, wants to know more. "Speaking of today, how much money would Coach have made today? Probably well over a million?"

"Only if he got an agent," says Kunstadt. "He could have made more back in the day, but he wouldn't demand it. He was vastly underpaid, and for the longest time UCLA didn't have good facilities either. Coach was paid $6,500 his first season at UCLA, and in his last season, twenty-seven years later, he was only paid $32,500. Today some coaches make that in one game."

"Okay. You guys make a great case for Coach," says Phillips. "That high-school coach today was definitely out of line."

"Coach is used to it," Kunstadt replies. "He was criticized a lot through the years."

"Seriously? By whom and for what?" asks Phillips.

Kunstadt explains. "Let's see. Some mocked his faith by calling him Saint John and judged him for not living up to their idea of what a Christian coach should be. He was criticized when he first got to UCLA because of his fast-break style—people said he couldn't win playing that way. I guess he proved them wrong. UCLA was picked to finish last in conference that first year, but they won the title. Then people said that Coach couldn't win the big one because he hadn't won an NCAA title his first sixteen years at UCLA. And his teams struggled for a few years before they went to the Final Four in 1962. They nearly won that year and almost won it in 1974 too. He might have won even more if he hadn't retired at age sixty-four because of mandatory retirement laws in the UC system. He had great players coming back and was still recruiting really well when he retired."

Phillips inquires, "Any other criticisms?"

Kunstadt goes on. "Coach told me he was criticized for putting his family first. People said that he didn't recruit well enough because he didn't want to leave his family to be on the road. Whenever UCLA lost, they said he hadn't scouted enough because he wouldn't leave his family at night to do so."

"But wasn't that true?" wonders Phillips.

Kunstadt continues to make the case. "Well, no one really knows, but putting his family first sure seemed to work out pretty well for UCLA. Coach said that his best recruiting tips and evaluations came from coaches who had played against an athlete he was looking at. He didn't scout as much as others because he believed in focusing on his team and what they needed to do to prepare. Teams knew what UCLA was going to do, but UCLA executed so well that teams weren't successful against them. He rarely even mentioned the other team in practice."

Desotell adds, "He also got criticized because his players prayed in the locker room before and after games. The UCLA administration made him stop doing that. So instead they had a moment of silence before they went out to play. He was criticized a lot when the title streak ended in a close game in 1974 when they lost to a great NC State team in double overtime. The eighty-eight-game winning streak had also ended earlier that year at Notre Dame.

All of a sudden, people said that the game had passed him by—he was too old, too old fashioned, his offense was outdated, and everyone had caught up to UCLA. And then UCLA won it again the next year as a total underdog, and Coach went out in 1975 on top."

"Coach Wooden—the great competitor getting the last word in," says Lokar.

Desotell continues. "And he did it through his actions, which is how he always answered his critics. His players could be critical of him too. Some made fun of the Pyramid and then admitted later in life how much it made sense and made a difference in their lives. He had some really tough guys to coach. One guy ripped him at the team banquet, and then Coach helped him get a coaching job in Europe right after that."

Scarano states, "That's Coach showing love and consideration in the face of adversity."

Desotell agrees and adds more. "Coach didn't play more than seven or eight guys, so you had some very good but unhappy players on the bench. He won a lot of the titles in the antiestablishment sixties, but he was so good, caring, and disciplined that his players were a disciplined and motivated team. They thank him for that now. Some of his most rebellious and stubborn players are the ones who now love him the most and are the most devoted to him."

I have one more thing to add. "That 1974 team was really tough to coach. Even USC coach Bob Boyd said he felt sorry for Coach that year. Boyd was a great coach who was never fully appreciated because he was in Coach's shadow. He had a great team with Paul Westphal, went 24–2, and didn't get in the NCAA tournament. And yet he felt sorry for Coach that year."

Feeling the camaraderie and nostalgia of this special week of camp, Lokar changes the subject. "How tough was it on Coach when his wife was sick and then after she died?" he asks.

"Coach absolutely loved her and still does," answers Kunstadt. "There is no way to ever begin to describe how hard that was on him. The family was really worried about him and maybe even wondered if he would survive long without her. A movie producer so admired Coach and Nell's relationship, their love for each other, that he wanted to make a movie about them. But Coach said no. He's too private for that."

I ask, "Didn't his sister die when she was young?"

"Both his sisters died within four months of each other when they were little, which was devastating to Coach's mom," replies Desotell. "Coach grew up on a farm during the Depression, and his family was not well off. But his dad was a rock for him. Right before Coach and Nell got married, there was a run on the bank, and Coach lost all the savings he had built up for their new life together. So Coach and Nell started out with nothing. A few years later Coach left his young family to serve in World War II. So yes, he knows the challenges, adversity, and pains of life. That is why he is so remarkable. He's the real deal—he lives what he talks about. His character has been tested by fire, and he learns from struggles and challenges and constantly grows. He is such a humble man of honor, grace, faith, and dignity."

There is not much that anyone can add to what Desotell has so passionately articulated. Michael Scarano simply says, "I love the guy," and in doing so speaks for all in the room. Lokar, who started the conversation, ends it. "Great talking, guys. See you in the morning. I'm going to go see if Wayne is back from his date yet."

All seems to be going well in the dorms until counselor Eric Hughes informs Hector and Hal that a toilet seems to have "exploded." Apparently a camper stuffed soda cans in it and kept flushing until something gave, and the bathroom flooded. Hector and Hal, as calm as ever, take a look at it, and tell the counselors to clean it up. They've seen just about everything in their many years at camp.

The last coach to go to sleep is David Myers. He is studying Coach's excellent book *Practical Modern Basketball*, looking for shooting drills that will transfer good practice shooting to games. By midnight he has found his answer and looks forward to telling Coach his plan in the morning.

9

Starting Our Last Full Day with Coach

As always, Hawk is honored to be the one who picks Coach up this Thursday morning. Coach Grayson is sitting in the backseat. Coach usually wants to know about injured campers, and today he asks how Kevin Tamura is doing. It is a rare light-traffic morning, and without realizing it Hawk finds that he is driving ten miles per hour over the speed limit. Coach notices and politely says, "You know, Steve, most people want to maximize their time with me. Is there a reason you are trying to get me to the gym in a hurry?" Coach Grayson suppresses a laugh, and Hawk smiles as he slows down.

Back at camp, counselors bang on doors to wake campers up. Fifteen dedicated campers rush to the gym to meet Coach Showalter for an optional morning rebounding clinic in the gym. Showalter is friendly, humble, and genuine and has a warm smile for the campers. He is an outstanding coach with a great passion and love for basketball, for teaching it, and for his players, so these dedicated campers will learn a lot.

The line at six forty-five is very short as campers are still dragging themselves to breakfast. One eleven-year-old camper, Dave White, is a camp veteran and has trouble sleeping in the dorms.

He has learned to get up early and read before breakfast while it is still dark outside. This week he is reading *Alive*, an inspirational story about survivors of a plane crash in the Andes, including the Uruguayan rugby team.

Coach Wooden greets Dave as he walks into the cafeteria and asks him how camp is going. Dave tells Coach about catching the soap bar in the shower last night. Coach tells his own story. "Sometimes when I took a shower, I would flip the soap from behind my back over my shoulder and try to catch it in front of my body." Dave asks Coach what else he can do to be a better ball handler. Coach says, "Sleep with your basketball. Make it your friend. Then it will become natural in your hand." With a big smile Dave enthusiastically answers, "Thank you. I'm going to try that."

Dave grabs a tray and a bowl of Fruit Loops. Coach has taught him this week to show initiative, so he walks over to Cowboys quarterback Danny White, who is sitting alone. "Excuse me. I'm a fan of yours. Would you mind if I ate with you?" The Dallas star kindly says, "No, I don't mind. Have a seat, little guy." Dave has a great breakfast and realizes after being around the ever-gracious Coach Wooden with all his accolades that he can hang out with anyone.

Making the Most of Meals with Coach

At the coaches' table Coach hands several articles to me this morning. At yesterday's coaching meeting, Coach Wooden told me about some past articles that he had written for *Medalist Sports News* and promised to bring a few of them. I have read much about Coach Wooden, but I have never seen these articles, and I treasure them.

Over breakfast Coach and Larry Lopez are discussing who the best baseball player ever is. Coach calmly says, "The best baseball player ever is Joe DiMaggio." Coach Lopez argues passionately that it is Willie Mays. Coach wins the argument in the eyes of the other coaches, who then ask about past UCLA basketball players and teams.

"Who is the best player you have ever coached?" one asks.

"Kareem Abdul-Jabbar is the most valuable player I have coached," replies Coach. "It doesn't necessarily mean the best player. I think perhaps Walton could do more things than Kareem, but Kareem is the most valuable player I've ever coached, and the most valuable player I've ever seen. If I was picking an All-Star team, I would start with Kareem Abdul-Jabbar."

"Who is the best guard you've ever seen?"

"The best all-around guard I've ever seen is Oscar Robertson," Coach says. Oscar Robertson played for the Cincinnati Royals and the Milwaukee Bucks. "He is the best basketball player I have ever seen. Not the most valuable player. Bigger players, centers, are more valuable. But Oscar could do more things well than any player I've ever seen. Jerry West would be my other guard," says Coach, referring to the Lakers player nicknamed "Mr. Clutch" for his many game-winning plays during his NBA career.

"Who was the smartest guard you ever coached?"

"I never had a smarter guard than Mike Warren. He was a five-foot-ten guard. He just didn't make mistakes out there. When a man got open, he hit the man, and he always had a high shooting percentage, because he never took a bad shot. He knew his limitations. Notice I didn't say he was the smartest player I coached; I just never had a smarter guard. Don Bragg—you wouldn't know him; he is the president of one of the biggest banks in America. He is very intelligent and played for me earlier at UCLA."

"What have some of your players gone on to do besides playing in the NBA?"

"Over thirty of my former players are practicing law in Southern California, eleven dentists, three doctors, I think. Most are in business of some sort or another. I'm proud of the Bob Archers—guys who graduate and do well after school."

"Do you think Dr. J is better than Larry Bird?"

"Pick Dr. J over Larry Bird today? Oh, no. Nobody can do that. Now I might consider taking Elgin Baylor over him. Now there's a great one."[1]

"Which is your favorite national championship team?"

"Oh, I can't give you an answer to that. Coach Showalter, how many children do you have?"

"Two, Coach."

"Which one is your favorite?" His answer brings a laugh from the coaches but also some insight.[2]

"Of my championship teams, three gave me the most enjoyment," Coach continues. "One would be the very first, because it is like your first child. We were undefeated, and it was the shortest team to ever win a title. We weren't picked by many to be in the top forty or fifty teams before the season started, and then we had an exciting pressing defense, and players played together about as well as is possible. So obviously that one gave me great satisfaction.

"And the last one. I had announced my retirement two days before, and you kind of want to go out a winner. There again we weren't expected to win a championship, because from the preceding year we had lost to graduation two superstars, Bill Walton and Keith Wilkes, and I'd also lost my two starting guards, Greg Lee and Tommy Curtis, and so we were starting with only one returning starter. We came back and won the championship. That gave me pleasure.

"And then I had another team that I called 'the team without,' and that was the team without Alcindor [Abdul-Jabbar]. He had just graduated, and a lot of coaches and some of the media had said, 'Wait until the big guy is gone. They're going to get their comeuppance.' And we did, because the next four years we won the national championship." The coaches laugh and clap.

"It is perhaps more gratifying to do the unexpected than to do the expected, and yet I had teams that didn't win national championships that I felt, in my mind, were just as successful as some that went undefeated. Now the alumni wouldn't agree with me on that, but it is what I feel that is more important."[3]

"Would you rather be the underdog?" someone asks.

"Oh, no. I'd rather be the favorite," Coach states emphatically. "If somebody knocks me down or I knock somebody down, which would I rather go up against? The one I knocked out. I'd rather be the favorite at all times." Coach is such fun to listen to with his great sense of humor, but there is also richness in everything he says.[4]

Hal walks by. "One more question, and then let's head to the gym."

"When I read old articles," a coach asks, getting in the final question, "people sometime refer to you as Johnny. Were you known more by that name then?"

This brings Coach's wonderful smile. "Yes, many people called me that. But did you also know that I was called 'John Bob' for the longest time? My Nell called me by that name a lot."[5]

It is a great way to end another special meal. We know not to take these times with Coach for granted.

Thursday Coaches' Meeting

No matter how much they try, Larry Lopez, Ed Tellez, Ray Tejada, and Bob Alaniz—the self-named "four Mexicans"—always seem to be a minute late to the morning coaches' meeting, even though they know how important it is to Coach that they are on time. Coach Mitrovich playfully looks at his Timex watch as the four arrive. Tejada quips, "Time Mex!" which brings a laugh from the coaches and big smiles from Hal and Coach Wooden.

Coach asks David Myers if he has come up with an answer to the challenge that Coach gave him at the lunch clinic yesterday: "Have you come up with an idea to increase transferability?"

"Yes, Coach," Dave says enthusiastically. "I'm adding shooting drills that come straight out of parts of our offense." Coach's warm smile affirms Myers.

At the meeting Coach stands with the other coaches as the camp directors go over the schedule. Hector and Hal encourage us to make it a good day, reminding us that it is the last full day of camp and the last day of stations.

Coach Wooden always seems to have a sense of which coaches were out late the night before by looking at their body language. A few from the El Torito crowd get a playful and good-natured needling by Coach. But he also has an important reminder for all of us: "Most of the youngsters here will not go on to play much beyond high school, if at all, but you can help them all become a little better today. Each one is important, so do the best you can with them, and help them get a little better."

After the meeting, as they walk into the gym to meet with the campers, Coach asks Ray Tejada about his talented player with the tough attitude. "He has been a little better each day, Coach," Ray responds. "Thanks for the encouragement the other day to just do my best with him."

"You're welcome, Ray. Keep working with him," Coach replies with a warm smile and a pat on the back.

Motivated by Coach

This morning's film is *Basketball Conditioning Drills*, an instructional fundamentals film sponsored by Coca Cola featuring Coach Wooden, his former assistants Denny Crum and Gary Cunningham, and the 1968 Lew Alcindor-led UCLA Bruins. The campers learn much from the video to reinforce and further explain what they are learning from Coach in the morning sessions. As he watches the film, Coach takes a long, refreshing drink from a Coca Cola bottle, which the campers, counselors, and coaches all find amusing.

While my group watches the film, I sit on the floor in the back and read the first of the special articles that Coach Wooden gave me at breakfast. It is titled "On Motivation":

In my opinion there is but little difference in the technical knowledge about the game of basketball among most experienced coaches, but there may be a vast difference in their ability to teach and to motivate, and knowledge alone is not enough to get desirable results.

Since young people of today are far more aware, inclined to be more openly critical, and more genuinely inquisitive than they used to be, leaders must work with them somewhat differently.

There was a time when the vast majority would follow blindly, even "into the shadow of death," but such is not the case now. Therefore we must always be on the alert for better ways to get ideas across and motivate.

Every individual under our supervision is a distinct and separate person from any other as no two people are exactly alike, although they may be very similar in some or many respects. Therefore, we should realize that we cannot expect maximum results from each individual if we treat them all alike. Each one must be given the treatment that he earns and deserves.

Some players need and respond only to the "pat on the back" and public criticism will harm rather than help them. Some need to be urged in a more stern or demanding way, while others need a concrete challenge in a competitive situation.

An important thing to remember is that criticism is not to punish, but to correct something that is preventing better results. Furthermore, test after test has proved rather conclusively that the "pat on the back" method is far more productive as a general rule than the "kick in the pants" or any method that causes loss of face before your peers.

There was a time when I gave all my players a rather extensive notebook. Later I decided too many of them really did not study it, so I decided to pass out a little information at a time. I found the latter method to be more productive, but, of course, it was necessary to use good judgment, not only in the material presented, but also in the timing as to when it was given to them.

Handouts pertaining to the following topics were passed out at what I considered to be appropriate times: goals, new rules, training suggestions, practice responsibilities, player essentials, attitude and conduct, normal expectations, academic responsibilities, criticism, game competition, individual offensive moves, fundamental hints (shooting, passing, receiving, rebounding, dribbling, stops and turns, pivoting, individual, team defense, team offense, when you do not have the ball, etc.).

Since I have been a collector of maxims, precepts, mottos, principles, and the like, I made it a practice to keep some posted on our player bulletin board at all times. I normally would not keep any one up too long and would try to find several that would be suitable for given situations such as the following:

For teamwork:

1. Happiness begins where selfishness ends.
2. Politeness is a small price to pay for the good will and affection of others.
3. The best way to improve the team is to improve ourselves.
4. It is amazing how much can be accomplished when no one cares who gets the credit.
5. Forget favors given, remember those received.
6. The main ingredient of stardom is the rest of the team.
7. True happiness, freedom, and peace cannot be attained without giving them to someone else.

For individual improvement:

1. When you are through learning, you're through.
2. I will get ready, and then perhaps my chance will come.
3. Ability may get you to the top, but it takes character to keep you there.
4. Discipline yourself, and others won't have to.
5. Do not mistake activity for achievement.
6. If you do not have time to do it right, when will you have time to do it over?
7. You may make mistakes, but you are not a failure until you start blaming someone else.
8. If you are afraid of criticism, you will die doing nothing.
9. The smallest good deed is better than the greatest intention.
10. The man who is not afraid of failure seldom has to face it.
11. Don't let yesterday take up too much of today.
12. Time spent getting even would be better spent getting ahead.

General:

1. There is nothing stronger in this world than gentleness.
2. You can do more good by being good than in any other way.
3. When success turns your head, you face failure.
4. Love is the medicine that can cure all the ills of the world.
5. There is no pillow as soft as a clear conscience.
6. Revenge is the weak pleasure of a little and narrow mind.

7. A good memory is one that can remember the day's blessings and forget the day's troubles.
8. The true athlete should have character, not be a character.
9. Your reputation is what others think you are; your character is what you really are.
10. The future may be when you wish you had done what you are not doing now.
11. Failure to prepare is preparing to fail.
12. Remember this your lifetime through—
    Tomorrow there'll be more to do,
    And failure waits with all who stay
    With some success made yesterday.
    Tomorrow you must try once more,
    And even harder than before.
13. The greatest conquest of man is conquering himself.
14. Talent is God given—be humble;
    Fame is man-given—be thankful;
    Conceit is self-given—be careful.
15. More often than we ever suspect, the lives of others we affect.

Once again I want to reiterate that, since no two players are exactly alike, some may not be motivated at all in this manner and very few to the same degree. However, it may help some and certainly should not hurt any. It might be compared to going to a coaching clinic or even going to church. You may not be able to put your finger exactly on where you were helped, but I am confident you would never be hurt by attending and always will be helped to some degree.[6]

I lean back against the wall in deep reflection, understanding that it will take a lifetime to understand the depth of these words and to try to live them out.

Intense Drills with Coach

As Coach begins the morning drills, a few coaches are dragging a bit after a late Wednesday night and perhaps one beer too many at El Torito. They are reminded that Coach does not miss anything when he asks Tom Gregory to demonstrate the dribble-out, jump-stop, reverse-pivot, pass-and-go drill. Gregory's head clears a little, and Coach enjoys his little tease. Some coaches in the past, unfortunately, have overdone their nighttime activities and have not been invited back to coach again.

Twenty minutes into the drill session, Coach directs the coaches to get two basketballs each. The next drill is dribbling forward on the move. One player starts dribbling and goes around his coach, who is quite a distance from the front of the line, and then dribbles back to the line. Soon after one begins, another camper starts dribbling toward his coach. Each camper needs to have his head up so that he does not run into the other player on the way back to line.

"Alright," Coach calls, "now the best offense is that change of pace, that stop and go. But you must use a low-bounce dribble. You're stopping and going because the defensive person is near you, or you wouldn't stop, you would keep going. Therefore you must keep the ball low. Do not let that ball in that particular situation come up higher than the knees. And then as you straighten up, the dribble comes higher, but when you go again, it is low. Go. Stop and go, stop and go, stop and go. Don't stop to make the bounce pass. Pass on the move. On the move."

Coach continues, "Straight lines, right hand, right side." After a while the players work on their left hand the same way. "Now with the left hand, with the left hand. Go to the left. Work together. Teamwork. Use the change of pace. Don't be careless. Jump-stop at the end."

After constant dribbling and movement, Coach stops the campers. It is rare that he will stop a drill to explain further, since normally he does so while the drill goes on. Today he is not pleased that they are passing sloppily, and he cares enough to want the drill done better. Coaches know that the goal is for campers to do these simple fundamentals over and over again, so ingraining them in players that the players can execute them quickly and without thinking about them. Much progress has been made toward that this week.

Coach knows that the campers can do better and corrects them with explanation, demonstration, and subtle scolding.

"Now it shouldn't be necessary to mention this again," reproves Coach, "but the most important part of the offense is the exchange of the ball from one to another. Never forget that offense is predicated on the exchange of the ball from one player to another, the exchange between teammates. Some of you are getting awfully careless. The jump stop and pass-off are equally important. Some of you make a good jump stop and then don't make a good pass."

The jump stops and passes get better.

Now Coach focuses on the ball handler protecting the ball with his non-dribbling hand. These are simple drills, but they focus on detail. "As you drive around the coach, put the off-arm back of the hand to the coach. Protect it, dribbling low and protecting it with the other hand. You must keep good balance."

Coach is silent for a while as he observes. Then he is back verbally cueing based on what he observes. "Go. Go. Stay low. Low bounce. Don't dribble so high. Keep working. Your head is up all the time. We want no collisions."

Utilizing the same drill, Coach now combines different dribbling moves.

"Alright now, around both coaches the same way, but now you are combining the crossover, change of direction, change of pace along with the stop and go. Now whenever mixing up the stop-and-go and the crossover, use the change of pace, change of direction. Always on the change of pace, make it with changing direction because of the defense. Otherwise you wouldn't have to really protect it with a low-bounce dribble when you make a change.

"Be quite clever, never fancy. Don't be a hot dog. Be clever—not a hot dog," Coach firmly instructs. "Be quick. As you come around the coach, make a good long bounce pass to the first one in line. The second one with the ball, be sure you are out of his way.

"Now I want the hard dribble straight toward the coach, the one-pump fake, and then take the imaginary shot, come around the coach, and get a good offensive tip, tipping that ball back into the basket at the line in front of you. You can't do it if you are tipping it sideways. It's forward. Go.

"Good balance—you can't jump if you're not on balance. Get those feet spread. All the way up to the line. Use your imagination. Let's get up there. Get to that line quickly."

Coach knows that the campers can do better and corrects them with explanation, demonstration, and subtle scolding. "Some of you are lazy after your shot. You're not getting to the line quickly and under control. Get to the line quickly and under control, and then jump up and get your tip. Get around that coach quickly. Eyes on the target. Keep your elbow straight."

The players aren't going far enough on their tip, so he stops to explain what he wants. Coaches at this point wonder if they should be doing a better job directing their own campers.

"Alright, I want everyone over here to point to this line here," Coach commands. "That's the line you come to before you make your setup. That's the offense tip. This line is right here, it's not back there. It's right here. Get all the way there quickly. After you take your shot, get to that line under control, then get a good tip there. Alright, go."[7]

Coach often smiles when he is this direct in his corrections. He is not mad but emphatic in his teaching points. His smile lets the players know that he cares about them, and they respond well. They run the drill correctly and enjoy the different aspects in the drill, including the imaginary tip-in.

Coach is working hard, and the campers are too. There is a wonderful chemistry between him and his campers, as they know that he cares about them. One older camper, a big and intimidating kid even to the counselors, knows that more than anyone. The first day of camp, he was out of control with his stubborn, defiant, lazy attitude. No one knew what to do with him. Coach called him into a side room in the gym Tuesday morning. No one knows what Coach said to him, but after five minutes the camper came out of that room a completely different person and has been an angel ever since. He has had another great workout today. All in a day's work for Coach Wooden.

The Final Stations

During his daily walks while stations are going on, Coach picks up pennies that he finds on the ground, and this morning he picks one up by the front courts. He explains to a few nearby campers that he started doing that during his Purdue playing days, during the Great Depression. "I can give it away or I can save it, but I can't spend it."

As he continues his walk with Hawk at his side, he observes how Coach Smelser has his sleeves rolled up, his shorts hiked way up his waist, and his hat on backward. Smelser and his players are having a good time as they practice. Coach turns to Jeff Dunlap, who is manning a station on the court next to Smelser, and says just loud enough for Coach Smelser to hear, "Jeff, do you know who my favorite American is?"

"Yes, Coach, it's Abraham Lincoln."

"Mr. Lincoln once said that you can learn something from every person you meet. Most of the time it is what not to do." It is hard to tell who smiles more—Coach Smelser or Coach Wooden.

Coaches quietly or verbally celebrate, or at least breathe a sigh of relief, at the conclusion of Thursday's stations. "Camp is over" is a frequent saying when stations end on Thursdays, but all that means is that the hardest work is done. There will still be one more speaker this afternoon after lunch, one more workout session with Coach tomorrow morning, and the filling out of player evaluations. But the rest of the time before going home will consist of games.

After working hard in the stations all week, coaches finish with a sense of peace and of accomplishment. We know that we have become better coaches during the week, having gained new teaching and communication insights and methods, new and better ways to connect and engage with campers, and improved ways of reaching individual athletes who might be struggling. Stations and games outside are a true labor of love on the part of the coaches and other staff, and the best reward is seeing the improvement made by so many campers. It is blacktop basketball in the summer sun, hard and invigorating work in sweaty camp clothes. Coaches are not allowed to take shirts off, but bad tan lines and all, it is a great feeling to walk off the station courts to go to lunch. Best of all, coaches know the satisfaction of hard work done out of a sincere desire to help campers improve and to honor Coach Wooden.

After stations Coach Grayson talks with Coach Wooden on the front courts. At one point it appears that Coach Wooden is upset with Grayson. When Coach Wooden leaves the area, the nearby coaches ask what Grayson has done to get Coach so uncharacteristically riled up.

"He's not mad at me," Grayson answers. "I asked him about the offensive hooking foul called on Keith Wilkes late in the game at Notre Dame that ended UCLA's eighty-eight-game winning streak in 1974. Coach said, 'Oh, that was a terrible call, especially since [Notre Dame player] John Shumate was going over our backs all game long, and then the ref calls that on Wilkes late in the game.'" We give Grayson credit for asking a bold question and appreciate Coach's honest response and competitive spirit.

Coach Wooden at Lunch—with Kids and Coaches

Coach is not at his usual seat at the beginning of lunch. Instead he is seated with the Showalter, Myers, and Kunstadt children, who are all very close in age. Melissa Showalter is the oldest, followed by Karin Kunstadt, Kelly Myers, Kerri Kunstadt, and Brent Showalter, who is the youngest. Coach makes time for them as if they were his own grandkids, and they love him with a pure love, since they have little understanding of what a famous coach he is. For Karin and Kerri Kunstadt, Coach is like the grandfather they never had, since both their grandfathers passed away long ago. During the week, he goes on walks with them, watches them swim at the pool, and might even invite them to his condo for dinner. Occasionally Lil Lopez's granddaughter joins this group. The children also take a picture with Coach every year, by which they can see their yearly growth the way other kids do by their school pictures.

Lil brings over a batch of freshly baked oatmeal chocolate-chip cookies for Coach and the children. Coach Don Showalter's wife, Vicky, thanks her. "Lil, you are so sweet to our children."

As they enjoy the delicious cookies, Coach pretends that he has something in his slightly closed fist. "I have a Muppet baby in my hand. Guess which one it is."

Kerri Kunstadt says, "Miss Piggy."

"No, it's Kermit," says Coach. "Do you see him?" Coach starts talking to a pretend Kermit the Frog in his fist.

Kerri Kunstadt says, "No, we don't see him."

"Oh, no. He must have gotten away." Coach starts looking all around for Kermit as his little buddies giggle with delight.

Coach says goodbye to his little friends and goes to eat lunch with the coaches and answer their questions.

"How much did you scout?" one begins eagerly.

"We didn't do a lot of scouting and did less than most every other team. We were more concerned about our team. We wanted to know some about our opponent, but we could get basic information, style of play, and tendencies from box scores, other coaches, and media reports.

"I actually did less scouting than any other coach I've ever heard about. I wanted our team to concentrate on what *we* could do—namely, try to execute our style of play to the best of our abilities."

"What was your approach when you played a rival like USC or Notre Dame?"

"I tried to motivate players the same every game. If it is a natural rival, the players motivate themselves. I stressed that we should play to our level of competency."

"What about your pregame routine?"

"Keep the format the same every game," Coach states matter of factly. "For warm-ups I disliked the standard two-line layup drill, but we did use it some. We might use a continuous two-man passing drill or offense without shooting. The first five to seven players need to shoot free throws until they feel right. That could be two or three; it could be five or six. The last five minutes before we go back out for the last time, we take care of bathroom needs. Then we go over matchups, the tip off, what defense we are in, what offense we are running to start the game."

"What about at halftime?" someone asks.

"I gather the assistants together, hear their notes, and talk to them as the players use the bathroom, get a drink, rest, and talk to each other," Coach explains. "I talk to individuals while the assistants talk on their area on the chalkboard. I would not use the chalkboard. I would talk last. I was sterner if we were doing things well."

"What if you were behind at halftime?"

"If we were struggling, I would pick them up. I might tell them to forget it. Play our game. Don't try to catch up the first five minutes of the second half. I might tell them there is no way they can play as well, or they play as badly in the second half. In the locker room or on the way back out, I might build up a player. I wanted to avoid embarrassing a player in front of his peers, although with some players I could do it in front of the team."[8]

The questions, as always, come thick and fast. "What would you do if a player was not playing at his highest level in a game?"

"Well, I had the greatest ally in the world—the bench," says Coach. "They could sit by me for a while, and I'd talk to them for a moment. I might give them a chance to try again, and if they didn't shape up, they'd be sitting back on the bench again. But remember, one of the greatest motivating things in the world is the pat on the back. It can also be a smile, a nod, a word. Every one of you likes to be patted on the back. And if you say you don't, you're lying," he says with a smile. "But sometimes the pat has to be a little lower and a little harder." This brings a laugh.

"But I think any person in leadership must get it across to those under his supervision that you care for them as a person, and about their family, and you talk with them about their problems," he continues. "You may not be able to solve their problems, but you can help. It is very important that it gets across that you care about them individually."[9]

"What about after the game?"

"The key is, did you play well, win or lose? There would be no chiding if they didn't play well. They were already down. Commend them. I might chide them after a win, especially if we didn't do well for a few games in a row and I can see trouble or complacency ahead. I did little raising of my voice. If we lost, it was not a good time to talk. Try to build them back up and make it short. If we win, then bring them down."

"How did you work on free-throw shooting?" another coach asks.

"Free-throw shooting is an art that one needs to practice a lot," answers Coach. "We shot free throws during breaks in practice. Later in my career and right before we won our championships, I felt like something was missing. We began to have the players who were not playing in the scrimmage go and shoot ten free throws on the side. When they were finished, they would come over to a coach and get subbed into the scrimmage. That helped us in many ways and, I think, contributed to our championships. We also shot free throws at the end of practice. We had different ways that also might help us end practice on a high note. A team had to make a certain number with each player shooting one each. Maybe one player has to make a one-and-one."

"What are the keys to great teams?"

"Great teams play tough team defense, are consistent, and persevere. Defense isn't as fun or spectacular, but defense should be consistent and is more of a common denominator than offense. It wins championships.

"Any person in leadership must get it across to those under his supervision that you *care* for them as a person," Coach tells his coaches.

"They also go to the boards on every shot," Coach continues, "play unselfishly on offense, and have strong chemistry and character. Play as a team—it is a team game. Accomplish things as a group. Louisiana State with Pete Maravich could have been national champs if they had played as a team.

"The coach's job is to develop the best team, not to keep everyone happy. As in all of life, have empathy but make decisions that benefit the team. Think in terms of the season and not the moment. I will get ready, and perhaps my chance will come. Sidney Wicks was the best forward on the team as a sophomore, but UCLA didn't have its best team when he was in the game. If he got away from the team game, he came out. With Lewis Alcindor we could do this. The next two NCAA titles were possible because Wicks learned discipline as a sophomore, and he became the MVP."

With that the coaches bus their trays and walk with Coach to the gym. As they walk, Coach Lokar uses the opportunity to ask one more question of Coach: "What do you do about teammates who don't get along?"

"Players must figure out how to use their talents for the good of the team. If you do well, there is plenty of credit for everyone. If you don't do well, there is not much credit for anyone. Competitive contact will cause some tension. Take pleasure in the spirited players. We were all made different by the good Lord. Keith Erickson was a spirited player who might have challenged me some, but I liked Keith. He was a spirited competitor, and he was the key to our press in '64 and '65."[10]

Our final camp lunch with Coach, as far as we know, has come to an end.

10

Respect and Thanks for Coach

Coach Wooden usually introduces the guest speakers. Today's guest speaker is Jamaal Wilkes, member of UCLA's '72 and '73 title teams, key player on the last seventy-three wins of the eighty-eight-game winning streak, Academic All-American, and three-time NBA champion with the Lakers and one-time champion with the Warriors. As he waits to speak, Coach Gregory asks him what it is like to speak at Coach Wooden's camps.

"I want to do well," Wilkes responds. "I have too much respect for Coach not to do my best. But I also want to try to say something profound, because the campers have been listening to Coach all week, and he's taught them everything they need to know."

Coach Wooden gives his warmest and most effusive introduction to Jamaal. "If I were to describe the ideal player," Coach tells the campers, "I would have the player be a good student, polite, courteous, a good team player, a good defensive player and rebounder, a good inside player and outside shooter. Why not just take Jamaal Wilkes and let it go at that? I would want Jamaal Wilkes on any team that I coach."[1]

Wilkes speaks briefly about how fortunate the campers are to be able to work under Coach Wooden and to learn the fundamental drills. "The fundamentals assimilate the movements in a game. Don't just go through the motions. Have a sense of urgency to do them right and to the best of your ability each time. Pay attention to detail. That is what I tried to do every day at UCLA."

Wilkes talks about offensive rocker-step moves as well as his shooting practice habits. He also emphasizes to the campers that they should work on weaknesses. "Work on what you do well but also on what you don't do well, like maybe learning to dribble with your left hand. That is how you improve. Listen to your coaches."

Wilkes next talks about his unorthodox shot and how Coach Wooden never corrected it. Coach knows that every player is different and should be treated differently. "After my first practice on the varsity as a sophomore, Coach Wooden called me over and asked me to shoot. He rebounded and passed to me. I have to say that I made just about every shot. Coach stopped me and then asked some things about my shot, like if the ball came off my fingertips correctly and with backspin. I said yes. Coach said okay and that I was dismissed. He just left me alone after that."

When Wilkes finishes, Coach Carlson asks Coach about the story about not changing Wilkes' shot. "I thought about changing his shot," remembered Coach, "but the start and finish were about perfect, even if everything in between was not. He shot very well, so I just left him alone, and I'm glad I did."

Thursday Afternoon Games

It is hot playing outside, but the campers love the competition of the camp games. Fourteen-year-old Branden Higa is a strong leaper, runs the floor and plays hard. He is beet red after his USC team beats Washington in a close game. Coach David Myers checks on him. "Great game, but are you okay?"

"Yes, I'm good. It's just really hot out here. I need to jump in the pool right away."

He rushes off to the pool where a few of his friends are already in the water showing off for lifeguard Rhondi Pinkstaff. Rhondi is an attractive 19 year old Cal Lu student who has a great summer job. She teaches swim lessons in the morning and then watches over the campers in the afternoon.

Despite the attention shown to her, Rhondi sees the campers as sweaty boys who turn the water dirty. Every hour she tells them to get out of the pool for ten minutes of "rest time." In reality, it is a chlorine break to keep the pool sanitary.

Michigan, led by eleven-year-old Darren Ranck, beats Minnesota on the outside courts. Afterwards, Darren rushes to the dorm lobby to buy a cold Gatorade. He has learned a lot in his three years at camp. He was his team's best player his first camp but did not win the Pyramid of Success award because he yelled at his teammates. That gave him the incentive to be a better teammate, which is true to how his parents raised him. He had a great attitude last summer, and he won the award. Coach Morgan is his coach now and has already decided he is going to win the award again this summer.

One of Darren's teammates fell and scraped his knee when he tripped at the end of the game. Coach Morgan is a certified trainer and wastes no words in his mandatory injury report. "Injury - bruised knee. Cause of injury - asphalt. Treatment - ice."

Free-Time Reflections

Thirteen year-old Jon Keller is on his way to the pool wearing a USC shirt. Coach Rivera playfully asks him, "Jon, why are you at this camp if you are such a big USC fan?"

"My grandfather went to USC but I love Coach Wooden and performing for him. I learn so much and the fundamental drills with Coach Wooden are great."

Darren elaborates when Rivera asks what else he is learning. "I thought I knew everything but when Coach showed us how to put on our shoes and socks it showed how smart he is and that I could learn a lot from him. And it was really cool that he wouldn't let Bill Walton get away with anything because it showed me we all have to do the right thing."

"That's a great attitude. Alright, have fun swimming. Try not to get wet." Coach Rivera is a beloved coach and quite funny.

Cowboy players take over the pool when camper swim time ends at four o'clock. A few players may also show off for Rhondi who makes sure the water gets a fresh dose of chlorine before they arrive. The players are there for their weekly body fat evaluation. One at a time they step into a big cage that is dropped into the pool for the trainers to measure their body fat. The water feels cool and invigorating for the players after two more hot and tough work-outs today.

Coach's ride home with Hawk includes an *LA Times* reporter sitting in the backseat. The reporter interviews Coach the entire way home, and as they near Coach's condo, he asks, "Do you think that you could have coached today's athletes with their tattoos, sagging shorts, trash talking, and jewelry?"

Coach answers. "Let me ask you something. When you were younger, did you wear bellbottom pants, experiment with drugs, rebel against authority, wear long hair or mutton chops, or protest against the Vietnam War? I coached in the sixties and seventies and dealt with all of that. Of course I could coach today's athletes." Hawk has been in the car during many such interviews, but this is a most memorable response and shows that Coach's competitive spirit is still strong.

The reporter has one more tough question for Coach: "What do you say about people who were impressed with your offense, defense, and press work but felt you didn't work enough on special situations like end-of-game strategy?"

Coach playfully answers, "That was true and very observant of them. We didn't plan on being in close games, and fortunately we weren't in that situation very often, and when we were, we usually won."[2] The reporter could not help but laugh and enjoy the response.

Counselor Eric Hughes and coach Ray Tejada catch part of the Cowboys' practice and cannot stop talking about Bill Bates. "Crazy Bill" has been a special team mainstay for the Cowboys since he made the squad as a free agent. Ray tells Eric, "He is just killing people out there. The guy just hits and works unbelievably hard."

For the fourth straight day, camper Tony Strickland is at the Cowboys' practice. Today after practice he holds footballs on the tee to help kicker Rafael Septién practice field goals. Tony is having a rich experience playing for John Wooden and also being an honorary member of the Cowboys.

Finally having some time alone for the first time all day, I sit down on my dorm bed to read the second article that Coach gave me this morning, "Need One Know Why":

> It was a delightful morning, cool and clear, for my daily five-mile walk around the UCLA track. After this sixty-five-minute exercise, I relaxed under a cool shower and then enjoyed a leisurely breakfast before leaving the Los Angeles International Airport to catch a plane for a trip across this great, wide, beautiful, and wonderful country of ours.
>
> Even though I have flown hundreds of thousands of miles, I never cease to marvel at this jet age in which we now live. How is it possible to place several hundred people in a huge hotel on wheels, take it thousands of feet into the air, and move it several hundred miles an hour under complete control toward another destination? I simply cannot comprehend how such a thing is possible. As I thought about this and gazed out the window at the beauty of the sea, the mountains, and the landscape below, I found myself caught up in a somewhat reflective and wondering mood about many things.
>
> I wondered, why—
>
> - are there so many who want to build up the weak by tearing down the strong?

- is it that many non-attainers are very quick to explain and belittle the attainers?
- are there so many who cannot seem to realize that winners are usually the ones who merely execute better, at least on that particular occasion?
- is it so difficult to realize that you cannot antagonize and influence at the same time?
- is it that we are so slow to understand that failing to prepare is preparing to fail?
- can't we realize that it only weakens those we want to help when we do things for them that they should do for themselves?
- is it so much easier to complain about the things we do not have than to make the most of and appreciate the things we do have?
- is it that so often we permit emotion rather than reason to control our decisions?
- is it so difficult to realize at times that nothing we can do will change the past, and the only way to affect the future is by what we do now?
- is it that it is so much easier to give others blame than it is to give them credit?
- is it that many who are quick to make suggestions find it difficult to make decisions?
- don't we realize that others are certain to listen to us if we first listen to them?
- aren't we more interested in finding the best way rather than having our own way?
- is it so difficult to develop the feeling that those under our supervision are working with us, not for us?
- is it much easier to be a critic than a model?
- is it so hard to disagree without being disagreeable?
- can't we understand that all progress comes through change even though all change may not be progress?

- is it that we often forget that big things are accomplished only by the perfection of minor details?
- do we dread adversity so much, when facing it is the only way to become stronger?
- can't we motivate ourselves when we know that results come through motivation?
- is it that some seem ashamed to let others know that they pray or read the Bible?
- should it be difficult to give thanks, express thanks, or merely say "Thank you"?
- can't we have patience and expect good things to take time?
- is it so easy to be quick to judge when possessed of only a few facts?
- is it that it is so easy to see the faults of others and so difficult to see our own?

I certainly do not have the answer for these questions, but I feel that the more I am aware of the fact that they do exist, the better chance I will have to face up to and possibly make them less of a problem.

Since I occasionally dabble in various verse forms to express some thoughts, I managed to come up with the following before we safely arrived at our destination.

Man in space,
A sea of clouds,
Huge jet engines,
Who can understand?

A baby's cry,
A hungry man,
A woman's tear,
Who can understand,
Or tell me why?

The East at dawn,
The West at dusk,
The stars at night,
The mountains tall,
The valleys green,
Need one know why?

Must we know why we are here on Earth?
Does wealth or station prove one's worth?
Is appearance made in three-score plus,
A way to measure one of us?

I truly want to find the way,
And know for this that I must pray,
And it won't matter what I say,
For He to whom I'll speak will know,
What is true and what is show,
To Him all things are very clear,
He knows exactly what we are,
And His judgment will be fair,
When we are all called together There.
Need one know why?[3]

As I finish reading, I marvel that Coach's ideas are as relevant today as they were when he first wrote them.

Coaches' Last Camp Dinner

Cowboys linebacker Ken Norton Jr. is one tough guy, but he is friendly too. He walks into the cafeteria carrying a towel with the letters "PE" on it. Camper John Caruso asks him what it means. "It means 'public enemy,'" Norton replies. John does not know whether to smile or run away.

Thursday night dinner is a time for the coaches to eat one more meal together before going our separate ways the next day, since as soon as camp ends, everyone will make a quick getaway to avoid the dreadful Friday afternoon traffic. Coaches and counselors linger over dinner as they savor memories and the opportunity to be with Coach very likely for just one more day. Coaches reflect on what has made Coach so special, unique, admired, and loved to each of them.

Wayne Carlson tells a story about being in the pressroom in San Diego when Coach announced his retirement after the last-second 75–74 win against Louisville in the 1975 national semifinals. "Since I played at San Diego State," Carlson says, "I was given a job as a media runner, and so I was there in the postgame press conference when Coach announced it. He has such strong principles and faith, and he lives by them. He showed them when he announced his retirement. I learned so much from the blocks in the Pyramid—also how to live a Christian life and the importance of family."

Counselor Steve Delaveaga talks about seeing Coach from a camper viewpoint. "You see him on stage, and he's just tough, commanding through the microphone and pushing us. Then as a counselor, you realize how easygoing he is and what a nice guy he is."

Counselor Greg Plutko is the son of Ray Plutko, a great coach who is one of the top administrators over high-school athletics in California and even in the nation. "I knew all about UCLA basketball," Greg says, "the attention to detail, the preparation, the hard work, all of it. Then I get to camp, and it is that way here. I've been a counselor at a lot of different camps, and this is the model for how they should all be run. It is Coach's camp, and he is active, involved, and caring. When he talks, I sit up straighter so that my campers and Coach will notice. I'm afraid to sprain my ankle in case Coach finds out that my shoes and socks weren't on correctly." Everyone at the table laughs but also agrees.

"His camps are authentic," says coach Ken Barone appreciatively. "At camps run by NBA players or college coaches, the campers don't see the headliners much, and the coaching isn't always good. Here you meet Coach Wooden and work with him, and he gets to know the campers. Through the years Coach has stayed the same—the drills and fundamentals and his dedication and compassion for everyone involved in the camps are the same every year. He is demanding and disciplined, but he treats players the way you would want your son coached. He is the man!

"We learn so much," Ken goes on. "So many little things. You can't even write it all down. The big picture for me is to 'teach what you know, and know what you teach.'"

Delaveaga continues the dialogue. "When I hear him speak, I think of the fact that many inspirational speakers can stir people up in the moment a lot more than Coach can, but what makes Coach so special and inspirational is who he is as a person. His consistency and steadiness and his daily moment-by-moment being true to himself separate him from everyone else."

Carlson adds, "And his humility, because he sees himself on a journey to keep striving each day to be better. He is honest and candid about sharing his own experiences, even admitting his coaching mistakes and the mistakes he's made dealing with various players throughout the years."

Coach Palarz speaks up next. "Camp mirrors that humility. Cal Lu is a small, comfortable, pleasant place, while Coach is this legend—we can say it. But he is so humble, personable, and hands-on."

"Yet he is also still a great competitor and fiercely independent," I add. "Two years ago I saw him at a UCLA game, and he must have thought I was talking to him as if he were an old guy, and he let me know by his tone that he didn't appreciate that. He was right to do that. I hadn't seen him in a few years, and I did kind of talk to him that way. I haven't since.

"I learn so much from him," I continue. "I make so many mistakes in how I treat kids and have nowhere near the on-court success he had, so I feel badly. But then Coach tells me about some of the mistakes he made, especially when he was younger, and they're mistakes that I have made. I realize that Coach is human, and I stop beating myself up for not being perfect, because he wasn't. Some of his wisdom comes from learning from his own mistakes, and that inspires me.

"He once told me, 'You are never a failure until you start blaming others,'" I share with the others. "Jim Harrick said that Coach gave him that advice as well, and it has been a tremendous help for him at UCLA. I struggled as a high-school coach using his system, and I couldn't understand why. Then I realized that you can't take Coach out of the system. Now I run less of his offense and defense and focus more on fundamentals, team spirit and conditioning, the principles in the Pyramid, and Coach's father's seven creeds, and my teams are consistently good and competitive each year."

"I call Coach when my team really struggles," says Hawk. "This past season I called him, and he said that I should go over the practice schedule I'd used for the past three weeks. 'I'll bet that you are doing too much five-on-five work and not enough fundamental drills,' he told me. 'Early in my career I made that mistake. The best plays don't work if your players can't pass, catch, and shoot.' Sure enough, he was right, and we played much better after we changed that."

Tom Gregory adds, "For years I have sat and listened to him. The basketball strategy is good, of course, but it is not brilliant. His genius is that he knows people and knows how to put them in places to succeed. He was a great teacher and model and a great competitor. Plain and simple, *I'm a John Wooden disciple—disciplined, up-tempo, fundamental basketball.*"

"As much as we listen to him, he himself is a great listener to us," Scarano adds. "He never interrupts, gives us his complete attention, and really listens when we speak. It is another example of modeling the right thing to do."

"I think the world of him and love him like a family member," Jeff Dunlap affirms. "He shows love to everyone, including the groundskeepers, cooks, janitors, and meal servers, and he makes them all feel appreciated."

John Saintignon tells his own poignant story. "I was head counselor, and while I was in his condo one day, the phone rang constantly. He didn't answer it, but I heard on the recording machine that the callers were former players, current college coaches, and, honest truth, a former US president. I finally asked if he was going to answer the phone, and he said, 'I'm with you now, and when we finish talking, I will call them.' It shows how much he cares about everyone and especially the person he is with at the moment. The greatest coach who ever lived makes time for each one of us. Each one of us has our own special stories with him."

Jaws walks by and is asked, "Jaws, what are your thoughts about Coach?"

With his warm smile he says, "Right now my mind is on getting the games started on time. But to give you a quick answer, Coach does such a good job with the kids and the staff here at camp. His attention to detail and fundamentals, his talk about the Pyramid, his poems, and his overall care for what goes on at camp speak volumes regarding what he is all about. That is even more important than all his records. Okay, I gotta get going," he finishes quickly. "Good luck in the games—and be nice to the refs."

Coach Dave Myers adds, "Coach has a tremendous influence by the things he says and with his poems as I listen to him on stage with that microphone. My family and I appreciate so much the influence he has had on us high-school coaches from Texas."

Coach Kunstadt agrees with Myers. "Yes, our families—the Showalters, Myerses, and Kunstadts—love to come every summer, although to be honest, Coach is second to Mickey Mouse in the kids' minds. But the older they get, the more that gap closes. Coach is so good to all our children, and they just love him. The greatest gift he may have given is how loving and good he has been to our kids."

Hal Mitrovich walks by and sums things up well. "Besides my family, the greatest influence in my life has been Coach Wooden. I feel as if we camp staffers are a part of Coach Wooden's family. We are a team. When you first meet him you feel stressed, but that goes away in the two seconds it takes for Coach to reach his hand out and say hello, and then you feel comfortable. It is a good stress when we work at camp, because it is family, and the paternal head of the family is Coach Wooden. The stress feels like the values of family—hard work, picking up trash. I stooped down the other day to pick up a penny, and I almost got hit by a truck." Coaches laugh.

"Those things were not just learned by Coach's speeches," went on Hal, "but by watching him. Some people want to see who is watching them before they do a good deed, but not Coach. He sees that piece of paper from as far away as he can see it, and he walks quickly over to it and picks it up. It teaches me the lesson that you have to do the right thing first. Coach passes all this on to us, and then we pass it on to our children, our students, and our players. We are part of the team with the greatest coach who's ever lived. I'm honored by it. Sometimes I feel as if I'm part of a pleasant dream. I'm very thankful."

Administrative director Chris Smith, who has stopped by the coaches' dinner table, particularly addresses the high-school coaches who have been speaking. "Coach loves being with all you high-school coaches as well. Deep down he is a high-school English teacher and a baseball, football, and basketball coach, and he loves being around children, especially the younger ones. Coach is always the same. There's nothing fake about him. He stays true to his character and nature, no matter who he is around or where he is, and here at camp he truly enjoys you coaches. When he is with family and people like you, he is happiest. Other than my brother and my dad, Coach has had the biggest influence in my life. Coach makes all of us feel special, as if we are a friend of his for life."

Don Showalter responds to Chris and wraps the discussion up perfectly. "We are so fortunate to be able to work for him. It's as if we all want to push ourselves to do well for him. So many coaches want to do what we are able to do. We are going to look back someday and realize how truly special this opportunity has been."

A Little Ribbing from Coach

Chris Smith has stopped by Cal Lu to say hello to the coaches and to take Coach to dinner. With him is longtime camp director Rick Eveleth. Hal goes with them and leaves Hector at camp by himself to watch over things.

The three men pick Coach up at his condo and take him to Lawry's in Beverly Hills. It is one of his favorite restaurants, famous for its prime rib and well known for a prime-rib-eating contest each year between the two Rose Bowl teams. As always, Coach insists on paying. The only way anyone else can pay for dinner is to get there before Coach and pay well ahead of dinnertime—and before Coach knows about it.

Chris, Rick, Hal, and Coach enjoy a great prime-rib dinner. After the meal Coach asks the waiter for a bag to put the many leftover bones in. Chris and Rick drop Coach off at home and then drive back to camp, where they give Hector the bag of bones. "Coach feels badly that you couldn't go with us, so he got you a to-go plate." Hector laughs the loudest of all of them and feels Coach's love.

The Games Go On

Tom Utsler, a five-foot-nine fifteen-year-old guard from El Dorado High School in nearby Placentia, has caught the eye of coaches the past two days for the number of charging fouls he takes. It does not matter if he is playing indoors or outside on the asphalt courts; he gets in others' way and is willing to be run over by the biggest, strongest, and most physical players. He takes the full contact and then jumps up right away, ready to play offense. A lot of cheering goes on when he does it, and sometimes it is his coach and counselors who shout the loudest. He takes a few more hits in tonight's game.

Coach Nash Rivera is the former coach at El Dorado High School, where he built a powerful basketball program before moving on to be an assistant coach with the UCLA women's team. Rivera is known for his funny sayings, like "Don't be bitter, reconsider." When asked who had the best chance to beat his team on a given night, Rivera would say, "The team we are playing, because that's the only team we are playing against." He is a beloved coach who can correct a player who has made a mental mistake by saying, "I'll bet your parents don't call you sonny, because you are not very bright."

Tonight before the game he tells his team, "This game is one of the last things you will do at camp. So what did the monkey say when he got his tail caught in the door? It won't be long now." His Michigan team won the game and had fun doing so.

Branden Higa and his teammates are excited. Most games are played outside, but Branden's team is in the gym tonight. Teams get motivated when they play inside—in the kind of atmosphere they are used to playing in. Coach Myers senses the player's excitement. "Hey, Branden," he says to his player, "you look like you're ready to jump out of the gym."

"This is fun, Coach. We're prime time tonight, playing inside with soft rims, so we're ready to go." His USC team plays well and defeats UCLA. That is allowed to happen at camp.

Camper Evaluations—and Antics

After roll call tonight the coaches work on each camper's player profile, an evaluation form that will be given to each camper at the closing ceremony tomorrow. We are careful to write positive comments and not to include the same things on every camper evaluation. Coaches grade each camper on a series of offensive and defensive areas and also on attitude. We need to be honest but also constructive in all that we write. The camp directors read these comments and occasionally ask us to rephrase things.

Coaches also write each camper's name neatly on a camp certificate, another document that each camper will receive before going home, and then sign it. Wayne Carlson has a better idea. He drives over to the nearby house in which cafeteria worker Laura Erwin rents a room with a few other Cal Lu students working there for the summer, as she is. On her typewriter she types the campers' names on Carlson's certificates. When he returns, his fellow coaches want to know if his time with Laura counts as another date. He explains that it was a chaperoned one, since her roommates were there as well.

"I thought it was so ridiculous on Sunday when Coach talked about how to put our shoes and socks on, but I get it now," says camper Mark Kailey.

"Which one of the roommates are you dating next?" someone teases.

"I'm not sure there's going to be a next date for Wayne," another predicts humorously.

Thursday night also means that the campers—most of them, anyway—have almost made it through the week without losing their keys. Of course, it takes time for anyone to untie his shoe, take the key off, open his room, and then put the key back on his laces, but a camper risks losing his key and paying a fine if he doesn't keep it tied onto his shoe.

Two campers from South Korea, Eddie and Jonathan Lee, have taken no chances at all. With shoes still on, one of them has lifted his foot up each night and unlocked the door with his key still laced onto his shoe. By now word has spread about their flexibility and ingenuity, and counselors and coaches watch with amusement and admiration as they do this one more time.

Later though, the mood changes dramatically. The head counselors are greatly concerned, because at the final bed check, they discover that a camper is missing. Counselors and even some of the campers search everywhere for him. Losing track of a camper is the biggest concern and fear at camp. After the counselors search the campus, gym, nearby streets, and every dorm room several times, they still cannot find him and are now deeply worried.

Meanwhile, campers Matt Lewis and Mark Kailey lie on their beds, tired but feeling good about camp, and reflect on the week. Kailey says, "I come from a tough neighborhood. I begged my parents to let me come to camp because I wanted to learn from Coach and show him how good I am. But I'm just not as good of a player as I thought I was."

Lewis interrupts, "But you seemed to have a great time. I didn't know this was so tough on you."

"It's not tough. Camp has been great. But where I come from, we just play, and there isn't much coaching or discipline. I thought it was so ridiculous on Sunday when Coach talked about how to put our shoes and socks on, but I get it now. The attention to detail in layups, shooting, passing, and everything else is really important. If I pay attention to details, the final result will be much better. The problem is, I'm going to be a senior next year, but I haven't prepared or worked hard enough to be a great player. So I have to adjust my goals now, because I realize that my future's not going to be in basketball. And it's good to know that. But the preparation, hard work, and details I've learned about here are going to be important in whatever I do in the future."

"Wow—that is really mature of you." With that Lewis slams a pillow at his unsuspecting roommate, who jumps up, slinging his own pillow in self-defense.

Jaws and Hawk have run out of ideas on finding the lost boy. They anxiously walk to Hector's room to tell him that they do not know where he is so that Hector can call campus security and the police.

As they are about to step into Hector's room, Jaws suddenly turns around and tells Hawk to follow him. Jaws runs to the boy's room and looks in the cabinets high up on the wall, where college students store their possessions. Standing on a chair, Jaws pulls back clothes to find the boy lying down inside the cabinet.

Jaws barks at him, "What are you doing up there?"

"Nothing. I was just hiding."

Jaws tries to be mean and stern but cannot suppress a smile as he helps the camper down. The boy should feel lucky that such a good-hearted person as Jaws has found him. "Go to bed, and don't leave your bed!" But the camper's smile shows that he has enjoyed the game.

The nightly headcount is no laughing matter to Hector. His number-one concern is camper safety, and he is tough on the head counselors in getting an accurate head count as soon as possible each night. He will not relax until he knows that all campers are in their beds, safe and asleep. Once they are, he might break out a cold one, which is the sign to the head counselors that it has been a good day.

As Jaws and Hawk walk into his room, Hector asks testily, "What took you guys so long?"

Jaws simply says, "Sorry."

Tonight that beer is opened very late, but it is a sign that camp life is all well. As the head counselors leave the room, Hector tells them, "Thank God that nothing really bad has ever happened at camp." Jaws and Hawk shoot each other a relieved look as they walk out.

Just Thinking

Meanwhile, I sit on my bed and read the last of my special Coach Wooden articles, "Just Thinking":

It has been said that you will be hurt occasionally if you trust too much, but you will live in torment if you do not trust enough. This statement could apply to both the youth and the adults in the uneasy society in our country today. Because of modern technology and the advances in all areas, our inquisitive youth are more inquisitive than ever, and this seems to scare their elders, because they do not have the answers to the problems that our young people want solved—right now.

Youth is a time of impatience, and they can't understand why the problems of society haven't been solved. They haven't lived long enough as yet to fully understand human nature and do not have the patience that eventually brings about more faith and better understanding. Good and worthwhile things take time, and that is exactly as it should be.

On the other hand, older people tend to become set in their ways, fear change, and quite possibly become too patient for problems to be solved. They sometimes forget that although all change isn't necessarily progress, all progress is the result of change.

Perhaps the breach between the youth and the adults of today is similar to the official-coach relationship in athletics. A few years ago I concluded an article in regard to this with the following statement: "In the final analysis, perhaps the main thing we need in all walks of life is more mutual trust and understanding of the problems of the other fellow. If we can acquire that, the coach-official relationship should no longer be a problem."

I am inclined to feel that our society as a whole has become so infatuated with material things that we have gotten away from the values that are everlasting. We are not seeking our happiness and peace from the things that cannot be taken away from us. As always, we should remember one of the great quotations from the greatest book of all, "Seek ye first

His kingdom and His righteousness, and all these things will be yours as well."

It is wonderful to see our young people so interested and as aware as they are today. They are truly concerned and are searching for answers to our problems. We older people should not judge them all by the few who get out of line through their impatience and immature judgment, but show the patience and understanding that should be the mark of maturity. As has been said, our young people need models more than critics. It has generally been proved that concrete example is usually a better teaching aid than word of mouth or written criticism, although there should be a place for all.

With all our problems, this should be a time of optimism, not pessimism. The very advances in technology and other areas that have contributed to many of our problems should eventually solve them. What the mind of man can create, the mind and heart of man should be able to control, and if advances in technology can be used for evil, surely they can be directed toward good.

I cannot presume to advise others, but I am confident that we all need help. Most of this we can get from talking to God through prayer and listening to Him by reading the Bible. We can gain further help from others, if we will only be receptive.[4]

As I kneel by my bed to say nighttime prayers, I offer a heartfelt prayer of thanks for Coach Wooden.

11

"The Reason I Teach"

Friday is a half day, and this Friday is unique in that it is most likely Coach Wooden's last Sportsworld camp day. It is tough getting out of bed for just about everyone, even for Michael Scarano and Nash Rivera, who always get up and go running. The line for breakfast is shorter than it has been all week.

As Coach Wooden enters the cafeteria, he notices eleven-year-old Lucas Silsbee with his left arm in a sling trying to balance his tray with his right arm. Lucas has spent much of last night at Thousand Oaks Hospital being treated for a broken clavicle, suffered in his Thursday evening game on the front courts.

"What happened, young man?"

"I broke my collarbone in my game last night."

"How did it happen?"

"I was running along the side trying to cut off a player. I reached in to steal the ball, and he ran over me, and I fell on my shoulder."

"I'm sorry that you were injured. But try to learn from it. That's why you play defense with your feet and don't reach. You learned a valuable lesson."

Lucas, the son of Hart High School's coach Craig Silsbee, has been to camp numerous times. He is mature enough to know that Coach always tries to find a helpful lesson in everything, and he takes Coach's words to heart.

Our Final Breakfast with Coach Wooden

Lil is in the cafeteria to greet Coach Wooden this morning, a man she truly loves and has helped through his toughest days. She is a blessing to him, and in turn she is very appreciative of all that he has done for her family, including her son, coach Larry Lopez.

Coach has special words for Lil this morning as she visits him one more time at his table with the coaches. "Thank you, Lil," he tells her, "for how well you have fed us. You have done a wonderful job, not just with the food, but with the friendship you have given all of us—coaches, counselors, and campers. I know that they all love you, and they have every reason to."[1]

Coach Carlson comments about Coach Wooden's daily breakfast oatmeal. "I was raised on oatmeal. My brothers—Maurice, Daniel, and Billy—and I had oatmeal for breakfast nearly every morning on our farm back in Centerton, Indiana. I raised my own children on oatmeal as well. Some things don't change; some lessons remain the same. Those my father taught many years ago may seem old-fashioned now, but like oatmeal, they still work."[2]

That leads to another question. "How else did your dad influence you?"

"My father set the course that guided me through my life—what I believe, what I do, and how I do it," Coach says simply. "He made everything happen by teaching us in word and deed that the simplest virtues and values are most important.

"My father died long before UCLA won a men's college basketball championship," he continues. "Do I wish he'd lived to see me coach a team to a national title? Yes, but his priorities were different. Material things and public notice meant little. Education was important. Family was important. Outscoring someone in a basketball game, even for a national championship, had much less significance. Dad lived long enough to see me accomplish what was important to him. Nevertheless, he was responsible for the good things that happened to me as a coach. He seldom attended games and was only slightly interested in results. His concerns and guidance were deeper.

"Dad's message about basketball—and life—was this: 'Johnny, don't try to be better than somebody else, but never cease trying to be the best *you* can be. You have control over that. The other you don't.' It was simple advice: work hard, very hard, at those things I can control and don't lose sleep over the rest of it. . . . Then he would usually add, as he talked to us at the kitchen table, 'Boys, always try to learn from others, . . . even if it's what *not* to do.'"[3] These are the secrets behind Coach's approach to basketball and to life.

"My father set the course that guided me through my life—what I believe, what I do, and how I do it," Coach says simply.

Someone else asks him, "How did you balance family and basketball?"

"I was criticized for how I balanced family and basketball," Coach replies. "I didn't leave my family to scout, and I was criticized if we lost. They said we lost because I didn't scout enough. I also didn't take basketball home with me, and I didn't allow basketball to take a night away from the family. Nellie went to conventions, scouting, speaking engagements with me when possible. As coaches, there are some things we have to do, but there are some things we do that we don't have to do. Coaches have to set life priorities. The Lord is first. I try to read at least a little bit from the Bible every day. You can learn something on every page. He should be first and the family second. I often put family in front and hoped and prayed the Lord would understand."

"This is totally changing the subject," one coach puts in, "but what do you suggest in regard to player/coach relationships?"

"The coach is human. He has to make decisions. He is not always right. Listen to the players, and then the players will probably get desirable results. Same with the players—listen to the coach, and most likely the coach will then listen to you.

"Learn to disagree without being disagreeable. I can't guarantee that personal likes and dislikes won't affect my decisions, although I try not to let that happen. But players should try to keep that in mind. Be agreeable. Not yes-men—you can ask questions. But the manner in which they are asked is important. And the coach should show interest in the players as people. That will pay off in the future."

"What about player/teammate relationships?"

"Show consideration for others, which is team spirit. Always thank teammates by pointing at them, acknowledging them with a nod, high-fiving not only the passer but everyone. Thank your teammate for screens, help, an outlet pass to start the break, a rebound, hustle, for calling out a screen. No teammate criticizes another teammate. That would be embarrassing to him and would create disharmony. You don't have to like each other, but you do have to show respect, consideration, and care. Be positive and helpful. Work toward group accomplishment. Players will have problems the coach doesn't know about. Players can help teammates by bringing these problems to the coach's attention. Players can also help with problems socially, help each other personally."

"And parents?"

"Parents should be interested but not interfering. You must bring problems up to parents without antagonizing them. Be amiable with parents but not intimate. Stay away from problem parents. Some parents are afraid to go to work because their son is not starting. Parents should be prejudiced; it would be unnatural if they weren't. But the coach is usually the most unprejudiced.

"If a parent is coaching him, the player gets caught between the coach and the parent. I had a player who was struggling because his dad was putting a lot of pressure on him from the home in Chicago. The player felt like he was letting his family down, and that pressure was hurting his performance. I wasn't aware of this until teammates made me aware. It is an example of the factors that we as coaches can't always control. We don't always know about the hidden reasons that a player is not performing to his ability level."

"I've always wanted to ask you something," a coach speaks up. "What do you think of Bobby Knight?" The questioner is referring to the highly passionate and immensely popular coach for the Indiana Hoosiers.

"He is quite a character and one of the finest teachers ever in the game. We are fellow Hoosiers, so we talk sometimes. I don't agree with some of his tactics, and I have told Robert that he doesn't need to use the language he uses. Now if I had to choose one person to coach a game that a team absolutely had to win, I would choose him. But I wouldn't allow my son to play for him."[4]

"What is your advice for dealing with referees?" another asks.

"You're going to get excited, you know. But I taught for forty years, and I had two technicals, and one I didn't deserve." Coach is in a great mood, and the coaches are really enjoying this. "I didn't mention the fact that there might have been many times I deserved one but didn't get it. But forget those."[5] The coaches laugh and continue to enjoy this last meal with Coach. "Never make it personal. Keep it professional. Be specific on what you want called."[6]

Ken Morgan smiles and asks a question that calls to mind the famous images of Coach during his UCLA days, when he paced the sidelines during games with a rolled-up basketball program under his arm. "Coach," he says with a bold grin, "I've heard that you occasionally said some not-so-nice things to the referees during games through your rolled-up program."

The other coaches look at Morgan with expressions that say, "I can't believe you just asked him that." Coach smiles in return and begins a long explanation. "I had a program in my hand, and

I had notes on this program, reminders of certain things. I might open it up and peek at it once in a while. No one seemed to notice that. They thought I just had it there as a megaphone to talk to the officials—which might have been true on occasion." The coaches laugh. "I said some things I wouldn't have liked if I were in their shoes, like, 'Don't be a homer.' 'Call them the same at both ends.' 'Watch the traveling.' 'Can you count to three?'" Coach is on a roll, and the coaches are really enjoying it.

"When I came to UCLA, we had an official in the conference who was a very, very poor official. Nice person. He was poor both ways. He wouldn't favor anybody. One game he made a horrible call against us, although he probably had made calls for us. As he came down the floor, I said, 'Lou, horrible call.' He ran by me and said, 'They like it at the other end,' and he kept going." The coaches all laugh. "How can you be mad at him? What is the saying? 'A soft answer turns away wrath'?"

Then Coach turns more serious. "In my other hand I had something as well. I went into the service during World War II, and my minister in Indiana gave me a cross. That was always in my hand in times of stress. That was in 1942, and I still have it in my pocket today. It is sort of worn out now, but I always had that in games. Some of my players knew that, but most people didn't."[7] With that Coach takes the cross out and shows it to the coaches, who are touched by the story.

This moves one to ask, "Will you please talk about love and balance and why they are so important to you?"

"Those are the two most important words in our language," Coach states. "Obviously 'love' is the most important word. If we had throughout this troubled world, to the extent we should have, love for one another, our problems would not be as severe. We'd have problems, of course, but they would not be as unmanageable if we just had more love and consideration for the other side, whatever it might be. Mother Teresa is one of my favorite people, and she showed love in wonderful ways.

"Now we must keep things in balance, in perspective. Don't get carried away if things are going too well or if things are going too poorly. Just keep making the effort to do the best you can in whatever you are doing. You must always be learning—learning from others to improve yourself in the activities in which you are involved, in whatever they might be."[8]

Hector walks by. "Okay, coaches. Let's get going."

Breakfast is over.

Meaningful Coaches' Meeting

The last coaches' meeting is earlier than usual, at seven forty-five, because of the shorter day today. Last night a few coaches dressed up to coach their games so that they could go out and socialize right after the games; Coach Wooden has heard about it and ribs the coaches some. "I heard that a few of you looked pretty good last night—like you were ready to coach in the NCAA championship game." All of us chuckle.

Coach Wooden has one more gift for me. It is a copy of the poem "Two Sides of War" by Grantland Rice that Coach Wooden has often recited to the coaches in the past. Coach says a few words about the poem, explaining that it helped him understand young people's opposition to the Vietnam War. He hands it to me and then recites it from memory:

All wars are planned by older men
In council rooms apart,
Who call for greater armament
And map the battle chart.

But out along the shattered fields
Where golden dreams turn gray,
How very young the faces were
Where all the dead men lay.

Portly and solemn in their pride
The elders cast their vote
For this or that, or something else,
That sounds the martial note.

But where their sightless eyes stare out
Beyond life's vanished toys,
I've noticed nearly all the dead
Were hardly more than boys.

I am again touched by Coach's kindness. I realize how far I have come in my own relationship with Coach from my first year at camp twelve years ago, when I was on edge—trying to do what was right, trying to earn the respect of the veteran coaches, trying to please Coach and earn the right to be asked back to coach future camps. I realize even more what a special person Coach is and how comfortable I am with him now.

During the meeting Coach Macias reviews today's different schedule and then hands out the individual pictures that were taken on Monday for the coaches to give to their campers. Mike Kunstadt then speaks on behalf of the coaches to express appreciation for Coach. "Coach, with camp I think of four things: the Pyramid, the 'A Little Chap' poem, your father's seven creeds, and how to give thanks. We are all so thankful for your inspiration to make each day our masterpiece. Thank you, and God bless you."

Coach replies, "I truly enjoy all these memories. It is difficult for me to show my true appreciation and thankfulness for all of it. I'm thankful for family and friends. I hope He knows how grateful I am. I'm not worthy. I know I'm not what I ought to be, what I want to be, what I'd like to be, but a lot of things have made me better than I would have been, and you're a part of it."[9]

The coaches move into the gym, touched beyond words. It truly brings into focus Hal's words from the night before: "This is family, and the paternal head is Coach Wooden."

Last Morning Workout with Coach

From eight to eight thirty, all the campers gather together for one last morning workout with Coach. This is most likely the last time that most of these coaches, counselors, and campers will have the privilege of working with Coach. They savor the opportunity, treasure Coach, and are even more attuned to Coach's voice and spirit than usual. Since most coaches signed up for the camp to be with Coach this one last time, a feeling of deep gratitude and a sense of being in the moment and seizing it for all it is fill the atmosphere. Everyone feels the extra enthusiasm, effort, focus, intensity, and energy in the gym as the campers work through the drills.

Even Coach himself seems to be sharper and more energetic than he normally is, as if that were possible. Following the ball-handling drills, Coach puts the campers through passing-on-the-move drills that involve two teams working together on passing back and forth on the move—parallel passing on the run: "Now I want the ball in every other line. First, third, fifth, seventh lines, get a ball. Coaches, back up to the center line now. You're going to work on the pass lead, getting the proper lead, the proper pass, pass back and forth. Go sideways. You run and pass forward, receiving the ball across the body. Go block the ball with the opposite side hand. Block and tuck. You must have a good exchange at the end. All is lost if you don't have good exchange at the end. Every pass is a good one. Never pass back. Always pass ahead of the player."

A counselor brings him a cup of water. Coach looks at his watch to make sure that he is on schedule and carries on: "Quicker, letter high," Coach insists, wanting the players to pass as high as the letters on the team jerseys are. "Pass on the move, learning how to lead your teammate, how to lead the receiver. Pass properly where he can handle it. All we want is the pass to be received. Keep those passes high. Move that ball, move that ball. I want a good exchange, a perfect exchange every time." The campers' clapping is as loud, crisp, and together as has ever been heard in the gym. The players are responding wonderfully in this special session.

"Now I want the bounce pass every time. That bounce pass can't come up higher than the waist. Pass above the knees, below the waist. The ball has to be close to the receiver's feet three quarters of the way to the receiver."

Coach now returns to an earlier dribbling drill. He has the campers dribble forward around their coach with right- and then left-hand dribbling again. This time he adds a long bounce pass back to the next person in line. "Go to the right of your coach, your right. Stay low. Now left-hand dribble—go to the left. Bounce-pass three quarters of the way. Bounce the ball below the waist. Come around him and make the pass—go. Good pass after you come around the coach."

The campers have just finished the next-to-last drill, and Coach decides to let them have some fun before the final drill in order to end this final, special session on a high note. "Come across the double green line, facing the coach all the time. I'm going to let you put on a show, do what you like to do," Coach calls, to the delight of the campers. "When I blow the whistle, I want you to go around your coach and go back to the line, because the next player is going to be coming out and putting on his show. Two balls in each line. Back up now. Back up from the line. Come out from your line, and put on a show. Next one in the line be ready."

Coach blows the whistle for each player to dribble any way he wants to. He smiles and encourages the campers' creativity. Generally he prefers a player to be clever and not a hot dog, but this one time players can act as if they are the Globetrotters if they want to. Coach seems to enjoy it as much as the campers, some of whom are very creative in their dribbling. A lot of spirited laughter, cheering, and joking with teammates fills the gym as each player does his own creative dribbling routine.

Coach blows the whistle for the last time to prepare for the final drill. "Roll the balls out behind you. Close in as you did at the beginning. Get your spacing. Straighten out your lines now. You should be in good straight lines. You should be directly behind someone in front of you. Face me. Hurry up, hurry up."

Coach will use this final quick drill to refocus the campers and to wind them down some. "Position for a jump ball. Get crouched, and I want intense spring. When you tip the ball, you do not bounce." Coach continually calls out a direction for the tip: "Front, front, back, left, right, right, left, right, front, front, back." He walks back and forth on the stage observing the campers for the last time. "Okay. Now two hands above your shoulders. Offensive rebound. Go. Go."

Finally Coach calls out, "On your stomachs." "Ughs" can be heard, and Coach has a big smile on his face. "Five fingertip push-ups. Up, down."

The campers call the number out. "One!"

"Down."

"Two!"

"Down."

"Three!"

"Down."

"Four!"

"Down."

"Five!"

The campers engage in loud, rhythmic, continuous, spirited clapping as they realize that they are now finished with this last workout. "Sit down, sit down. Lie down, lie down, hands behind your head. Feet up, relax, close your eyes. Quiet. Not a peep. Perfectly relaxed, every muscle relaxed. Everything relaxed. Eyes closed, ears in tune, however. You have had a pretty good workout, young men. Listen to the instructions you will receive from Coach Macias."[10]

Coach has wisely and effectively quieted and calmed the campers so that they are ready to hear Hector the Director and then transition to the next activity. In doing so he has given some a chance to savor the moment and to say a silent prayer of gratitude and appreciation.

Without any fanfare Coach Macias quickly announces, "Okay, everyone up. Let's go."

Camper Evaluations

From eight thirty to nine, the teams meet with their coaches one last time. During this time coaches speak to each camper personally for individual reviews of their camp report card. Campers are also given their camp certificates and the individual photos with Coach Wooden that were taken on Monday. Each camper receives an eight-by-ten copy of the camp picture as well, which for years were black and white but are now in color. Since some teams—those that happen to be tied in the games so far—will play for a championship before leaving today, this final meeting also serves as a pregame meeting for their last game.

Camper Harvey Mason meets with his team, which has been coached by Ken Stanley. “Harvey, I really enjoyed coaching you. You improved in every aspect this week. I’m also impressed that you played basketball all the time during free time this week. What is the main thing you learned here at camp?”

Harvey’s answer shows remarkable insight for an eleven-year-old. “I learned that you have to use your mind more and be a student of the game. I used to just go out and play, but now I know that I need to be patient, in control, and aware of things. Coach taught me that. I learned that little details are important, like the angle of my cuts, where to put my feet, how to bend my knees coming off screens. Things like that. And Coach made me feel really good when he told me I am a good athlete.”

Jim Nielsen’s team has really enjoyed playing for him this week, and as a gift they give *him* an evaluation—as a player! Jim is honored by their affection.

Fifteen-year-old Lance Haliday is really down when he meets with Coach Scarano. “I don’t want to go home. Things are so chaotic there. Here things are structured, and I learn so many important things, not just about basketball. I know that if I do the right thing, everything turns out well. It’s not that way at home.” Coach Scarano encourages Lance to remember Coach’s definition of success—controlling those things that he can control and having peace from doing that. Lance smiles for the first time all morning.

One Thing Coach Can't Do

Larry Lopez's son Adam, the five-year-old grandson of Lil, is too young to be a camper, but Coach has let him participate in the morning sessions and also during free time. Coach notices that he has not seen Adam all morning and asks Larry if he is okay. Lopez replies, "He's tired from playing so much basketball this week. He just didn't want to get out of bed this morning."

Coach says, "Let's go get him." They walk to Adam's room, where Coach does all he can to motivate him to get up, but Adam stays in his bed. As they walk back to the gym, Coach tells Larry, "I could get Bill Walton to do things, even if I had to threaten him at times, but I can't get Adam to get out of bed."

Championship Games and Checkout

Friday morning games are a bit shorter than the forty-minute Wednesday and Thursday games, and they include a few championship games. (There are no all-star games at a John Wooden camp.) This shorter game provides coaches a good opportunity to give campers some final personalized instruction to improve their basketball skills as well as their mental and emotional skills. Certainly that has been a main emphasis of the camp.

The younger gold division plays their last game, while the older blue division meets to go through the camp checkout procedure; afterward the groups switch places. Many parents come early to pick up their sons so that they can watch them play their final game. One boy's parents, who have dropped him off for four straight weeks and given specific instructions that he only play guard at camp, are now back to watch the final game. Because there is not much height on his team, Coach Grayson plays the boy a few sub rotations at forward. The parents are irate about this and let Grayson have it after the game.

To his credit Grayson resists employing his usual sarcastic humor to throw out a few choice comebacks. Instead he listens politely and then offers a simple apology to the parents and a brief explanation. He ends by sincerely praising their son for being a pleasure to be around, while resisting adding the caveat, "much different than his parents."

Photo Fun

Coach patiently, politely, and graciously signs many pictures for campers as well as for staff. Usually he writes "Thank you for your interest" or "Thanks for coming to camp." He might write "Thank you for your friendship" on the pictures of veteran coaches. Whatever he writes, it is easily readable, because he has very clear penmanship. Coach signs pictures, books, hats, posters, T-shirts, and balls. The better Coach knows coaches, the more he personalizes their pictures, and the more humor he uses as well. Coach once signed a Pyramid certificate for Chris Smith that said, "This will look good at the bottom of your parakeet cage." Chris didn't notice what Coach had written until it was on the wall in his office. On Larry Lopez's picture today, Coach writes, "Thanks for taking a picture with an old coach."

Tom Gregory and Coach became very close when Tom began coaching camps in 1976. One year Coach's sixteen-year-old granddaughter Cathleen had been at camp on Sunday with some of her friends. When the twenty-nine-year-old Gregory had been introduced at the parent orientation meeting, Cathleen and her friends had screamed and cheered loudly for him. Coach wrote on his picture at the end of the week, "To Tom Gregory, who attracts the ladies, both younger and older, and is the envy of many."

Coach Brad Barbarick is stirred when Coach writes on his picture today, "Best wishes always and in all ways." I was moved and honored one summer when Coach wrote on my picture, "This depicts the contentment so prevalent in those who truly are UCLA grounded. Best wishes, Greg. John Wooden." My mom was so touched by it that she had it enlarged into an eight-by-ten picture for me. For Lil Lopez, whom Coach treats with such love and respect, Coach simply writes, "You grace us with your beauty."[11]

A Quick Lunch

The last camp meal is an early lunch from ten forty-five to eleven thirty. Some parents purchase meal tickets and enjoy lunch with their sons and perhaps their friends. During this time coaches, counselors, and campers check out of their rooms. They turn their keys in to the counselors in the lobby and breathe a sigh of relief that they have made it through the week without losing them.

It is a quick meal for most, so there is little time for the coaches to talk. But they would not have had much time to talk with Coach anyway, because he has a very special guest with him. Melissa Showalter is celebrating her twelfth birthday today at camp, as she has with just about every other birthday so far. She used to sit on Coach's lap when she was little and feel his love. She is too big for that now, so she has given that seat up to the younger children. Instead she talks to Coach as a young lady and shares a special birthday cake with him that Lil has brought out from the kitchen just for her. Melissa is like her dad in that she pours her sincere heart into everything she does, and this is just one more memory that she is sure to cherish for the rest of her life with her adopted grandfather.

Closing Awards Ceremony

At noon everyone is in the gym for the closing awards ceremony. Hal Mitrovich stands behind a long table at half court facing the bleachers filled with parents and campers. He introduces the coaches and counselors one more time and then passes out the awards. Championship teams receive awards, as do individual camp winners like John Brooks, who receives a Pyramid of Success award for best attitude.

After the awards are handed out, Hector addresses the campers and family members. He is not normally one to show his emotions, but he clearly speaks from the heart and with deep appreciation and love for Coach Wooden. Hector's simple but touching tribute to Coach speaks for all the coaches. "This could be the last John Wooden Camp. For seventeen years thousands of campers have had the genuine, one-of-a-kind model teaching them the sport of basketball and also a way of life. With the closing of the John Wooden Basketball Fundamentals Camp, there will be a need to fill to offer young athletes similar opportunities to improve their skills. No one will do it like the master.

"Honesty, loyalty, friendship, cooperation—all the qualities in the Pyramid of Success—Coach Wooden has them." Coach starts to walk toward the middle of the court as Hector continues to talk.

"Coach Wooden is one of a kind. We have loved and admired him and will continue to do so. His magic is unequaled. We like to come back, the coaches love to come back to work with him, hoping that something will rub off—every year. Please welcome—a coach for all seasons for forever and ever—Coach John Wooden." Everyone in attendance gives Coach a rousing standing ovation, just as they do at the end of every camp, but this one is especially passionate.

Coach Wooden shakes Hector's hand and pats him on the side in a show of appreciation for Hector's words and affection for Hector himself. Hector is touched by the moment and by Coach's gesture.

"Thank you very much. Thank you. Thank you." Coach appreciates the ovation, but he has also learned to talk over it in order to end it. It is one more sign of his humble nature.

Although I dislike ever saying never, it's unlikely that I'll be participating in the camp this time again. And I'm going to miss it very definitely. One of the reasons I'm going to miss it is people like Coach Macias and these coaches over here, with whom you've had the great pleasure of working, and the counselors. But most of all, the wonderful young people with whom we've all had the opportunity of being able to associate during a period of time. I am reminded of a line from a favorite poem of mine: "They ask me why do I teach, and I reply, where could I find such splendid company?"

I can't help but think a little bit about it. Campers and coaches—it takes teamwork. We must have teamwork in every area. We have it here. The people of California Lutheran, oh, just every area, we have it. It reminds me a little bit of a part of Henry Wadsworth Longfellow and his "Hiawatha," which most of these youngsters have never read but some of you older people have read, and I expect there's some of you who maybe are not old enough. We used to have to read and memorize "Hiawatha." There's one part where he states:

So unto the man is woman.
Though she bends him, she obeys him.
Though she draws him, yet she follows,
Useless each without the other.

How true it is as far as camps are concerned. The campers without the coaches aren't going to get too much. The coaches without the campers certainly aren't going to be able to give. And that sort of reminds me a little bit of that. I don't know why that happened to come to me, but it did.

When I think of the camp, I hope the youngsters have gained something that will help them as far as playing basketball is concerned, but I hope it will also help them in areas other than basketball, which are really more important. Basketball is an extracurricular activity that they should get joy from and something that might in some cases direct their future. But it is other things that are certain to be involved in their future, and I hope that they get satisfaction and pleasure from having played basketball this week. I hope the youngsters this week have, and I hope they all remember. In order to try to say something that might be meaningful to them, what has happened is now past, and in no way is that to affect what is to come. It is what you do at the very moment, the present, that can affect your future. Don't live in the past, look forward to the future and prepare yourself for the future.

When Socrates was unjustly imprisoned and was facing imminent death, his jailers, tough and cruel at times, could not understand the serenity and the peace that he was undergoing when they felt he should be scared to death and prepared somewhat for his imminent execution. And they asked him how he could be so serene and peaceful, and he said, "I've been preparing for death all my life."

We hope that this week has helped these youngsters prepare a little bit for basketball, but we hope that it has also helped prepare them a little more for the life they must lead from now on.

I'm most grateful to all those who have been associated with camps with me. I want to particularly thank Coach Macias and Coach Mitrovich, directors for the week, coaches, and again the counselors and the wonderful people here at California Lutheran who have made camps here so much nicer than it could be when you don't have cooperation. Lil Lopez, what a wonderful job she has done with the cafeteria, feeding us through the years. But all the others too have made us feel comfortable and at ease, and that is probably more important than anything else.

I had not intended at all to close the remarks I would make this last time that I'll ever do this with the poem that generally has been for the younger group—not so much for the older group of campers. But maybe I'll just make it for the parents, and maybe that's just who it should be for anyway.

I decided some years ago I would never do it unless I was requested, and I think about fifteen times this week those who knew that this would probably be my last camp have said, "Are you going to give the poem? I want to be sure that you are asked."

So I will close my remarks with the poem that has been very meaningful to me. It is meaningful because I first saw it and received it in 1936, when my son was born. If it were my daughter, I wouldn't give the date, but my son doesn't mind.

The parents laugh. Coach continues,

I had been doing work for Harcourt Brace and Company. I taught English, and I was doing some editing of some books for them. And at the completion of the project, I received a check, which was the only reason I was doing it, as a matter of fact. We just called it extra work to pay the bills, and now they call it moonlighting or something of that sort. I finished it, and they sent a set of encyclopedias, the check, and a picture, which I had framed and have kept near since that time. The picture is of a man walking along the seashore, in the sand, and there's a little fellow coming behind him, his son, and he's trying to step in the footprints of his father before the wind wisps the footprints away.

And the words along the side are entitled "A Little Fellow Follows Me." And now that I'm going to give it, I'll probably forget half as much, but I'll see if I can:

A careful man I must always be;
A little fellow follows me.
I know I dare not go astray
For fear he'll go the self-same way.

I cannot once escape his eyes;
Whatever he sees me do, he tries.
Like me he says he's going to be,
This little chap who follows me.

He thinks that I am good and fine,
Believes in every word of mine.
The base in me he must not see,
This little chap who follows me.

I must be careful as I grow old
Through summer sun and winter snow,
Because I am building for the years to be
This little chap who follows me.

I hope that we here at the basketball camp at California Lutheran have set the type of example that would be helpful for your youngsters. But in the final analysis, ladies and gentlemen, it is the environment at home that will be the most prominent part of the lives of your young people. And if we set the proper example, we have no worries, and if we don't, we have plenty of worries. But let's not leave it to the other person to do it. Let's try to do it ourselves.

As Coach winds up his speech, he reminds people with his characteristic humor, "Please drive carefully on the way home. I'm often told by our out-of-state coaches in particular, although some of them—I don't want to exactly refer to San Diego as being out of state, but maybe it is." The crowd laughs. "It has often been mentioned to me about the crazy drivers in this area of the state, so please be careful on your way home. And thank you very much for being here and—"[12]

Coach Wooden's final words are drowned out by the loud, enthusiastic standing ovation of campers, staff members, and parents whose lives have been forever changed by the kindness and love of this great man.

EPILOGUE

Coach's Camp Legacy

It was time to journey home as well as to journey into a future that would no longer include camp with Coach Wooden. Hurried goodbyes were said as parents, campers, counselors, and coaches quickly left Thousand Oaks before they found themselves snarled in the notoriously crowded Southern California Friday traffic. Many passengers from camp fell asleep on the way home, and some coaches and counselors, like Brad Barbarick, pulled off the freeway and took a nap to keep from nodding off on their long drive.

It would hit each in his own way and time that this was the last time he would ever coach, help, or play under Coach at camp again. All would realize the truth of Don Showalter's statement from Thursday night: "We are going to look back someday and realize how truly special this opportunity has been." Former camper and counselor Steve Delaveaga speaks for many when he says, "The times spent with Coach were some of the best times of my life."

Fortunately for many, the future would include more personal interactions with Coach, and his influence would continue to help them be successful in their professional and personal lives. As Mike Kunstadt says, "The common thread for all of us is Coach Wooden."

Former Campers

Some campers went on to be outstanding high-school, college, and professional basketball players. Luke Walton was a star on great University of Arizona teams, played on LA Lakers NBA title teams, and is now the Lakers head coach. Don McLean became the all-time Pac-12 leading scorer and played in the NBA. His camp competitor Jerry Simon had a long professional basketball career in Israel after starring at the University of Pennsylvania. One of Sportsworld owner Max Shapiro's favorite former campers is Steve Kerr. Kerr was the ball boy for UCLA while I coached there and later went on to a distinguished career as an Arizona Wildcat and in the NBA. He is now the head coach of Shapiro's favorite team, the NBA champion Golden State Warriors.

Harvey Mason also excelled at the University of Arizona and then went on to become a multiple-time Grammy Award-winning record producer. Mason represents the many campers who have applied basketball and life lessons to success in medical, educational, legal, entertainment, political, and business fields. John Brooks became chief financial officer of Trinity Classical Academy in Santa Clarita, California, where he also served as head coach of a state finalist program. John Caruso went on to be chief operating officer of Sydney Evan, a jewelry company. Dan Fapp is vice president of L. E. Peabody & Associates, Inc., while Darren Ranck, who played basketball at Cal Lu, owns and runs his own attorney-services business. Kevin Tamura still has his Pyramid of Success award plaque from camp and applies camp lessons in his career as an executive vice president in commercial real estate and in raising three wonderful children. Many Pyramid of Success winners proudly display their awards on their office walls or desks along with their individual pictures with Coach.

One of those who do so is former camper Jamey Power, who used to help run his family's business, J. D. Power and Associates, where, amid several responsibilities, he had the job of developing the company's international division. He is now a marketing consultant, public speaker, and author of a book about customer satisfaction, and he is involved in a lot of philanthropy. "The Pyramid continues to serve as a reminder of his timeless values and principles, which my parents valued so much that they sent me to camp," Jamey says now. "The basketball fundamentals emphasis carried over to an awareness of the importance of business fundamentals."

The Pyramid is displayed to young people even more prominently—at Castaic Middle School north of Los Angeles—because of Coach's influence on coach Craig Silsbee and his camper son, Lucas. Lucas, the boy who broke his collarbone at camp, is a physical therapist helping others overcome injuries. His mom, Beverly, is a beloved former superintendent of the Castaic Union School District. Coach Wooden, out of respect for Coach Silsbee's family, spoke at Castaic Middle School's dedication. In honor of Coach Wooden and his enduring principles, a big painting of the Pyramid adorns the school's gym wall.

Another special Pyramid winner, Mike Dunlap, eventually became head coach at Cal Lu on his way to an impressive career winning titles on the collegiate and international levels. Eventually he became head coach of the NBA's Charlotte Bobcats.

Little camper Ken Ammann grew to love basketball and was a starter and Academic All-American at Stanford University. He is currently the head coach at Concordia University, Irvine, California, where he has won two National Association of Intercollegiate Athletics (NAIA) national championships, but he humbly says that his achievements are nothing "compared to Coach Wooden's *ten* titles!" He tells a poignant story: "When I was an assistant coach at Pepperdine, our head coach, Lorenzo Romar, knew Coach Wooden so well that our whole staff went to Coach's house to meet with the legend himself. I reminded Coach Wooden of the story of when I was a child at his camp and we had compared items in our pockets. He laughed and said, 'Why, yes, when I was a young man, my minister gave me a cross, and it has been in my pocket ever since.' He reached in to find the cross and discovered that he had misplaced it for the first time in almost eighty years! Well, Coach was not going to visit with us any longer until he found it. He tore apart his condominium for at least thirty minutes while my fellow coaches gave me stare downs. 'Nice story!' was all they would say for weeks. He eventually found it, and we had a memorable talk with him. He is the most amazing person I have ever met, and it began when he took the time to care about a six-year-old at his camp."

Camp lifeguard Rhondi (Pinkstaff) Durand continues to watch over kids as a junior high principal. "At the time I didn't fully realize what a legend Coach was. But he was so friendly. He willingly signed an autograph for my dad who definitely knew what a legend Coach was and treasured the autograph."

Novian Whitsitt, former camper, nighttime special-program performer, and Stanford University student athlete, became a professor of African American Studies at Luther College in Decorah, Iowa, while his brother Damon is in management with Google. "The years at camp and with Coach Wooden were irreplaceable years and memories," says Novian. "I grew up at camp every summer and learned so much at the feet of Coach. There never was and never will be a legend like him. Even in his late seventies at camp, he was modeling discipline and regimen in his personal life. He taught us to work hard in basketball and in every part of life. I have memorized the entire Pyramid of Success and did so at a young age, so it definitely impacts all I do."

Camper Mark Kailey prepared, understood, and paid attention to detail to become a leader in national security matters. "The lessons Coach taught prepared us to win at life and be fulfilled in life," Mark says. "I use one of his sayings at the bottom of every e-mail I send. The current one is 'Be more concerned with your character than your reputation.' With the high political scrutiny of today, it is a great reminder to just focus on doing the right thing and trust that things will turn out best."

Camper Branden Higa is the head women's volleyball coach at California Baptist University, where camp coach Michael Scarano is a well-liked and highly respected assistant athletic director. He played volleyball at Pepperdine University for Marv Dunphy, the gold-medal winning US Olympic coach who patterned his coaching after his good friend Coach Wooden. Higa says, "It is humbling to realize that I am a part of an extensive Coach Wooden coaching tree. As campers, we knew of Coach's great success, but we didn't really understand how special it was until much later. We were enjoying playing basketball all day and wondering what was for dinner and if we should take a shower that night. But it was also my first realization that sports is about much more than just playing the game and learning the skills. Coach Wooden seamlessly and naturally integrated personal development inside skill development. That is the magic of Coach Wooden. As a coach, I'm trying to catch up and live up to his high standards." Many camp coaches and counselors who are also part of Coach's coaching tree would say an "Amen" to that.

Former camper, head counselor, and current North Carolina State assistant Jeff Dunlap says, "I grew up in awe of Coach Wooden and UCLA basketball and was fortunate to play at UCLA. But when I first came to camp, I wanted to be around Coach Wooden, the celebrity, and learn everything there was to know about UCLA basketball. He was so humble and didn't act at all like a celebrity. It was much bigger than his greatness in basketball. It was about greatness of spirit, love, passion for life and family. It reshaped me, put me on the right track, and made me want to impact others through coaching."

Former Counselors and Coaches

Many former camp counselors and coaches have been very successful. The first camp director, Jim Harrick, went on to be one of the top college coaches in the country. While at Pepperdine University and then later at UCLA, he ran each university's first-ever sports camp, both of which are now largely successful multi-sport camps. After a distinguished career Harrick passionately states, "The Wooden system is not the only way to play in the world, it is just the best. This is the way to coach." Coach continued to have fun with Harrick. Harrick's 1995 squad was the first UCLA team to wear the now-standard long shorts. Coach told him, "I don't like them; they look like bloomers," with that unmistakable twinkle in his eye.

Eric Hughes has been a longtime college and NBA assistant coach and is currently an assistant with the Milwaukee Bucks. Bernie Bickerstaff, former camp coach, became a longtime NBA head coach. Jack Currier has been successful in educational resource sales. Jack was playing in the informal morning game in which NBA great Pete Maravich collapsed and died, sadly, from a heart attack. John Hayes put his refereeing work to good use. He is now a fulltime youth and high-school referee for multiple sports. Hayes says, "There was a time at the lowest point of my life where someone challenged me and said 'I thought you were a follower of Coach Wooden.' That resonated strongly and impacted my change and resurgence. My personal contact with Coach fifteen years earlier was a huge key in turning my life around."

Counselor Greg Plutko was an assistant coach at one of California's powerhouses, Glendora High School, under coach Mike LeDuc, where Plutko coached future NBA players Tracy Murray and Casey Jacobson. Plutko became a head coach and then moved up the school and district administrative levels. He is now superintendent of the Huntington Beach Unified School District. "I have a picture of Coach that is above my head on a wall in our conference room," Plutko says. "I quote from memory his sayings, and our own saying 'Go slow to go fast' is like his 'Be quick but don't hurry.' My staff quotes Coach Wooden back to me. Coach was engaged, paid attention to detail, cared about his students and staff, was constantly teaching, and showed grace under pressure. That is a wonderful model for me to try to emulate."

As part of the coaching tree that Branden Higa articulates so well, many coaches have excelled in college jobs, such as Brad Barbarick, longtime head coach at Concordia University in Portland, where he hired his former camp coach, Shim, as his assistant. Former head counselor Steve Hawkins is a Division I head coach at Western Michigan, where Larry Farmer is his valuable assistant. Hawkins, who has led his program to the NCAA tournament, has a tattoo on his upper right arm displaying Coach's definition of success and his signature. Howard Fisher became only the second head coach at College of the Canyons in Santa Clarita, California, where he replaced his mentor, camp coach Lee Smelser, when Smelser retired after a long and distinguished career. In 2002, Smelser was elected to the California community college coaches Hall of Fame. Mike Thibault's dedication to basketball and to hard work has led him to great success as a pro head coach, which includes CBA and WNBA championships.

Ken Barone was a UCLA assistant for Jim Harrick and a longtime high-school and junior-college coach. As a further example of Coach Wooden's coaching tree, Ken himself mentored younger camp coaches, like me, and at one time six of eight coaches in a local high-school league were his former players.

Jim Nielsen coached high-school basketball at Van Nuys High School. He later worked as a principal at three different high schools before becoming the director of secondary education for the Las Virgenes school district. Jim continued to coach at camp even after he became a principal in exchange for camp tuition for his young son Jasen. Jasen is now a criminal lawyer. "I was blown away by the tight and efficient camp organization," Jasen recalls, "the high expectations, and the high respect everyone had for Coach. I also remember how warm Coach was toward me and my dad and how special he treated us. As I got older, I realized that he treated everyone that way."

"I was so blessed to have the experience of working with Coach Wooden," Jim says today. "I didn't realize at the time how much it helped me personally and professionally. When I played in Europe, he even wrote long, handwritten notes to me in his perfect penmanship. I wish I would have tried to use what I learned from him earlier in my life, but it is only after hearing it over and over again that it makes more sense and is able to be applied."

Coaches have also been leaders in their states. Mike Kunstadt, for example, runs Texas Hoops, a key scouting service promoting

Texas high-school basketball players, and was instrumental in creating the first Texas summer basketball opportunities for these rising athletes. Ray Lokar, Greg Plutko, and I have each served as president of SCIBCA, the Southern California coaches' association. Lokar also holds a key leadership position with the Positive Coaching Alliance. Coach Bill Fleming's Iowa high-school squads were ranked in the top ten in the state for an astounding twenty-seven years, and he was inducted into the Iowa Basketball Hall of Fame in 2006. Over sixty of his former players and campers have become coaches themselves, and they carry on Coach Wooden's teachings that they learned from Coach Fleming.

Don Showalter is a coach with USA Basketball and one of the nation's most accomplished high-school coaches. He has been recognized many times by numerous state and national organizations for his achievements and dedication to the game. Many other high-school coaches, such as Tom Gregory, Wayne Carlson, Kevin Barbarick, Jon Palarz, and Yutaka Shimizu, have had distinguished careers, and most camp alumni run their own highly successful camps patterned after the Wooden Camps. At eighty years old, Mickey Perry, one of the very first camp coaches, still runs his own summer camps. For twenty-two years Jeff Dunlap and former NBA player Jack Haley ran the distinguished Complete Player Basketball Camp. Southern California (SCIBCA) Hall of Fame coach Wayne Carlson is the longtime co-director of Snow Valley Basketball Camp, one of the longest-running and most successful camps in California.

Speaking of Wayne Carlson, he had quite a few more dates with cafeteria server Laura Erwin. His question to her at our Sunday camp dinner as to whether she would go out with him was eventually followed by another big question—whether she would marry him. She said yes again, and they have been happily married for well over thirty years with two fine sons.

Camp personnel credit much of their success to what they learned from Coach. They also benefit greatly from listing him as a reference on their résumés. John Saintignon became an exceptional and innovative high-school, college, and international coach. He was hired at Bonita Vista High School in San Diego after the disbelieving principal was finally convinced that the person who had called to recommend John really was Coach Wooden. However, that principal was more trusting than the Arizona principal who later hired John but only after calling basketball coach Lute Olsen at the University of Arizona, who convinced him that the celebrated Wooden really did make those types of personal calls. Saintignon correctly states that "Coach spent a lot of money making numerous calls on behalf of camp personnel."

Coaches also became award-winning teachers, and they credit Coach with teaching them how to be a teacher of any subject and any sport. Many coaches have been accused of talking too much about Coach Wooden, a charge that each is honored to plead guilty to. They are known by the three-by-five index cards that they use for practice planning and carry around following Coach's example. Hector the Director Macias retired from teaching, coaching, and athletic administration at University High School to work with at-risk youth from San Diego County, which he did into his eighties. In doing so he followed Coach Wooden's example of continuing to get better with age.

Coach Ray Tejada became Dr. Ray Tejada and is a professor at Cal State Channel Islands teaching kinesiology and leadership. "Coach's great teaching and example of organization and preparation are the foundation of my own teaching. I present a PowerPoint on the Pyramid of Success to my senior leadership students, many of whom have gone on in educational leadership and have taught the Pyramid's principles to their own staffs and students." Dr. Tejada has also used Coach's organizational and leadership principles as a key leader in the League of United Latin American Citizens (LULAC).

Ken Morgan has taken teams all over the world, including to the former USSR. Don Showalter does clinics all over the world for USA Basketball. In 2012 I was privileged to coach the first US team ever to play in North Korea. It amazed me that the only English some people in North Korea knew was "John Wooden."

Camp visitor Steve Tucker, a lifelong admirer of Coach, has won four straight ABA professional titles and as of the writing of this book is on a ninety-two-game winning streak, the longest in professional basketball history. He constantly quotes and credits Coach Wooden.

The camaraderie built at camps was incredible. Chris Shalby, in his position as executive director of various nonprofits, says, "The most enjoyable part of camp, besides being around Coach so much, was being with all the good people. When you enjoy the people you are with, you enjoy your work and are productive. I look for that now, and I also apply Coach's little gems and what he taught us about discipline, preparation, repetition, teamwork, and ultimately, true success."

The camaraderie continues to grow today. Brad Barbarick says, "Most of my closest friends in coaching are still those from camps." Steve Hawkins recollects, "What I remember as much as anything else is the family that we were as coaches and counselors. It is unbelievable to this day. It was a very special time." Steve Hawkins was a groomsman in Erik Hughes's weddings and Jeff Dunlap's best man in his wedding. All three are best friends today and meet every year at the Final Four, as do others from camp.

Coach Wooden's Continuing Influence

Amazingly, Coach Wooden remembered everyone's names, no matter how long it had been since he had seen them. I had not seen Coach Wooden in many years when I approached him before a game at UCLA's Pauley Pavilion in 2004. My two grade-school daughters wanted to meet him. I told them, "Now girls, he knows a lot of people, and I haven't seen him in a few years, so he might not remember me." However, Coach recognized me right away and said, "Hello, Greg, I was just talking about you today over lunch with Debbie [Willie] Haliday." My daughters were impressed, to say the least, and I was amazed. Mickey Perry simply says, "How does he remember who I am? I'm just a peon. But somehow he does."

Ken Barone tells a similar story. "When Coach was in his nineties," Ken remembers, "I saw him at a UCLA game. Since he knows so many people, I said to him, 'Hi, Coach. I don't know if you remember me, but I'm Coach Barone.'"

With a warm smile Coach replied, "Ken, you don't have to remind me. I know who you are. How is your wife, Marian, and how are your grandchildren?"

"He was a great man," Ken says. "When we were working with him, we didn't really understand how special it was."

Coaches were able to stay in touch with Coach Wooden because he made time for people and worked to build friendships. In 2001 Mike Kunstadt organized a special camp reunion. Everyone met in Van Nuys, California, on Saturday, August 4; we enjoyed the opportunity to see Coach and to express appreciation for him, and he willingly signed many items for us. Coach Wooden's signature is not something you can sell and make money from, because for decades he willingly signed so much for so many for free.

The Showalter, Myers, and Kunstadt kids were all at the reunion, except now they are all wonderful adults, led by Dr. Melissa (Showalter) Kahler, the "big sister" of them all. Coach seemed to enjoy seeing them most. Don Showalter was one of many who spoke at the reunion. "Coach made it a wonderful family experience for us," he said. For years the children stayed in touch with Coach, and he sent birthday, graduation, wedding, and birth-of-children cards to them. Each of the children heard astonished friends say later in life, "Wow. You really know Coach Wooden?" but in the kids' minds he was still the sweet "grandfather" they had loved dearly. In their hometowns some people thought that they actually were his grandchildren.

The coaches' wives cherished memories of time with Nell by the pool or of shopping with her and of Coach himself. Gerri Kunstadt says, "He was just a sincere, loving person and such a pleasure to be around." To this day she is touched by what she saw on a visit to his former condo. "The family Bible is open to the same page from which Coach Wooden read to Nell on her last day alive."

Vicky Showalter cherishes family memories of camp. "We were so honored to be involved with camps as a family," she says. "Coach was always so humble, down to earth, and welcoming. It was so clear how much family was a priority to him, and he made it that way with our families. We have a professionally framed collage of all our pictures from camp, from the first year when Don went by himself and then through the years as our family grew. We were truly blessed to be with Coach all those years, and Don continues to benefit from having worked with Coach at such a young age."

Jim Nielsen recalls, "My wife, Linda, is an English teacher and a Canadian, and she didn't know much about who John Wooden was when she and I first met. But she became a big fan of his because of his love for English and poetry—and for the amazing person that he was."

Showalter's fellow Texan David Myers is still powerfully impacted by Coach's words and examples. "He stressed balance in every aspect of his life," says Dave. "He emphasized that you can't say one thing but then under pressure say or do something else. He was truly a great competitor who reveled in the thrill of a close game, when often his team would spurt at the end to win. He told us, 'You won't like all your players the same, but you must love them all the same.' Oh, and 'I pick up pennies and put them in my left shoe. I can't spend them—only save them or give them away.'" At the camp reunion Myers gave Coach a shoe full of pennies—with a key in the shoelaces.

David's daughter, now Kelly Wigley, has become a coach, and when one of her former players wrote and thanked her for the big influence she'd had on her life, Kelly thought, *Oh my goodness. In a really small way I understand the huge influence that Coach had on his players and campers.* Kelly's former player is now an athletic trainer, and she wrote Kelly, "When I get flustered, I hear you say, 'Be quick, but don't hurry.'" Indeed, another example of the ripple effect of Coach Wooden's influence.

Coach had one more lasting influence on Kelly. She still loves crunchy bacon, and when she is with her family, she requests that they cook it "John Wooden crispy."

Customers at Vip's Cafe in Tarzana do the same. Coach shared breakfast there regularly with many who wanted to talk with him, and today visitors can sit in his booth and order the "John Wooden Breakfast"—item number two on the breakfast menu, which consists of crispy bacon, two eggs, an English muffin, and hot tea. Others honor Coach by ordering a simple bowl of hot oatmeal.

Coach Wooden continued to inspire, guide, and help coaches and camp leadership in many ways. He made coaching appearances at Craig Impelman's camp well into his eighties and nineties, where he would teach the game and life lessons to young players. From the indescribable suffering he went through at the loss of Nell, he found the grace and love to comfort and console Tom Gregory at the passing of his mother at a special banquet that Tom attended the night after her funeral. Coach changed his planned script to read "God's Hall of Fame" in honor of Tom's mom, which greatly comforted Tom. Words cannot describe the gratitude Chris Smith has for Coach after he helped Chris through the loss of his beloved wife, Mae. Ann Meyers Drysdale, who had been a source of comfort for Coach in his darkest days, was comforted by "Papa" in a similar way when her husband, Don, died of a sudden heart attack in 1993.

Coach also influenced the parenting of many. Pat (Yount) Maldi explains, "One of Papa Wooden's sayings that I used religiously when raising my daughter, and I still quote it just about every day, is 'Never do for your child what they could—and should—do for themselves.' I also learned that it is not okay to tell your kids 'because I told you so.' My daughter Natasha just turned twenty-one, is a senior at Dartmouth College, and is currently in Morocco studying Arabic. So it seems to have worked well, although when she was six, she told Papa Wooden that she was going to become an author, 'just like you, Papa.'" Little did Natasha know that Coach Wooden knew a lot more about basketball than he did about writing.

Through his example Coach influenced others to have strong family values. Steve Delaveaga cut a professional career in Australia short because of his commitment to his wife and children. Larry Lopez coached Delaveaga as a camper at camp and later at Cal Lu, where he was the nation's third-leading scorer. "He had an amazing work ethic and attitude, even as a camper," remembered Lopez, "and he got every ounce out of his ability and epitomized what Coach talked about in the Pyramid. That is one reason Coach was so fond of Steve and enjoyed their time in the car so much. And that is where Coach influenced Steve so much, including family values."

Camper Rob Caulfield played professional football in Brisbane, Australia, and now is an executive recruiter with Bank of America and proud father of three children. He played basketball for a year at Cal Lu and met his wife, Lorena, there, where she was an athletic trainer. Rob says, "I returned to campus years later and sat in the gazebo, where I vividly pictured Coach encouraging me to apply my basketball enjoyment to every aspect of my life, including family. He told us, 'The best thing a father can do for his children is love their mother.' That impacted me, and I think that is why my wife likes me so much! I can thank Coach for that." When he returned to Cal Lu, now California Lutheran University, he found that it had impressive new academic and athletic facilities, with the old gym having been turned into a center for theater arts.

Coach influenced many in their faith as well. "His faith was foundational to everything," remembers Jim Nielsen, "but he showed it in such a subtle way."

Larry Lopez is now a deacon in the Catholic Church. "My wife laughs and said I went from one obsession to another—basketball to the church. His biggest faith influence on me is because of how he lived his faith. You have to practice what you preach, but I'm not perfect, so just like Coach carried his cross, I wear a crucifix and the Miraculous Medal to remind me. Through basketball Coach taught and reinforced the same principles I had learned from a special Jesuit priest when I was six years old and also what I had learned as a thirteen-year-old Eagle Scout. Everything he taught us carried over to every aspect of life, such as teaching, coaching, family, and faith." By the way, Larry's little sleepy son, Adam, became good enough to walk on at UCLA.

Camper Dave White became a UCLA cheerleader and is now a college basketball referee and a pastor. "My faith was not as strong when I was a camper as it became later. Coach's own faith and his cross that he personally showed me at camp had a great influence on me choosing the Christian faith. I also received the hustle award, which showed me that hard work is rewarded. It still hangs on my office wall. Coach was a sage, a grandfather to me."

Coaches could tell many stories about being with Coach through the years since camps ended. Tom Desotell, who was selected to the Wisconsin Basketball Coaches Association's Hall of Fame in 2014, explains, "In 2002 Coach invited me to come out to see the World Series in Anaheim. 'They want me to throw out the first pitch', Coach mentioned. I couldn't get out there, but I did get a World Series baseball from Coach a month after the game. He signed it 'To Coach Tom Desotell, from John Wooden, World Series participant.' When asked how it felt to throw out the first pitch, he exclaimed that he had thrown a perfect strike. 'I knew it because it rolled right across home plate,'" he chuckled with characteristic Wooden humor.

Desotell also reflects on one of the gifts Coach gave him. "On another recent visit to his condo, Coach ordered me to go into the bedroom and bring out a pair of shiny black shoes next to the sliding door. The black dress shoes fit me perfectly. 'My daughter, Nan, was disappointed that I couldn't ever break them in and that they continually pinched me in the heel," said Coach. "She'll be so happy that they fit you, because I told her that you'd be coming out and had the same size I do.' I thought, *Wasn't the last time we mentioned my shoe size nearly thirty years ago?!*"

What is true for all the coaches and counselors and perhaps for the campers as well is that when any of us deals with a tough life challenge, such as a problem on the job, a relationship struggle, or the loss or illness of a loved one, we often remember Coach's words, or we wonder what he might say to us if he could speak to us today.

Ken Morgan visited with Coach a month before he passed away. "He was frail, but even at ninety-nine he was as sharp as could be, and he remembered everything. He still had his sense of humor and still made me laugh when he teased me. I asked if he remembered the book that I had written awhile ago, and he said, 'Yes, that was very boring, wasn't it?' with that same twinkle in his eye."

Coach was invited to numerous weddings but rarely attended, simply because he did not want to be a distraction and especially did not want to take any attention away from the bride. But he still made the couple feel his love and support. John Saintignon brought his fiancée, Angelica, to Coach's condo before the wedding. "He talked with her for two hours straight and ignored me the whole time. Of course, that was him having fun with me and also approving of my future wife. He also wrote individual letters to each of my groomsmen."

He also stopped going to Final Fours because it was too hard for him to be there without his beloved Nell, with whom he had shared so many special memories there. But he did go to the 1995 Final Four to watch his protégé Jim Harrick lead UCLA to its eleventh title. In typical fashion he left his seat right before the end of the game so as not to take the focus away from the players and coaches.

Former camper Tony Strickland describes Coach's impact so well. Strickland went on to play college basketball, played with great players like UCLA's Tyus Edney, and is a Dallas Cowboys season ticket holder even though he still lives near his boyhood home in California. "I still cry when they lose," he says. At a young age Strickland became a member of both the California State Assembly and the State Senate and recently lost a close race for a seat in the United States House of Representatives. "We all learn more from losing than from winning. It is how well you get back up after being knocked down that matters. That is one of many important lessons I learned from Coach Wooden.

"Many people who have been around Coach have become successful in many different fields and in all aspects of life," Strickland reflects. "Everything I learned at camp transfers to every aspect of life and transfers well to the next generation. Coach's Pyramid is on the wall of my office and on my children's bedroom walls. Before we say our nighttime prayers, we talk about a few of the precepts in the Pyramid. I have met every president from Richard Nixon to George W. Bush and become close with a few of them, and I talk about meeting Coach Wooden in the same context as meeting those presidents."

Coach continued to grow personally and perhaps to impact even more people after his basketball camps ended. He wrote books; made life-changing speeches; appeared on numerous TV and radio shows; reconnected with UCLA athletes through the Wooden Academy, a leadership development program for Bruin student-athletes; and generously opened his home to countless visitors from all walks of life who sat in his den and were informed, entertained, and enlightened by him. Some, like 18 year old David Stroud, were dealing with a life-threatening illness and received encouragement, strength, and love from Coach. In addition, Coach wrote countless thoughtful handwritten notes in response to letters he had received asking for basketball and personal advice. He spent a lot of money on postage and did all this without a personal secretary.

Many of the most avid readers of books written by and about Coach Wooden are those associated with the camps. Camper Jon Keller, still a lifelong USC fan, is one of them. "I have read every one of Coach Wooden's books," he says, "and was blessed to hear him speak many times." Branden Higa states, "It was through his writings and my personal visits later in life that what I learned as a camper really started to make sense. I came to appreciate that Coach is one of the last truly great American legends."

Coach's Lasting Legacy

Indeed, Coach long ago stopped being just a UCLA treasure and became a national treasure. He was valued for his faith, family commitment, character, wisdom, and love. He belonged first and foremost to his family, which included a whole new generation of wonderful great-grandchildren. But somehow he made everyone seem like a friend.

Many do not know much about Coach Wooden, especially among the youth. But whether they know of him or not, people are still influenced by his legacy and by those who love and honor him. Many know him as the great UCLA basketball coach. But in reality, that success became a platform for Coach to build a much greater legacy than that of winning NCAA championships. Coach Wooden once said, "Winning scores and great reputations are meaningless in the eyes of the Lord, because He knows what we really are, and that is all that matters."[1] His ultimate legacy is one of love, which he said is the greatest word in the human language. He became a man defined by love for God and for his fellow human beings. For the tens of thousands who came into contact with him through his camps, his voice and his spirit live on and touch the lives of countless people. His words are in the minds and hearts of millions.

Coach died at age ninety-nine on June 4, 2010. Some of his coaches were in gyms running their own basketball camps when they were told the news. It somehow seemed fitting that they were told in a gym, where his voice was always in their heads, his love in their hearts, and his lessons forever ingrained in their souls. For many the real sadness hit the next Sunday while sitting in church, since so many were inspired and uplifted by the living example of Coach's faith. The first camp director and eventual NCAA championship coach Jim Harrick describes what Coach meant to him: "He was my teacher, mentor, advisor, and friend and the man I admired most in the world." Pat (Yount) Maldi says today, "My spirit was renewed each summer being with Coach. He is the closest thing I know of to a living saint, and I loved, respected, and admired him."

Campers, counselors, coaches, and Sportsworld and Cal Lu personnel were recipients of Coach's love in the summers of our youths. We teach, coach, and live with thankful hearts for our time with Coach Wooden, his immeasurable influence on us, and most of all his love for us.

To paraphrase the poem that Coach ended camp with:

A careful man you'd always be;
Many people still follow thee.
You knew you dare not go astray
For fear we'd go the self-same way.

You could not escape our eyes;
Whatever we saw you do, we tried.
Like you, we say we're going to be
Grateful folks who follow thee.

We think that you are good and fine,
Believe in every word of thine.
The base in you we do not see,
Admiring folks who follow thee.

You were careful as you grew old
Through summer sun and winter snow,
Because you were building for the years to be.
Blessed folks who follow thee.

Acknowledgments

My love and appreciation for Coach Wooden grew even deeper in the process of writing this book, and his words came alive to me in new and fresh ways. It is amazing how rich his words and example are twenty-five years after the last camp! I should have written this book a long time ago. My students and players would have had a much better teacher and coach because of all the things I learned and relearned!

My fellow camp coaches and counselors agreed that one of us who regularly attended Coach's fundamentals camps needed to write this book, because no one else could really understand what camp with Coach Wooden was like. Their tremendous insight and encouragement were a huge help to me in the book being written, and I tried to express the best I could their words, stories, thoughts, and feelings. In the process old friendships were renewed and new ones discovered. My love and appreciation for the generosity, goodness, and talent of Coach's many camp coaches, counselors, and campers grew as I wrote. Coach Wooden attracted really good and talented people and then drew out the best in them. Those same people told me great stories, articulated wise insights, made me laugh, inspired and encouraged me, and gave me confidence to complete the mission. Each could write his own book, so I am humbled and thankful for their support and affirmation in my efforts to tell our story.

My sincerest thanks to the following for contributing to the book: Ken Ammann, Brad Barbarick, Kevin Barbarick, Ken Barone, John Brooks, Karin (Kunstadt) Canipe, Wayne Carlson, John Caruso, Rob Caulfield, Mark Coffman, Jack Currier, Steve Delaveaga, Tom Desotell, Troy Dueker, Jeff Dunlap, Mike Dunlap, Rhondi (Pinkstaff) Durand, Dan Fapp, Howard Fisher, Bill Fleming, Joe Fuca, Douglas Golden, Gary Grayson, Tom Gregory,

Debbie (Willie) Haliday, Jim Harrick, Steve Hawkins, John Hayes IV, Rick Hayes, Branden Higa, Eric Hughes, Melissa (Showalter) Kahler, Mark Kailey, Jon Keller, Gerri Kunstadt, Mike Kunstadt, Ray Lokar, Larry Lopez, Lil Lopez, Robert Lopez, Hector "Hector the Director" Macias, Pat (Yount) Maldi, Harvey Mason, Butch Mettinger, Hal Mitrovich, Ken Morgan, David Myers, Greg Newell, Jasen Nielsen, Jim Nielsen, Iran Novick, Jon Palarz, Bud Pell, Mickey Perry, Greg Plutko, Jamey Power, Darren Ranck, John Saintignon, Chris Shalby, Max Shapiro, Brent Showalter, Don Showalter, Vicky Showalter, Lucas Silsbee, Jerry Simon, Lee Smelser, Leroy Smith, Chris Smith, Zach Stillwell, Tony Strickland, Kevin Tamura, Ray Tejada, Ed Tellez, Cathleen Trapani (Coach's granddaughter), Steve Tucker, Kerri (Kunstadt) Westmoreland, Dave White, Novian Whitsitt, Kelly (Myers) Wigley, Jamaal Wilkes, and Tom Williams.

A special thanks to Wayne Carlson, Michael Scarano, Chris Smith, and Pat (Yount) Maldi for offering valuable help at critical times by providing me stories, contacts, information, and encouragement to move ahead.

The book is written in loving memory of Van Bye, Hal Mitrovich, Yutaka Shimizu, my former El Dorado High School coach and mentor Nash Rivera, Craig Silsbee, and Tom Williams.

Thanks to Max Shapiro for his support and encouragement to write this book. Thanks too for your vision and courage to convince Coach Wooden to do the camps and then to keep doing them!

A huge thank-you to Valencia High School students in Santa Clarita, California, whose typing skills more than made up for my lack of those same skills. Thank you for typing well, patiently, and willingly: Bridget Beebe, Kayla Brennan, Elaine Bunyan, Rachel Council, Davis Ender, Nicole Gibson, Melissa Gonzalez, Ashley Hawn, Kelly Lee, Sally Lee, Natalie Lloyd, Harrison Martin, Kaitlyn McCarthy, Cat Mesick, Rachel Miller, Alaina Nichols, Briana Perkins, Michael Rosati, Ashlynn Rossi, Maria Sepulveda Jaramillo, Sahara Soliman, Miranda Torres, Caitlyn Tuzon, Lauren Vennero and Korbin White.

A very special thanks to the members of my soccer team, the Lady Vikings, for rooting me on in the process of writing. I'm hopeful that you were in some small way positively impacted by Coach Wooden through my coaching.

I will forever be grateful for my two years on Coach Gary Cunningham's staff at UCLA. He remains one of the finest men I have ever known as well as a great coach. Jim Harrick has been a mentor to me ever since those days, and Larry Farmer became my big brother in coaching by providing me a chance to assist Craig Impelman on UCLA's JV team. Those were rich, exciting, and fulfilling times, and coaching with Craig is one of the highlights of my life. He was so good to me. We share so many memories, including the times when Coach Wooden wished us good luck before games as we sat on his bench in his Pauley Pavilion.

Thanks to Steve Lawson for contributing to another book honoring Coach Wooden. He spent so much time with Coach and writing about him that he mirrors the best qualities of Coach. I have heartfelt and deep appreciation for his professional expertise and guidance and for his personal gifts of service, humility, generosity, patience, wisdom, faith, and love.

Steve put a great team together for me. Becky English was my MVP as she poured her heart, soul, and impressive skill into the manuscript. Rob Williams showed his professionalism and creative brilliance on the book cover and internal design and did so with patience, poise, and a friendly touch. Thank you to Jennifer Cullis for excellent proofreading and to Jason Chatraw for his work with the e-book formatting.

Ann Higginbottom is a sincere, kind, giving, and gracious writer. Her personal touch made the publishing of this book a reality. And she put me in touch with Steve! I think Clayton Kershaw should be known as the brother-in-law of Ann more than for anything else.

Thanks to Ingrid Boydston, Dr. Ed Frierson, and Joel Govea for giving me encouragement and tips from their own writing pursuits. Thanks also to Wooden book author Steve Jamison for his practical advice and to Athletes in Action writer and tour teammate

Kathy Kaiser Harl. I am grateful to Ken Tuttle for valuable resources about Coach.

Two of the most inspirational people in my young teaching and coaching career were Connie Grosse and Larry Hoekman. Connie was one of the best teachers in the country when she taught at El Dorado High School. Larry, another teacher of mine and later a mentor coach, gave me my first big break in coaching, and his mentoring of me made coaching at Coach Wooden's camps and other special coaching opportunities possible for me. Forty years after my coaching career began, Larry humbly served as my assistant coach on a semi-pro team that played in China. Connie's and Larry's insights and reflections on the manuscript for this book were invaluable as has been their constant encouragement.

Thank you to *LA Times* prep sports editor Eric Sondheimer for great contacts. Former *Orange County Register* sportswriter Randy Franz also provided me with strategic and insightful feedback. I've known Randy since I coached him as a little kid, when he was the smartest and best player around. He became my coach with the book.

One of the greatest honors of my life is to be the godfather of Delaney Patricia Hayes, who brings me great joy and has a special place in my heart.

My son-in-law, Tim VanName, spent valuable hours on the train home from his job as a biomedical engineer to provide me with valuable feedback, suggestions, and encouragement about the manuscript. He is one of the smartest people I have ever met, and not just because he chose to marry my daughter Megan.

Megan is often on night shift as a nurse at Johns Hopkins Hospital. She spent many non-working nights trying to stay on a night schedule reading the manuscript and providing invaluable suggestions and improvements. Her generosity, goodness, determination, and beautiful spirit inspire me.

Megan and her younger sister, Kara, make me better in ways that only precious daughters can. Kara pushes me to adventure and to do so with a can-do spirit. With her talent and beautiful spirit, she will always be my favorite singer. I was only able to write so much this summer because she was away helping young girls in Yosemite all summer; otherwise I would have wanted to be with her. Thanks to Jan for the gift of our two amazing daughters, the greatest blessings in my life.

My beautiful mom, Patricia Kennedy Hayes, believed in me more than anyone. She was a saint in life and is now a saint in heaven. Her indescribable love continues to touch and inspire our family.

My dad, John Hayes III, sacrificially paid my way through UCLA and gave me a love for sports and for reading. He also taught me the importance of prayer. Like Coach Wooden, he gets better with age. Dad, through your perseverance and love, you keep Mom alive for us.

My sincerest thanks to the extended Wooden family, who shared Coach Wooden with the world. We still pinch ourselves that he would call us his coaches, counselors, and players, care so much for us, and give us so much.

Most of all, thanks be to God, the source of all the good in my life, for rich summers with Coach.

Notes

Introduction: The Untold Story of Coach Wooden's Camps

1. In 1971 then twenty-nine-year-old Max Shapiro of Sportsworld signed Coach Wooden to run day camps for boys at Pacific Palisades High School near UCLA. Shapiro originally wanted Coach to run overnight camps and offered him a significant amount of money to do it, but Coach said no because, as head men's coach at UCLA, he felt he needed to be at the university every day in the summer. The Coach Wooden camp became Sportsworld's headliner camp.

   Because of the popularity of the camps, once Coach retired from UCLA in 1975, he began doing overnight camps. These camps were originally held at pristine locations like Point Loma Nazarene University in San Diego, Pepperdine University in Malibu, University of California Santa Barbara, and California Lutheran College in Thousand Oaks. Eventually an advanced camp for the better high-school players was added as well as a girls' camp and an adult camp. In later years Cal Lu became the main campus because it was so close to Coach Wooden's Encino condominium.

   In 1988 Coach began to think his camp days were finished, but he rallied after the camp staff put on a "Just Say Maybe" campaign in the summer of 1987 in the hopes that Coach would at least consider returning. He did, and in summer 1988 he came back for what Coach and everyone else expected to be his last camp. This is the year that the camp in this book was centered on. Despite planning to quit, Coach did come back a couple years later and did two or three more camps in the early nineties, but 1988 really marks the pinnacle of his overnight camps.
2. Sportsworld's John Wooden Basketball Fundamentals Camp brochure, 1975.

Chapter 1: Meeting a Legend

1. Greg Hayes's personal camp notes.
2. Karen Rudolph Drollinger, "Master at the Mid-Court," *Second Look*, vol. 1, no. 2, 1987, 14–16, http://issuu.com/sportsspectrum/docs/orelhershiser (accessed October 2015).
3. Greg Hayes's personal camp notes.
4. Coach Wooden's speech to campers and parents, summer 1988, as recorded on Greg Hayes's personal video.
5. John Wooden Basketball Fundamentals Camp Players' Notebook.
6. Ibid.
7. Camp brochure, 1975.
8. Ibid.
9. Greg Hayes's personal camp notes.

Chapter 2: Focus on the Fundamentals

1. For readers who are unfamiliar with basketball terminology, I have included a glossary at the back of the book defining various terms. Hopefully this will help you untangle the difference between screens, suicides, and swishes!
2. John Wooden Basketball Fundamentals Camp Coaches' Handbook; Greg Hayes's personal camp notes.
3. John Wooden, *The Difference Between Winning and Succeeding* (TED, January 2001), online video, http://www.ted.com/talks/john_wooden_on_the_difference_between_winning_and_success (accessed October 2015).
4. Coach Wooden's Monday morning workout with campers, summer 1988, as recorded on Greg Hayes's personal video.

Chapter 3: Getting Acclimated

1. All quotes in this section above this note from Greg Hayes's personal camp notes.
2. John Wooden, interview by Tim Tassopoulos, "Goodbye to a Legend: Coach John Wooden," Focus on the Family, June 28, 2010.
3. John Wooden, interview by Dennis Rainey, "True Success: A Personal Visit with John Wooden," FamilyLife Today, June 7–8, 2010, http://familylifetoday.com/series/true-success-a-personal-visit-with-john-wooden/ (accessed October 2015).
4. Greg Hayes's personal camp notes.
5. Wooden, "Goodbye to a Legend."
6. Karen Rudolph Drollinger, "Master at the Mid-Court," *Second Look*, vol. 1, no. 2, 1987, 14–16, http://issuu.com/sportsspectrum/docs/orelhershiser (accessed October 2015).
7. Camp reunion DVD, personal home video, July 2001.
8. Greg Hayes's personal camp notes.
9. Wooden, "True Success."

Chapter 4: Tuesday Morning with Coach

1. For the story of Coach's day camps in Pacific Palisades, see note 1, introduction.
2. Camp reunion DVD.
3. John Wooden, *The Difference Between Winning and Succeeding* (TED, January 2001), online video, http://www.ted.com/talks/john_wooden_on_the_difference_between_winning_and_success (accessed October 2015).
4. All quotes in this section above this note from Greg Hayes's personal camp notes.
5. Greg Hayes's personal coaching clinic notes.
6. Greg Hayes's personal camp notes.
7. Coach Wooden's Tuesday morning workout with campers, summer 1988, as recorded on Greg Hayes's personal video.

Chapter 5: Coach Wooden's Pyramid of Success

1. Coach Wooden's Pyramid of Success talk to campers, summer 1988, as recorded on Greg Hayes's personal video.

Chapter 6: Coach and Friends

1. Greg Hayes's personal coaching clinic notes.
2. Greg Hayes's personal camp notes.
3. Greg Hayes's personal coaching clinic notes.
4. Greg Hayes's personal camp notes.
5. Karen Rudolph Drollinger, "Master at the Mid-Court," *Second Look*, vol. 1, no. 2, 1987, 14–16, http://issuu.com/sportsspectrum/docs/orelhershiser (accessed October 2015).
6. Greg Hayes's personal camp notes.
7. John Wooden, interview by Dennis Rainey, "True Success: A Personal Visit with John Wooden," FamilyLife Today, June 7–8, 2010, http://familylifetoday.com/series/true-success-a-personal-visit-with-john-wooden/ (accessed October 2015).
8. All quotes in this section above this note from Greg Hayes's personal camp notes.
9. Wooden, "True Success."

Chapter 7: Rainy-Day Adjustments

1. John Wooden, *The Difference Between Winning and Succeeding* (TED, January 2001), online video, http://www.ted.com/talks/john_wooden_on_the_difference_between_winning_and_success (accessed October 2015).
2. All quotes after note 1 from Greg Hayes's personal camp notes.
3. Wooden, *The Difference Between Winning and Succeeding*.
4. All quotes after note 3 from Greg Hayes's personal camp notes.

5. Greg Hayes's personal camp notes.
6. Coach Wooden's Wednesday morning workout with campers, summer 1988, as recorded on Greg Hayes's personal video.
7. Coach Wooden's spontaneous talk to campers on his favorite maxims and his father's creed, summer 1988, as recorded on Greg Hayes's personal video.
8. Greg Hayes's personal camp notes.

Chapter 8: Let the Games Begin!

1. Greg Hayes's personal camp notes.

Chapter 9: Starting Our Last Full Day with Coach

1. All quotes in this section above this note from Greg Hayes's personal camp notes.
2. John Wooden, interview by Tim Tassopoulos, "Goodbye to a Legend: Coach John Wooden," Focus on the Family, June 28, 2010.
3. Ibid.
4. Ibid.
5. Greg Hayes's personal camp notes.
6. John Wooden, "On Motivation" (Xeroxed copy of article given to Greg Hayes by John Wooden, n.d.).
7. Coach Wooden's Thursday morning workout with campers, summer 1988, as recorded on Greg Hayes's personal video.
8. All quotes in this section above this note from Greg Hayes's personal camp notes.
9. Wooden, "Goodbye to a Legend."
10. All quotes after note 9 from Greg Hayes's personal camp notes.

Chapter 10: Respect and Thanks for Coach

1. John Wooden, interview by Dennis Rainey, "True Success: A Personal Visit with John Wooden," FamilyLife Today, June 7–8, 2010, http://familylifetoday.com/series/true-success-a-personal-visit-with-john-wooden/ (accessed October 2015).
2. Ibid.
3. John Wooden, "Need One Know Why" (Xeroxed copy of article given to Greg Hayes by John Wooden, n.d.).
4. John Wooden, "Just Thinking" (Xeroxed copy of article given to Greg Hayes by John Wooden, 1976).

Chapter 11: "The Reason I Teach"

1. Camp reunion DVD.
2. John Wooden, *My Personal Best: Life Lessons from an All-American Journey* (New York: McGraw-Hill, 2004), p. 1.
3. Ibid, p. 4.
4. All quotes after note 3 from Greg Hayes's personal camp notes.
5. John Wooden, interview by Tim Tassopoulos, "Goodbye to a Legend: Coach John Wooden," Focus on the Family, June 28, 2010.
6. Greg Hayes's personal camp notes.
7. John Wooden, interview by Dennis Rainey, "True Success: A Personal Visit with John Wooden," FamilyLife Today, June 7–8, 2010, http://familylifetoday.com/series/true-success-a-personal-visit-with-john-wooden/ (accessed October 2015).
8. Greg Hayes's personal camp notes.
9. Camp reunion DVD.
10. Coach Wooden's Friday morning workout with campers, summer 1988, as recorded on Greg Hayes's personal video.
11. Quotes are from actual pictures that Coach Wooden signed.

12. Coach Wooden's supposed final camp speech to campers, parents, and staff, summer 1988, as recorded on Greg Hayes's personal video.

Epilogue: Coach's Camp Legacy

1. John Wooden, interview by Dennis Rainey, "True Success: A Personal Visit with John Wooden," FamilyLife Today, June 7–8, 2010, http://familylifetoday.com/series/true-success-a-personal-visit-with-john-wooden/ (accessed October 2015).

Glossary of Basketball Terms

- **back pick**—occurs when the screener sets a screen away from the ball on the defender's back
- **block and tuck**—a way of catching a pass
- **block-out or screen out**—when a player uses his body to stay between an opponent and the basket and thus gets into better position for a rebound
- **center**—a taller player who plays close to the basket
- **change of direction/change of pace**—changing speeds and direction, with or without the ball
- **cut**—running to the basket to try to get open for a pass or layup
- **defensive slide**—when a defender moves side to side or at angles without crossing his feet
- **drive**—dribbling away from the basket to try to get a very close shot or a layup
- **Forward, or wing**—an offensive position played to the sides of the basket near the key area and out toward the sideline along the baseline
- **full-court press**—when a team plays defense for the entire length of the court (rather than just on the half court)
- **guard**—a smaller player who dribbles and shoots away from the basket
- **guard backdoor play (aka the "blind pig")**—when a guard cuts hard by the forward on the same side who passes to him, cutting hard to the basket for a layup
- **guard cut**—a smaller player starts away from the basket and cuts to it looking for a pass to score a layup
- **jump shot**—a shot taken after a player jumps in the air

- **jump stop**—coming to a complete stop by landing on balance, low and on two feet at the same time
- **low post play**—an offensive player starts with his back to the basket and very close to try to score
- **one-and-one**—an offensive player with the ball tries to score against a single defender
- **pick, or screen**—when an offensive player legally blocks the path of a defender to open up another offensive player for a shot or to receive a pass
- **pick-and-roll**—one of the most common offensive plays, which occurs when a player dribbles around a screen or block by a teammate, who then runs to the basket looking for a pass; either player can score
- **pivot**—keeping one foot planted on the ground while stepping in one or more directions with the other foot
- **pump fake**—faking a shot close to the basket
- **reverse pivot**—a pivot backward away from a player
- **rocker step**—faking with one foot to drive by a player or take a shot
- **screen, or pick**—when an offensive player legally blocks the path of a defender to open up another offensive player for a shot or to receive a pass
- **shot fake**—a feigned attempt at a jump shot, restrained before the feet leave the ground
- **suicides**—a demanding conditioning drill for players running back and forth from different spots on the court
- **swish**—making a basket without hitting the rim but only touching the net
- **tip-in**—tipping a missed shot into the basket
- **two-hand rip**—grabbing a rebound with two hands and snapping it to the chin with the elbows out
- **UCLA duck move**—a part of the UCLA offense where a big player cuts in front of the basket looking for a pass from a player at the free throw line

- **UCLA high-post offense**—the offense run by many of UCLA's title teams
- **V-cut**—a way of getting open to receive a pass
- **zigzag**—a player running or sliding at angles up the court and changing directions every three to four steps